PERSPECTIVES

ON THE DOCTRINE OF GOD

PERSPECTIVES

ON THE DOCTRINE OF GOD

4 VIEWS

PAUL HELM · BRUCE A. WARE

ROGER E. OLSON · JOHN SANDERS

EDITED BY BRUCE A. WARE

NASHVILLE, TENNESSEE

Contents

Contributors

Paul Helm

Paul Helm is a Teaching Fellow at Regent College, Vancouver, BC, Canada. He is a graduate of Oxford University, and among his published writings are *Eternal God, The Providence of God* and *John Calvin's Ideas*.

Roger E. Olson

Roger E. Olson is Professor of Theology at George W. Truett Theological Seminary of Baylor University, Waco, Texas. He holds the Ph.D. from Rice University, and among his published writings are *The Story of Christian Theology, The Westminster Handbook to Evangelical Theology*, and *Reformed and Always Reforming*.

John Sanders

John Sanders is a Professor of Religion at Hendrix College, Conway, Arkansas. He holds the Th.D. from the University of South Africa, and among his published writings are *The God Who Risks, No Other Name*, and as editor, *The Openness of God*.

Bruce A. Ware

Bruce A. Ware is Professor of Christian Theology at The Southern Baptist Theological Seminary, Louisville, Kentucky. He holds the Ph.D. from Fuller Theological Seminary, and among his published writings are *God's Lesser Glory*, *God's Greater Glory*, and *Father, Son, and Holy Spirit*.

List of Abbreviations

EvQ	*Evangelical Quarterly*
FP	*Faith and Philosophy*
HAR	*Hebrew Annual Review*
HBT	*Horizons in Biblical Theology*
IDB	*The Interpreter's Dictionary of the Bible*
JBL	*Journal of Biblical Literature*
JBMW	*Journal for Biblical Manhood and Womanhood*
JETS	*Journal of the Evangelical Theological Society*
LCC	Library of Christian Classics
NIDNTT	*New International Dictionary of New Testament Theology*
NPNF	*Nicene and Post-Nicene Fathers*
TDNT	*Theological Dictionary of the New Testament*
TDOT	*Theological Dictionary of the Old Testament*
TOTC	Tyndale Old Testament Commentary
TynBul	*Tyndale Bulletin*

Introduction

BRUCE A. WARE

Recent decades have witnessed a renewed and vigorous interest in the doctrine of God within evangelical theology. Theologians from the broad evangelical spectrum have produced both differing and innovative reformulations in understanding just who God is and how he relates to the world he has made. Only a moment's reflection makes clear that revisiting this doctrine amounts to a reconsideration of the foundations of the Christian worldview itself, taken at its largest and most comprehensive level. Everything in theology and life is affected by just how one understands the nature of God himself and the nature of God's relationship with the created order, particularly with his own people. A. W. Tozer could not have been more to the point: "What comes into our minds when we think about God is the most important thing about us." Therefore, evangelical pastors, Christian leaders, and educated and concerned laypersons would benefit much from being aware of some of these proposed understandings of the God of the Bible coming from different evangelical scholars and communities.

The purpose of this book is to put before readers a sampling of some of the most important proposals for understanding the doctrine of God from within evangelical theology. Certainly the four positions described and defended in this book do not exhaust the work being done, but these chapters provide a helpful understanding of key points along the spectrum of viewpoints that evangelical theologians are currently advocating. A careful reading of these chapters will go a long way to informing readers of some of the most prominent proposals of the doctrine of God offered today within the broad movement known as evangelicalism.

The design of this book is to offer two pairs of viewpoints on how God and his relations to the world should be understood, one pair of chapters coming largely from the Reformed camp, and the other pair from the movement of free will theism, more commonly thought of as the broad Arminian camp. Of course, both within Reformed and Arminian traditions, significant differences can be detected, such that neither camp is by any means monolithic. Because of this, we thought it best to represent both a more classical or traditional Reformed and Arminian perspective while also presenting more modified versions of each of these traditions as these have been developed in recent years. One will find, then, two Reformed perspectives and two free will theist (Arminian) perspectives in the four chapters of this book. In each case the defenses of the traditional views are coupled with some innovative modifications of these traditions which, while still Reformed and Arminian respectively, represent something of a modification of aspects of each of these traditions.

Paul Helm leads off the book, arguing for a classical Reformed understanding of the doctrine of God and of divine providence. He puts forward his A-team representatives in support of his Reformed understanding, purporting to show how Augustine, Anselm, and Aquinas argued for and prepared the way for expanded developments in Calvin and others who followed him. As indicative of the heart of the Reformed understanding of God, Helm focuses attention on the concept of predestination in his endeavor to demonstrate a uniform understanding in the doctrine of God through the whole history of the church that was embraced and advanced within the Reformed tradition. In light of this proposal, Helm then finds troubling all three other perspectives presented in this volume, seeing each of them, to lesser or greater extent, to deviate from this uniform classical tradition. In the latter part of his chapter, Helm then endeavors to show what he sees as some of the deficiencies of these other views, all of which depart, as he understands it, from the historical doctrine of God embraced in the Reformed tradition.

My own contribution endeavors to be faithful to the Reformed tradition, and in this respect I affirm much of what Helm has argued. But my deeper concern is faithfulness to the biblical revelation of God, which must ultimately direct the doctrines that we advance within the evangelical church. Ultimate allegiance to Scripture means that we must be willing to modify the traditions we inherit even while respecting greatly their wisdom and insight. My own Reformed model shows some modifications of divine attributes such as immutability and eternity and makes use of what appears in Scripture to be examples of divine middle knowledge in endeavoring to represent Scripture's portrayal of God's own nature and of the ways in which he relates to his human creation. Readers will find fundamental commitments of the Reformed doctrine of God are retained along with some significant modifications, all in an endeavor to be as faithful as I can be to the whole of God's self-revelation.

Roger Olson presents a clear and forthright case for a classical Arminian, or free will theist, understanding of God and his relations to the world. Olson endeavors to explain and defend a truly classical free will theist perspective rooted in the teaching of Jacob Arminius and John Wesley while acknowledging that other viable variations have been proposed in more recent years. For Olson a commitment to the love of God for the world that he has freely made, along with a recognition of God's sovereign decision to grant his moral creatures libertarian freedom, ultimately grounds the classical Arminian tradition in upholding its understanding of God and divine providence. Olson defends his perspective against a number of criticisms and provides biblical, historical, and philosophical support for his classical free will perspective of God.

Finally, in his chapter John Sanders provides one of the clearest short defenses available anywhere of what has come to be known as the open theist perspective of God and divine providence. Sanders highlights many significant points of common commitment with the broader Arminian tradition, endeavoring to demonstrate the legitimacy of his perspective as one that is rightly and genuinely within the free will theist tradition. But he also describes some of the reasons his openness view has departed both from the broader classical theist and, more narrowly, from the classic Arminian understandings of God. Providing sustained biblical and philosophical argumentation, Sanders argues forcefully for his perspective, answering many objections along the way. He ends with a short section in which he reflects on the debate of the past decade and tries to clear up some of the confusion, as he has seen it.

Readers, then, will find here a stimulating set of chapters, all of which are meant both to inform them of the contours of some of the discussion on the doctrine of God within evangelical theology and to provide argumentation they can assess in their own endeavors to understand the God of the Bible rightly. Clearly not all of the views reflected in this book can be correct. They disagree with one another at some fundamental levels. But the reader will be instructed and encouraged to think more carefully and to consider factors he may have otherwise overlooked by a careful probing of these four perspectives on God and his relations to our world. May God be merciful to us all and use resources like this one to guide us ultimately to know the truth, which alone can set each and all of us free.

CHAPTER 1

Classical Calvinist Doctrine of God

PAUL HELM

But if Scripture indubitably opposes our understanding, even though our reasoning appears to us to be impregnable, still it ought not to be believed to be substantiated by any truth at all. It is when Sacred Scripture either clearly affirms or in no way denies it, that it gives support to the authority of any reasoned conclusion.—Anselm

I begin with a confession. Despite the title of this contribution, I reckon that there is no such thing as the "Classical Calvinist Doctrine of God." This "doctrine" is none other than the mainstream Christian doctrine of God. It is the same, give or take some details, as that set forth by Augustine, Anselm, and Aquinas—the A team—three of the formative Christian theologians in the period before the Reformation.

In revisiting and refreshing the biblical basis of Christian doctrine, John Calvin and his followers pursued an essentially conservative course, reforming or attempting to reform only what they judged by Scripture to need reforming. That is why Calvin's

Institutes, considered as a work in systematic theology, is such an uneven book. Thus the doctrines of divine simplicity, eternity, and immutability, together with divine freedom, omniscience, and omnipotence, were left undisturbed. Calvin also affirmed the orthodox view of the Trinity and the Incarnation and gave those doctrines a central place in his theology where the emphasis fell mainly on soteriology. And as we shall see, even the doctrine for which Calvin is best known and often reviled, predestination, he took from the A team because he held that what they believed was apostolic and dominical. Predestination is a central implication of the doctrine of prevenient grace as it was affirmed by the Second Council of Orange in 529.[1]

If this is so, then the "perspectives" on the doctrine of God offered by the other three contributors to this book must be regarded as deviating from the main spine of Christian theism. If those setting forth the core of Christian theology can be shown to concur over predestination and the doctrine of God that it implies, then the onus of proof must be on the shoulders of those who wish to affirm that Calvin held a perspective on the doctrine of God distinct from that of the mainstream tradition (hereafter "the tradition"), one that can be discussed side by side with other more recent perspectives.[2] In this connection the use of perspective is questionable because it presumes that any serious perspective is and ought to be regarded as a live option for Christians.

Reference to tradition, however hallowed, does not settle theological issues. And appeal to tradition ought not to be taken as an indefeasible argument for the truth of some Christian doctrine. Nevertheless, the views of the A team, and particularly the biblical grounds they offer for those views, create a presumption in favor of those views. Nothing more than this but also nothing less. I do not deny that there are other early voices in the church such as those of Origen or Ambrose or Jerome. Nevertheless, on

---

1. Council of Orange, *Creeds of the Churches*, ed. John H. Leith (New York: Doubleday Anchor, 1963). However, the Council affirms nothing directly about predestination or about the particularity and irresistibility of grace.

2. The emphasis placed on the doctrine of predestination in this chapter is not to be taken as an endorsement of the view that it is a central dogma of either John Calvin, Calvinism, or, for that matter, of mainstream Christian theology.

any account of the development of Christian doctrine, particularly in the Western church, theirs cannot be said to have become the default position.[3]

I intend this chapter to undermine the presumption of parity between the tradition and the three other perspectives offered in the book. In terms of the Reformation and afterwards, and considered in historical order, Arminianism rejects the Augustinian doctrine of efficacious grace and its doctrinal underpinnings and consequences and affirms the power of the human will autonomously to cooperate with God's grace. These positions are substantially similar to those by which Pelagius and the Semi-Pelagians rejected Augustine's view of grace. Arminius himself rejected the Augustinianism of the Reformation on rationalist grounds and in developing his own response employed among other things the doctrine of middle knowledge newly devised by Molina and Fonseca.[4]

Later on the Wesleys and most of the Methodist movement avowed a more evangelical form of Arminianism,[5] thus sparking off controversy with Calvinists such as George Whitefield and Augustus Toplady. The Wesleyan style of Arminianism has influenced the doctrinal stance of more recent denominations and movements such as the Church of the Nazarene and Pentecostalism. With its espousal of a God who is in time, mutable, liable to be surprised and frustrated, who cannot foreknow the future free actions of humanity since there is no such future for Him to know, open theism is a further development of Arminianism. It is what follows when libertarian freedom, coupled with the belief that such freedom and God's knowledge of the future are irreconcilable, is made the central pillar of Christian theology. Open theism has precedents in an earlier

---

3. Such theologians did not devise a "third way" between Augustinianism and the varieties of Pelagianism, but (for example) on the relation between divine foreknowledge and merit they are recognizably Pelagian, though of course independently of the influence of Pelagius. For a brief discussion see Herman Bavinck, *Reformed Dogmatics*, vol. 2, *God and Creation*, trans. John Vriend, ed. John Bolt (Grand Rapids: Baker, 2004), 348.

4. As Richard A. Muller has shown in *God, Creation, and Providence in the Thought of Jacob Arminius* (Grand Rapids: Baker, 1991), chap. 9.

5. For an interesting discussion of these differences see J. I. Packer, *Honouring the People of God: Collected Shorter Writings of J. I. Packer*, vol. 4 (Carlisle: Paternoster Press, 1999).

deviation from the classical Christian position, the Socinianism of the sixteenth and seventeenth centuries and (interestingly) in the antifatalistic metaphysics of Cicero to which Augustine reacted so robustly in *The City of God*.[6] Finally, insofar as the modified Calvinist perspective represents a clear and distinctive position, it seems to be somewhat unstable as between the tradition and Arminianism. Ultimately it must find its resting place in one of the other of these two positions.

In what follows I shall endeavor to make good each of these claims and their implications for the doctrine of God. I shall highlight the traditional Christian view of predestination and its Scriptural sources and note the doctrine of God that it entails. There is of course no reverse entailment since predestination is God's free decree.

I shall first attend to the views of the A team and then to Calvin himself. Then we shall, as Calvin did, revisit the biblical basis of predestination. I shall show how the three other perspectives clearly deviate from or, in the case of modified Calvinism, are inclined to deviate from this position and the consequences such deviations have for the doctrine of God. A philosophical side to all this will emerge, a distinctive position that is implied by the classical Christian view of God and its basis in Scripture, and a philosophical lesson from the story of the deviations therefrom. It has to do with the philosophical attitude to the mysteriousness of the relation between God and his creation, and thus with the important question of whether, for the Christian, theology or philosophy has priority in the articulation of Christian doctrine.

Predestination and the Tradition

Augustine of Hippo (354–430)

We shall look at only two representative writings of Augustine. First, his letter to Simplicianus, Ambrose's successor as Bishop of Milan (published in 396, shortly after

---

6. Augustine, *The City of God*, vol. 9.

Augustine became a bishop), shows that Augustine's views on grace and predestination were not the product of the mind of a morose and hard old man but were clearly present much earlier. Augustine deals with two passages from chapters 7 and 9 of Paul's letter to the Romans that were critical in the later Pelagian controversy. We shall examine his remarks on Romans 9. The second writing is his later *On the Predestination of the Saints* (429) which refers back to Augustine's earlier treatment of Romans 9 in his letter to Simplicianus. Three themes are prominent in these writings: God's grace is unmerited; it is efficacious; and in freely choosing to give grace to some and not to others, God acts righteously.

In his letter to Simplicianus, Augustine at once raises the question of whether the "according to election" of Rom 9:11 refers to a choice based on the foreknowledge of Jacob's faith even before he was born. Augustine responds:

> If election is by foreknowledge, and God foreknew Jacob's faith, how do you prove that he did not elect him for his works? Neither Jacob nor Esau had yet believed, because they were not yet born and had as yet done neither good nor evil. But God foresaw that Jacob would believe? He could equally well have foreseen that he would do good works. . . . The reason for its not being of works was that they were not yet born, that applies also to faith; for before they were born they had neither faith nor works. The apostle, therefore, did not want us to understand that it was because of God's foreknowledge that the younger was elected to be served by the elder. He wanted to show that it was not of works, and he stressed that by saying, "When they were not yet born and had done neither good nor evil." He could have said, if he wished to, that God already knew what each was going to do. We have still to inquire why that election was made. It was not of works, because being not yet born they had done no works. But neither was it of

faith, because they had not faith either. What, then, was the reason for it?[7]

He develops the point.

> But the question is whether faith merits a man's justifi-cation, whether the merits of faith do not precede the mercy of God; or whether, in fact, faith itself is to be numbered among the gifts of grace. Notice that in this passage when he said, "Not of works," he did not say, "but of faith it was said to her, the elder shall serve the younger." No, he said, "but of him that calleth." No one believes who is not called. God calls in his mercy, and not as rewarding the merits of faith. The merits of faith follow his calling rather than pre-cede it. So grace comes before all merits. Christ died for the ungodly. The younger received the promise that the elder should serve him from him that calleth and not from any meritorious works of his own. The Scripture "Jacob have I loved" is true, but it was of God who called and not of Jacob's righteous works.[8]

The discussion then introduces the idea of effective calling.

> If he [Paul] said "It is not of him that willeth, nor of him that runneth, but of God that hath mercy," simply because a man's will is not sufficient for us to live justly and righ-teously unless we are aided by the mercy of God, he could have put it the other way round and said, "It is not of God that hath mercy, but of the man that willeth," because it is equally true that the mercy of God is not sufficient of itself, unless there be in addition the consent of our will. Clearly it is vain for us to will unless God have mercy. But I do not know how it could be said that it is vain for God to have mercy unless we willingly consent. If God has mercy, we also will, for the power to will is given with the mercy itself. It is God that worketh in us both to will and to do of his good pleasure. If we ask whether a good will is a gift of God, I

---

7. "To Simplician—on Various Questions," trans. John H. S. Burleigh, in *Augustine: Earlier Writings,* Library of Christian Classics (London: SCM Press, 1953), 389–90.

8. Augustine, "To Simplician," 391.

should be surprised if anyone would venture to deny that. But because the good will does not precede calling, but calling precedes the good will, the fact that we have a good will is rightly attributed to God who calls us, and the fact that we are called cannot be attributed to ourselves. So the sentence "It is not of him that willeth, nor of him that runneth, but of God that hath mercy" cannot be taken to mean simply that we cannot attain what we wish without the aid of God, but rather that without his calling we cannot even will.[9]

The position is clear. Whatever part divine foreknowledge may play in the granting of grace, that foreknowledge is not based on foreseen faith or works, but faith, love, and other graces come as a result of the efficacious calling of God, the outworking of the predestinating will of God based on the knowledge of his own mind.

In Augustine's work *On the Predestination of the Saints,* he refers to this exchange with Simplicianus, and many of the themes of the earlier work recur. But Augustine takes the argument a stage further to stress that behind the giving of grace is God's election and that men and women are thus predestined to the grace that they enjoy. Much of his language simply paraphrases Paul:

> Therefore God chose us in Christ before the foundation of the world, predestinating us to the adoption of children, not because we were going to be of ourselves holy and immaculate, but He chose and predestinated us that we might be so. Moreover, He did this according to the good pleasure of His will, so that nobody might glory concerning his own will, but about God's will towards himself. . . . Because He Himself worketh according to His purpose that we may be to the praise of His glory, and, of course, holy and immaculate, for which purpose He called us, predestinating us before the foundation of the world. Out of this, His purpose, is that special calling of the elect for whom He co-worketh with all things for good, because they are called according to His

---

9. Ibid., 394–95.

purpose, and "the gifts and calling of God are without repentance" (Rom 11:29).[10]

There are a number of references to reprobation in this work and others. For example, "He saved them [the elect] for nothing. But to the rest who were blinded, as is there plainly declared, it was done in recompense. 'All the paths of the Lord are mercy and truth.' But His ways are unsearchable. Therefore the mercy by which He freely delivers, and the truth by which He righteously judges, are equally unsearchable."[11] Such references are understandably muted, but for Augustine reprobation is not simply inferred from predestination but grounded in the biblical data, and the grounds for condemning the reprobate differ from the grounds for blessing the elect. All events are under God's providential control, but the term *predestination* is reserved by Augustine for the destining of men and women to salvation. God foreknows what he himself does not (and cannot) do—that is, acts of evil. He does not predestine such acts, but they are part of his providence.[12]

One further point. In warmly embracing the Pauline ideas of Romans 9, Augustine faces head-on the question of divine equity in God's choice of some and not of others. Not for him an arbitrary God, however. Commenting on Rom 9:14 in his letter to Simplicianus, he says:

> Let this truth, then, be fixed and unmovable in a mind soberly pious and stable in faith, that there is not unrighteousness with God. Let us also believe most firmly and

---

10. Augustine, *On the Predestination of the Saints*, chap. 37, trans. Robert Ernest Wallace, in *Saint Augustin's Anti-Pelagian Works: A Select Library of the Nicene and Post-Nicene Father of the Christian Church*, ed. Philip Schaff (Grand Rapids: Eerdmans, 1971), 516.

11. Augustine, *On the Predestination of the Saints*, 11:504. See also, for instance, Augustine, *De Anima*, 4:10 and Augustine, *City of God*, 22:24.

12. Augustine, *On the Predestination of the Saints*, 19:507. One way that Augustine has of preserving the asymmetry between God's attitude to evil and to good is to understand foreknowledge as causal in the case of good actions but as noncausal in the case of evil actions. "For a man does not therefore sin, because God foreknew that he would sin, Nay, it cannot be doubted but that it is in the man himself who sins when he does sin, because He, whose foreknowledge is infallible, foreknew not that fate, or fortune, or something else would sin, but that the man himself would sin, who, if he wills not, sins not. But if he shall not will to sin, even this did God foreknow" (Augustine, *City of God*, vol. 10). Nevertheless, all falls within the order of his providence (v. 11).

tenaciously that God has mercy on whom he will and that whom he will he hardeneth, that is, he has or has not mercy on whom he will. Let us believe that this belongs to a certain hidden equity that cannot be searched out by any human standard of measurement, though its effects are to be observed in human affairs and earthly arrangements.[13]

In his work *On the Gift of Perseverance*, Augustine also maintains, in accord with Paul's teaching in Romans 8, that not all who are given grace are given the grace to persevere but that by his inscrutable will God grants perseverance to some and yet not to others. So it is not possible for a person to know with certainty that he is called "until he has departed from this world."[14] This may seem to be in strong contrast with Calvin's later emphasis on assurance, and yet Augustine's teaching on this point has parallels with Calvin's own recognition of "transitory faith . . . that lower working of the Spirit."[15]

Anselm of Canterbury (1033–1109)

About 600 years later Anselm wrote his last major work, *De Concordia* (*The Compatibility of God's Foreknowledge, Predestination, and Grace with Human Freedom*),[16] which provides good commentary regarding his views on predestination. He shares some of Augustine's peculiarities—an attachment to the privative notion of sin and evil, the use of the idea of merit,[17] the possibility of falling from grace,[18] the view of justification as moral renewal,[19] and the strange idea that the number of the elect exactly corresponds with the number of the fallen angels.[20]

---

13. Augustine, "To Simplician," 397.

14. Augustine, *De Dono Perseverantia*, trans. Robert Ernest Wallace, in *Saint Augustin's Anti-Pelagian Works*, chap. 33.

15. John Calvin, *Institutes of the Christian Religion*, ed. John T. McNeil, trans. Lewis Battles (London: S.C.M. Press, 1960), 3:2, 11.

16. Anselm, *De Concordia*, trans Thomas Bermingham, in *Anselm of Canterbury: The Major Works,* ed. with an introduction by Brian Davies and G. R. Evans (Oxford: Oxford University Press, 1998). Page references are to this translation.

17. Anselm, *De Concordia*, 455, 452, 470.

18. Ibid., 456.

19. Ibid., 453.

20. Anselm, *Cur Deus Homo* 1:18 (Cf. Augustine, *Enchiridion* 29; *City of God* 22:1).

But there are differences: Anselm's concise, analytic style as well as his concern to harmonize foreknowledge and predestination with free will lead to the almost complete absence of a sense of mystery or of the struggle that Augustine had with the idea of predestination.

It would be rash to assume that Anselm was attempting the reconciliation of foreknowledge and predestination with *libertarian* freedom.[21] Much that he says is consistent with compatibilism if he is understood as defending the part that the will plays in the reception and expression of divine grace against the view, which he explicitly refers to a number of times, that human beings are totally passive and treated by God impersonally.[22] We will touch on this issue briefly below, though our main aim is to expound Anselm on predestination. We shall see that he follows Augustine fairly faithfully, even if their styles are dramatically different.

Divine foreknowledge is infallible and extends to all future things including the free actions of all his creatures (this mindset is what generates the problems that Anselm is addressing in *De Concordia)* and including those people whom God predestinates, as Paul teaches in Rom 8:29.[23] God's foreknowledge is not caused by what exists: "If God owes his knowledge to things, it follows that they exist prior to his knowledge of them and that their existence is not owed to God. For they cannot owe their existence to God if God does not know them."[24] Consequently, if God foreknows evil acts, then it seems that he causes them, a central problem addressed in *De Concordia*.

Predestination is the carrying into effect of what is foreknown. "It is, of course, beyond question that God's foreknowledge and predestination do not conflict, rather, even as God

---

21. Such an assumption underlies the work of Katherin A. Rogers. For example, "Anselm's Indeterminism" in *The Anselmian Approach to God and Creation* (Lewiston: Edward Mellen, 1997), and "Does God Cause Sin? Anselm of Canterbury versus Jonathan Edwards on Human Freedom and Divine Sovereignty," *Faith and Philosophy*, 2003.

22. Anselm, *De Concordia*, 452, 466. (See also *Cur Deus Homo* I.10).

23. Ibid., 450.

24. Ibid., 447.

foreknows, so he predestines."[25] "Predestination is the equivalent of pre-ordination or pre-establishment; and therefore to say that God predestines means that he pre-ordains, that is to bring about that something happen in the future."[26] Therefore God's predestination embraces both good and evil acts.[27] The difference between foreknowledge and predestination is basically the difference between God's mind and His will. Predestination is the purposing of certain individuals to grace and glory, namely those individuals "foreknown" by God. What Anselm has to say about grace throws light on the nature of predestination, in particular that its ground is not the foreseen merit or good standing of the one predestined.

As already noted, in his discussion of the place of the human will in the operation of divine grace on the soul, Anselm is combating two extremes: those who claim that the will has no part to play in this operation, and those who give autonomy to the will.

> Therefore since we come upon some passages in sacred Scripture which seem to recommend grace alone and some which are considered to uphold free choice without grace, there have been certain proud individuals who have decided that the entire efficacy of our virtues rests upon our free choice alone and in our own day there are many who retain no hope whatsoever of the very existence of free choice.[28]

The latter are not so much compatibilists as passivists, even fatalists, holding that divine grace is imparted apart from the will, not through the will renewed by grace. It is unwarranted to assume that by "free choice" in such a passage Anselm means libertarian freedom. Divine grace does not operate apart from the will, nor does the will independently receive divine grace, but grace works on and through the will. In the case of adults, "grace always aids one's innate free choice by giving it the uprightness which it may preserve by free choice, because without grace it

---

25. Ibid., 450–51.
26. Ibid., 449.
27. Ibid., 450.
28. Ibid., 453. See also 452, 466.

achieves nothing toward salvation."[29] It may seem, then, that the will autonomously cooperates to receive God's grace, for perhaps the gift of uprightness can be rejected. But no.

> And even if God does not give grace to everyone, for "He shows compassion to whom he wills and hardens those he wills to harden" (Rom 9:18), still he does not give to anyone in return for some antecedent merit, for "who has first given to God and he shall be rewarded?" (Rom 11:35). But if by its free choice the will maintains what it has received and so merits either an increase of the justice received or power by way of a good will or some kind of reward, all these are the fruits of the first grace and are "grace upon grace" (John 1:16). It must all be attributed to grace, too, because "it is not of the one who wills, nor of the one who runs, but of God who shows mercy" (Rom 9:16). For to all, except God alone, it is said: "What do you have that you have not received? And if you have received it all, why do you boast as though you had not received it?" (1 Cor 4:7).[30]

Anselm, no less than Augustine, notes the fact of reprobation, as in these words: "In fact he is said to harden people when he does not soften them and to lead them into temptation when he does not release them from it. Therefore there is no problem in saying that in this sense God predestines evil people and their evil acts when he does not straighten them out along with their evil acts."[31] Once again the familiar Augustinian (and Pauline) themes are rehearsed; the same New Testament passages are relied upon.

Thomas Aquinas (1224–1274)

We shall briefly consider two places where Thomas discusses predestination: *Summa Theologiae* 1.23, and Article 6 of his *De Veritate*.[32] The treatments are similar. Thomas's thought is gov-

---

29. Ibid., 455.
30. Ibid., 455. See also 452–53, 456.
31. Ibid., 450.
32. Translated by Robert Mulligan in *Thomas Aquinas: Providence and Predestination* (Chicago: Henry Regnery, 1953). All page references are to this edition.

erned by two ideas. The first is that predestination is an eternal act, and the second is that it has those temporal effects intended by God, who plans[33] and "sends" predestination, in the way an archer sends an arrow. In these respects predestination is an aspect of providence.[34]

> Clearly predestination is like the plan, existing in God's mind, for the ordering of some persons to salvation. The carrying out of this is passively as it were in the persons predestined, though actively in God. When considered executively in this way, predestination is spoken of as a "calling" and a "glorifying;" thus St. Paul says, *"Whom he predestinated, them also he called and glorified."*[35]

Election and predestination are interrelated. The following extract summarizes the overall position.

> By its very meaning predestination presupposes election, and election chosen loving. The reason for this is that predestination, as we have said, is part of Providence, which is like prudence, as we have noticed, and is the plan existing in the mind of the one who rules things for a purpose. Things are so ordained only in virtue of a preceding intention for that end. The predestination of some to salvation means that God wills their salvation. This is where special and chosen loving come in. Special, because God wills this blessing of eternal salvation to some, for, as we have seen, loving is willing a person good, chosen loving because he wills this to some and not to others, for, as we have seen, some he rejects.[36]

---

33. Thomas Aquinas, *Summa Theologiae* vol. 2, *The Mind and Power of God* (part 1, ques. 14–26), gen. ed. Thomas Gilby (Garden City, NY: Image Books, 1969), Ia.23:2, 164.

34. Aquinas, *Providence and Predestination*, 101.

35. Aquinas, *Summa Theologiae*, Ia.23.2, 164.

36. Ibid., Ia.23.4, 168. Note the comments of Fergus Kerr. "For Thomas, God is the cause that enables all agents to cause what they do. . . . There is no problem He cites Isa 26:12 ('O Lord, . . . you have done for us all our works') . . . together with John 15:5, 'Without me, you can do nothing'; and Phil 2:13: 'It is God who worketh in us to will and to accomplish according to his good will.' For Thomas, evidently, Scripture settles it; there is no need for theoretical explanations of how divine freedom and human freedom do not, or need not be thought to, encroach on each other. . . . Thomas only excludes certain tempting views: yes, God does everything, God is not a partner in the existence

Thomas also provides a full and clear account of reprobation.

> The causality of reprobation differs from that of predestination. Predestination is the cause both of what the predestined expect in the future life, namely glory, and of what they receive in the present, namely grace. Reprobation does not cause what there is in the present, namely moral fault, though that is why we are left without God. And it is the cause why we shall meet our deserts in the future, namely eternal punishment. The fault starts from the free decision of the one who abandons grace and is rejected, so bringing the prophecy to pass, *Your loss is from yourself, O Israel* (Hos 13:9).[37]

Even if predestination were granted in accordance with the foreseen merit in the ones predestined,[38] such merits are themselves the product of divine predestinating grace. So predestination is not on account of any merits foreseen, but they are the cause of it only in the sense that they are part of the ordained divine sequence which begins in the calling of men and women and ends in their glorification.

> The fact that God wishes to give grace and glory is due simply to His generosity. The reason for His willing these things that arise simply from His generosity is the overflowing love of His will for His end-object, in which the perfection of His goodness is found. The cause of predestination, therefore, is nothing other than God's goodness.[39]

---

and activities of the world; God does everything, however, in such a way that the autonomy and reality of created agents is respected. Above all: the effect is not attributed to a human agent and to divine agency in such a way that it is partly done by God and partly by the human agent; rather, it is done wholly by both, according to a different way, just as the same effect is wholly attributed to the instrument and also wholly to the principal agent—but now Thomas is referring us to an analogy, and either we see it or we don't. In the end, he excludes certain views and leaves us simply with the mystery of the relationship between divine creativity and human autonomy. . . . Thomas has nothing more basic to offer than these observations." Fergus Kerr, O.P., *After Aquinas: Versions of Thomism* (Oxford: Blackwell, 2002), 44–46. I'm grateful to Mark Talbot for drawing attention to this discussion.

37. Aquinas, *Summa Theologiae*, Ia:23. 3, 167.
38. Aquinas, *Providence and Predestination*, 144.
39. Ibid., 116.

And so what about the place of free will?

> God does not act on the will in the manner of one neces-
> sitating; for He does not force the will but merely moves it,
> without taking away its own proper mode, which consists
> in being free with respect to opposites. Consequently, even
> though nothing can resist the divine will, our will, like every-
> thing else, carries out the divine will according to its own
> proper mode. Indeed, the divine will has given things their
> mode of being in order that His will be fulfilled. Therefore,
> some things fulfill the divine will necessarily, other things,
> contingently; but that which God wills always takes place.[40]

John Calvin (1509–1564)

In the *Institutes* Calvin said that predestination is that "by
which God adopts some to hope of life, and sentences others to
eternal death."[41] God is the author of predestination; and, since
God is eternal, predestination is "God's eternal decree, by which
he has compacted with himself what he willed to become of each
man. For all are not created in equal condition; rather, eternal life is foreordained for some, eternal damnation for others.
Therefore, as any man has been created to one or the other of
these ends, we speak of him as predestined to life or to death."[42]
So each person is born already destined to life, or to death.

Predestination is an aspect of divine providence. (The fact that
Calvin treats providence and predestination in different places in
the *Institutes* ought not to mislead us. Providence as he treats
it is intertwined with the destiny of the church.) Predestination
here covers both predestination to grace and glory and reprobation. Election and predestination in the narrower sense seem to
be used more or less interchangeably. For example, in *Institutes*
3.21.7 Calvin used "election" and "predestination," first as
regards the nation of Israel, then of the chosen remnant within
Israel, which the New Testament church is in the line of—that

---

40. Aquinas, *Providence and Predestination*, 131.
41. Calvin, *Institutes* 3:21.6.
42. Ibid. 3:21.6.

is, individual men and women destined not merely for temporary privileges but for eternal salvation:

> Although it is now sufficiently clear that God by his secret plan freely chooses whom he pleases, rejecting others, still his free election has been only half explained until we come to individual persons, to whom God not only offers salvation but so assigns it that the certainty of its effect is not in suspense or doubt. These are reckoned among the unique offspring of God mentioned by Paul (*cp.* Rom 8:8; Gal 3:16 *ff.*). The adoption was put in Abraham's hands. Nevertheless, because many of his descendents were cut off as rotten members, we must, in order that election may be effectual and truly enduring, ascend to the Head, in whom the Heavenly Father has gathered his elect together, and has joined them to himself by an indissoluble bond.[43]

More exactly, predestination in the narrower sense is the "handmaiden" of election.[44] Not only is God the author of predestination; he is the source of it; that is, Calvin is emphatic that who are predestined does not depend on anything in them that God foreknows and that makes them deserve his mercy. As he put it, commenting on Rom 8:29, the foreknowledge of God "is not a bare prescience . . . but the adoption by which he had always distinguished his children from the reprobate." And again in his comment on Rom 11:2 ("God has not rejected his people whom he foreknew"[45]), Calvin said, "By the verb *foreknow* is not to be understood a foresight, I know not of what, by which God foresees what sort of being any one will be, but that good pleasure, according to which he has chosen those as sons to himself, who, being not yet born, could not have procured for themselves his favour." These are the remnant, chosen by grace (v. 5).[46] Here, for Calvin, such foreknowledge is not simply causative but also graciously causative.

---

43. Calvin, *Institutes* 3:21.7.
44. Ibid. 3:22.9.
45. Unless otherwise stated, biblical quotations are taken from the ESV.
46. John Calvin, *Commentaries on the Epistle to the Romans*, trans. John Owen (Calvin Translation Society reprint, Grand Rapids: Baker, 1979), 317, 410.

The divine plan of salvation was founded on "his freely given mercy, without regard to human worth." God does not predestine a person to salvation because he foreknows that person's meritorious works, or faith, or anything else that is "worthy" about that person that might provide a reason God would discriminate in the person's favor. Such discrimination is grounded in God's judgment although that judgment is "incomprehensible,"[47] not in the sense that it is incoherent, but in the sense that it is unfathomable, and perhaps necessarily unfathomable, by us. The sense of mystery, vividly present in Augustine (and of course, in the apostle Paul), but muted in Anselm and Aquinas, returns in Calvin. So predestination is "secret," and thus a person cannot know whether he is predestined to life by *a priori* reasoning, or by directly divining God's will, but only *a posteriori*, through one's relationship to Christ.[48]

God's unchangeable plan in willing the end of the salvation of the church also wills the means, which is "intrinsically effectual unto salvation for these spiritual offspring alone."[49] Those on whom God has eternally planned to show such mercy are, in time, called and justified. Calvin emphasizes that the "golden chain" of Romans 8 is unbreakable. "Among the elect we regard the call as a testimony to election. Then we hold justification another sign of its manifestation, until they come into the glory in which the fulfillment of that election lies."[50]

In one of the few explicit references to Thomas Aquinas, Calvin took issue with him over a "subtlety."[51] Thomas claimed that there is a sense in which God predestines glory on account of merits, namely if these merits are themselves seen as the fruit of divine grace. Calvin called this an "absurd affection," a distraction from the main point, which is that in election we are to "contemplate nothing but [the Lord's] goodness." In any case the basic fact is a person's election to life. Predestination arises from election. Election to glory is the cause of predestination to

---

47. Calvin, *Institutes* 3:21.7.
48. Ibid. 3:24.5.
49. Ibid. 3:21.7.
50. Ibid. 3:21.7.
51. Ibid. 3:22.9.

grace, an order that we would be foolish in any way to qualify, as (in Calvin's view) this quibble of Thomas's was inclined to.[52]

Calvin always acknowledged a dark side to predestination, reprobation. In electing some, God "passes over" others. As with Augustine, this passing over is not inferred from the fact of predestination; Calvin believed it is clearly taught in Scripture in its own right. The God who reprobates is not the fictional God of "absolute might," for "the will of God is not only free of all fault but is the highest rule of perfection, and even the law of all laws."[53] Though the "passing over" is due only to God's will, nevertheless the ground of condemnation of those passed over lies in their own guilt. "Their perdition depends upon the predestination of God in such a way that the cause and occasion of it are found in themselves."[54] Why are those who are elected favored over those who are reprobated? "He who here seeks a deeper cause than God's secret and inscrutable plan will torment himself to no purpose."[55]

Predestination and Scripture

The Christian church has confessed belief in divine predestination in the sense discussed not because it seemed like a good idea or because it could be proved by reason or because believing it would make life easier, but because it was found to be an integral and important feature of God's divine revelation of the gospel of God's grace in Christ.

Scripture teaches that the salvation has its source in eternal election. Predestination is not simply a logical corollary drawn by certain theologians from some other idea—say, the idea of grace—but is explicitly taught in its own right. Its origin is found

---

52. It may be thought that Calvin was himself quibbling at this point since Aquinas said (for example) that "we may say that God pre-ordains that he will give glory because of merit, and also pre-ordains that he will give grace to a person in order to merit glory," nevertheless, when we consider predestination "in its whole sweep . . . the effect of predestination in its completeness cannot have any cause on our part" in *Summa Theologiae* Ia.23.5 Reply (172). But Calvin was appalled by any reference to "merit," however circumscribed.

53. Calvin, *Institutes* 3:3.2.

54. Ibid. 3:23.8.

55. Ibid. 3:24.12.

in Israel's own election by an all-powerful, gracious God who disposes all things, including good and evil human agency, according to his purpose. As we have noted, however, the tradition concentrates on two texts in Paul, Romans 8–9 and Ephesians 1. Let us first consider these.

Predestination is personal and purposive, the destining of individual men and women to grace and glory through Jesus Christ. It is *pre* because this destining was divinely intended and fixed—"purposed in Himself" (Eph 1:9 NKJV)—"before the foundation of the world" (Eph 1:4 NKJV). Believers are predestined in Christ to the full enjoyment of the salvation he has obtained, through the application of the benefits of that work to them by the Spirit ("to the adoption as sons," Rom 8:23). It is a fully Trinitarian destining, motivated by grace and love, and not, as it is sometimes portrayed, the whimsical act of an arbitrary despot. This predestination according to God's electing purpose of those whom he foreknew issues in the so-called golden chain of Romans 8, where Paul argued that whom God foreknew he predestined to become conformed to the image of his Son: "And those He predestined, He also called; and those He called, He also justified; and those He justified, He also glorified" (v. 30). This led Paul to exclaim, "If God is for us, who is against us?"—predestination to the end, but also of all the means that are necessary to accomplish that end, the chief of which is Jesus' death by crucifixion. Thus it is part of the apostolic witness that Christ's death at the hands of wicked men was accomplished by "God's determined plan and foreknowledge" (Acts 2:23 HCSB; cp. 4:28).

As Paul makes clear, in predestining both the end and the means, the Lord predestines the elect to adoption and to holiness, the renewal of Christ's image in them. Election in Christ and all that this entails is both necessary and sufficient for attaining such states or goals. God's grace expressed in election and predestination must therefore be sufficiently powerful or efficacious to ensure these ends. So election provides not merely necessary causal conditions, for necessary conditions do not guarantee that anything comes to pass. God's grace provides necessary and sufficient causal conditions not only effectively to call the person in question out of spiritual death but also never subsequently to allow him to be separated from God's love (Rom 8:39). In the New Testament this is expressed as efficacious "calling" (1 Cor 1:26–28). It is irresistible and will overcome any opposition on the part of those who are predestined to enjoy the benefits of the golden chain. This irresistibility is to be understood chiefly in logical rather than psychological terms although it may have a psychological aspect. It is not that those whom God efficaciously calls never resist the workings of grace, never feel constrained, or never put up a fight. Rather, God's grace ensures that their minds will be renewed. (Of course, Scripture teaches that not all who are outwardly called, through preaching and testimony of various other kinds, are inwardly and effectively called in this sense.)

On these issues, Paul does not stand alone. In the sixth chapter of John's Gospel, after feeding the 5,000 and proclaiming himself to be the bread of life (John 6:35), Jesus probed the motives of those who were following him, noting that there were those who had seen him and yet had not believed (v. 36). He stated, "Everyone the Father gives Me will come to Me, and the one who comes to Me I will never cast out" (v. 37). He confessed the unity of his will with the Father's, and finally announced, "This is the will of Him who sent Me: that I should lose none of those He has given Me but should raise them up on the last day. For this is the will of My Father: that everyone who sees the Son and believes in Him may have eternal life, and I will raise him up on the last day" (vv. 39–40 HCSB). The certainty and assurance of Jesus' statements—that all those the Father gives him *will* come to him, that He *should* lose none of those, and that he *will* raise them up on the last day—indicates sovereignty over the minds and circumstances of particular men and women.

Then there follow claims that are fundamentally important concerning the efficacy of divine grace, the efficacy of the call. At first it may seem that what Jesus went on to teach is that the divine "drawing" (v. 44) is only a necessary condition of a person's coming to Christ. "No one can come . . . unless the Father who sent me draws him" (v. 44 HCSB, see also v. 65). But there is more: "Everyone who has heard and learned from the Father"—

learned in the "drawing" of them, presumably—"comes to me." The certainty is based on the Father's activities—making known, drawing, and teaching—activities that are causally sufficient for a person's coming to Christ. They ensure that the person comes. Many are (outwardly) called; few are chosen. So not only Paul but John as well teaches the efficacy of the divine calling.[56] This language recurs throughout the New Testament. At one point in his narrative of the apostolic preaching in Acts, Luke noted, almost laconically, "As many as were appointed to eternal life believed" (Acts 13:48), and that Lydia received Paul's teaching because the Lord opened her heart (Acts 16:14).

Predestination bespeaks the eternal knowledge, power, goodness, and pervasive control of God, as well as his right to discriminate, efficaciously calling some and leaving others. What kind of God can be a predestinating God? In writing of God's preservation of his people in his grace, Paul stated that God causes all things to work together for their good, relating these things to one another so that they ensure rather than thwart his purpose for his people. This implies control over all contingencies that do or could affect the divine purpose, including the plans and actions of people hostile to or indifferent to it, as in the case of Christ's crucifixion. The Lord works these contingencies together, freely giving us all things (Rom 8:32–39). Even if we were to imagine that all these powers were *not* under God's direct control, Paul stated that God's power and wisdom and goodness and love are such that they are able to ensure that these things nevertheless do not separate believers from God's love. But of course they *are* under the direct control of God, for they are each creaturely powers, created things, upheld and bounded by the Creator. After having set out the scope of the gifts with which the believers have been blessed "with every spiritual blessing in the heavens, in Christ" (Eph 1:3 HCSB), Paul stated in Ephesians 1 that these blessings are "predestined according to the purpose of the One who works out everything in agreement with the decision of His will" (v. 11 HCSB), a sovereign Lord in full control of everything

---

56. For more on the sovereignty of God in John's Gospel see the helpful treatment by D. A. Carson, *Divine Sovereignty and Human Responsibility* (Grand Rapids: Baker, 1994).

that happens in the cosmos that he has created and sustains, and who has subjected all things to Jesus Christ (v. 22). This account of predestination thus entails what is sometimes called a meticulous or "no risk" view of providence.

But what about God's foreknowledge? Is what God foreknows the ground of predestination? Does not the customary juxtaposition of foreknowledge, predestination, and election (see Acts 2:23; 4:28; Rom 8:28; 1 Pet 1:1–2) point to this? We need to distinguish between what William Hasker has called "simple foreknowledge" and "the traditional view." "Simple foreknowledge" is the "foreknowledge that embraces all *actual* free choices, including those that are yet to be made."[57] On such a view God knows by being informed from the occurrence or potential occurrence of all events, knowing the actual future event like a human spectator. By contrast Paul affirms that the source of predestination lies in God's foreknowing what he himself wills, as in Rom 11:2: "God has not rejected His people whom He foreknew." Such foreknowledge is the source of predestination and perseverance, informing and guiding both.

So in the biblical view predestination is not based on what God foreknows that others shall choose to do but on his knowing what he himself purposes. Yet alongside the spine of the church's teaching on predestination there have been those who have claimed that predestination is based on God's foreknowledge of what use people will make of his grace, or (in more evangelical versions of the objection) on his foreknowledge of their faith in Christ. They no doubt want to pay some respect to the idea of predestination as it is to be met in the pages of the New Testament, but they also want to give prominence to the idea of human autonomy. Foreknowing these decisions, whether they are meritorious or not, God then predestines them. But how can this be when Paul states that the purpose of predestination is to recreate in the image of Christ those who otherwise are dead in trespasses and in sins? As Augustine argued, this is Paul's precise point in his account of the different destinies of Jacob and Esau

---

57. William Hasker, *God, Freedom and Knowledge* (Ithaca, NY: Cornell University Press, 1989), 55. Emphasis in original.

in Romans 9. In the womb each had done neither good nor evil, and so in order that God's purpose might stand, not of works, but of him who (effectively) calls (v. 11), the elder was destined to serve the younger. As Calvin succinctly put it, "If he chose us that we should be holy, he did not choose us because he foresaw that we would be so."[58]

What view of human agency does this Pauline and Johannine view of predestination imply? Here opinions differ. Some, perhaps the majority of those who accept this view, have seen compatibilism to be more consistent with predestination, harmonizing both with the idea of an all-encompassing divine decree and with the efficacious work of God's grace in regeneration and sanctification. Others, perhaps the minority, who may have not only the biblical teaching of predestination in mind but also the entrance of evil in a world made good by God, have been libertarians. Hence the long history of discussion as to whether divine foreknowledge and human freedom are compatible. What is important for our purposes is not to attempt to arbitrate in that debate here since it involves an issue in anthropology rather than in the doctrine of God, but to note that this difference of opinion reflects the fact that the Bible does not teach a doctrine of human agency that clearly falls either into the libertarian or into the determinist family in the way that it clearly teaches the doctrine of predestination. So Christians are free to adopt, as their opinion, either compatibilism or libertarianism about human agency in a way that they are not free to deny Paul's teaching on predestination.[59]

Alongside the biblical teaching that God is pervasively sovereign are abundant biblical references to a more anthropomorphic view of God who "comes down," learns, and "repents." What are we to make of such language? Is the Bible at odds with itself,

---

58. Calvin, *Institutes* 3:22.3.
59. Among Calvinists who have favored indeterminism are J. L. Girardeau, *The Will in Its Theological Relations* (Columbia, SC, 1891), and William Cunningham, "Calvinism, and the Doctrine of Philosophical Necessity," in The *Reformers and the Theology of the Reformation* (1862, reprinted London: Banner of Truth Trust, 1967). For a strong doctrine of divine sovereignty coupled with the affirmation of libertarianism, see Hugh McCann, "Divine Sovereignty and the Freedom of the Will," *Faith and Philosophy* (1995), and "The Author of Sin?" *Faith and Philosophy* (2005).

on the one hand teaching eternal election and predestination, on the other portraying a God who changes His mind?

We should note three points. First, a strong doctrine of divine sovereignty undergirds the biblical narratives in which such language occurs. Examples are the patriarchal narratives in Genesis. Second, the "real time" impact of what God says to Abraham, Jonah, Hezekiah, and others tests them to elicit their faith and increase their self-knowledge. This means that what God has decreed for them can only be revealed little by little. Third, words such as those of God to Hezekiah, which from a grammatical point of view seem to be unconditional predictions, are better understood as implicitly conditional divine speech-acts that warn rather than predict.[60]

The Other Perspectives

Having set out a historical overview of the spine of Christian belief about predestination, along with its scriptural basis, we shall now look at the various "deviant" positions, how they understand predestination, and what doctrine of God each of these deviations implies.

Open Theism

In keeping with our emphasis on predestination as a test case for a doctrine of God, we shall confine our attention to John Sanders's treatment of divine sovereignty in chapter 7 of his book *The God Who Risks: A Theology of Providence*[61] and then examine his interpretation of the key texts in Romans 8–9 and Ephesians 1.

The sharp difference of approach when compared to that of the tradition is at once apparent. Sanders stresses that he is not interested in a "preconceived" notion of God[62] but in one that

---

60. I have discussed these points at greater length in "God in Dialogue," in *Interpreting the Bible: Historical and Theological Studies in Honour of David F. Wright*, ed. A. N. S. Lane (Leicester: Apollos, 1997), and in connection with John Calvin, in *John Calvin's Ideas* (Oxford: Oxford University Press, 2004), chap. 7.

61. John Sanders, *The God Who Risks: A Theology of Providence* (Downers Grove: InterVarsity, 1999).

62. Sanders, *God Who Risks*, 208.

corresponds to the types of relations that God has freely chosen to establish. He thinks God wants mutual fellowship and so had to create a world that involves reciprocal relations between personal agents, that is, between all personal agents, including God Himself. While the relation between God and ourselves is personal and reciprocal, it is not equal because God does much more than we do in establishing and maintaining the relationship. Nonetheless, Sanders asserted, "I suggest that God has sovereignly established the rules of the game for personal relations of fellowship, not manipulative or contractual relations."[63] Libertarian freedom is "a necessary condition for a loving relationship."[64] Sanders's reasons for adopting this reciprocal view are that it alone does justice to certain portrayals of God in Scripture, of God as being grieved, changing His mind, resorting to alternative plans, being open and responsive to what men and women freely do, and so on. He denies what he calls God's "specific sovereignty," that "God always gets precisely what he desires in each and every situation."[65] But as we shall see, it is Sanders's view that is "preconceived," driven by a nonnegotiable affirmation of libertarian freedom. It is a paradox of this view that although God wishes to establish personal relations with men and women, he cannot unless these creatures "admit" him. If creatures alone can open and close the door, they, not God, have sovereignty. Election therefore remains an abstraction, an unfulfillable possibility—no one is ever elected.

A fallacy lurks in Sanders's language at this point. To say that the traditional view of divine sovereignty is that God always gets precisely what he desires in each and every situation is extremely misleading. As seen in our discussion of the A team, Calvin, and Scripture, what God wills is the total order of things, but this does not imply that he desires, in exactly the same sense, each separately identifiable part of that order. That would be like sup-

---

63. Ibid., 211.
64. Ibid., 223.
65. Ibid., 213.

posing that each thread of my tartan tie must be tartan, or that each daub of a beautiful painting must itself be beautiful.[66]

Sanders's own proposal is that God exercises "general sovereignty,"[67] establishing certain structures—an overall framework—within which he and his human creatures freely interact. "God desires a relationship of love with his creation and so elects to grant it the freedom to enter into a give-and-take relationship with himself,"[68] which is a relationship of risk for God, for he might not get what he wants. Within this framework of macromanagement, God also, from time to time, micromanages and thus brings about specific events such as the exodus of Israel and the incarnation of the Son. But otherwise we live in a world in which there is pointless evil, in which much happens that is not a part of God's plan.[69]

As noted, central to Sanders's conception of such general sovereignty is a libertarian or indeterminist account of human freedom.[70] His model requires it; it is indispensable to his system. He put the point strongly. "Libertarian freedom is understood as the infrastructure of covenantal love. It is a necessary condition for a loving relationship, since love cannot be forced: material freedom presupposes libertarian freedom."[71] According to this view, it is within an agent's power with respect to any given free action either to perform the action or to refrain from it. He says that if we are to take the language of Scripture seriously, then another view of human freedom (than compatibilism) must be affirmed.[72] But as we have noted, Scripture does not affirm this view of freedom any more than it affirms compatibilism. Nevertheless, it is clear that Sanders's development of a model of divine human

---

66. For more on this, see Paul Helm, "All Things Considered: Providence and Divine Purpose," in *Comparative Theology: Essays for Keith Ward,* ed. T. W. Bartel (London: S.P.C.K., 2003).

67. Sanders, *God Who Risks,* 213.

68. Ibid., 213.

69. Ibid., 214.

70. Ibid., 44; see also 12.

71. Ibid., 223.

72. Ibid., 221. He concedes that "the Bible does not speak in the precise philosophical language of compatibilism or libertarianism" (223). Nevertheless, he holds that libertarianism must be affirmed if we are to make sense of Scripture.

relations in terms of reciprocal personal relations is controlled or governed by a philosophical doctrine.

As a consequence of his commitment to libertarianism, Sanders avows that God cannot know all of the future, despite the many biblical statements to the contrary. For example, Isaiah 42:9 tells us, "New things I declare; before they spring forth I tell you of them" (NKJV). Isaiah 44:7 affirms, "Who is like Me? . . . Let him proclaim and declare it; . . . and the events that are going to take place" (NASB). In Isaiah 46:10 God states that He is "declaring the end from the beginning, and from ancient times things that are not yet done, saying, 'My counsel shall stand, and I will do all My pleasure'" (NKJV). Sanders claims that sometimes, such as when human beings still have a choice to make, there is no definite future for God to know. Once again, the plain assertions of Scripture are being modified or reinterpreted, this time in terms of a philosophical doctrine about time that Sanders calls "presentism."[73] According to presentism only the present moment is real, and so God knows the past and the present but there is no exhaustively definite future for God to know.[74] Instead, God attempts to "know the future" by knowing the past and the present and by trying to forecast the future from his knowledge of the present situation.[75]

If God exercises only the kind of general sovereignty that Sanders indicates, then there appears to be some question whether, given that God has certain "overarching purposes,"[76] they will be fulfilled. Despite his claim that God can "micromanage," since he cannot do this too often and leave us free, why can't his will be continually thwarted? Even if God is omnicompetent and resourceful,[77] replacing plans which fail with other plans, there is no guarantee that these other plans will succeed.[78] Must his improvisations in the face of human freedom enjoy greater

---

73. Ibid., 129.
74. Ibid., 305, n. 121.
75. Ibid., 73–75; see also 125–32.
76. Ibid., 234.
77. Ibid., 234.
78. Ibid., 235.

success than his original plans?[79] Perhaps the answer is yes, if those objectives are sufficiently vague. God brings the Gentiles into the people of faith,[80] but he cannot bring any particular Gentile into the faith, and he cannot guarantee that any Gentile at all will be among the people of faith. God's purposes have an "ultimate direction."[81]

In several places Sanders borrowed the language of the tradition to which he is not entitled, given his views about human freedom and God's providence. Thus to say that "Christ has brought about our redemption, changing lives and societies"[82] is to use the language of efficacious grace but to use it in a setting which in fact denies the possibility of such unilateral redemption. His claims that God fulfills his promises of redemption also come from the tradition that he repudiates.[83] Similarly, in stating that we may have faith in God's promises, it is not at all clear what such faith is grounded in.[84] As he said, in words that are more consistent with his overall position, "God is working within the rules of the game he established to overturn the results of sin, and so it is quite possible that God may not get everything he wants."[85]

Sanders offers little or nothing by way of a positive interpretation of divine predestination or divine foreknowledge, even when this is understood as limited to God's knowledge of a future much of which is outside his control. The nearest he comes to an interpretation is an excursus on predictions and foreknowledge as part of his discussion of the New Testament data.[86] According to Sanders, divine foreknowledge has to do exclusively with the

---

79. Sanders says that "in Genesis 3 the totally unexpected happens" (*God Who Risks*, 46). The Lord expected the humans he created to trust him and to believe that he had their best interests in mind (45), yet with their "rejection of the divine wisdom, the implausible . . . occurred" (47). There was no good reason for Adam and Eve to reject God's blessing and provision (47), and yet they did. He also believes that "the Bible does not attribute some mistakes to God" if we say that "God would be mistaken if he believed that X would happen . . . and, in fact, X does not come about" (132).

80. Ibid., 232.

81. Ibid., 233.

82. Ibid., 234.

83. Ibid., 125–29.

84. Ibid., 235.

85. Ibid., 230.

86. Ibid., 129; see also 137.

incarnation and with the electing of a people of God, not with exhaustive foreknowledge of future contingencies. "When God is said to have foreknowledge, the object of the divine knowledge is either Jesus Christ or the people of God (as a group)."[87] But given the tenets of open theism even to claim this much seems unwarranted.

How does Sanders handle those passages in which divine election and predestination and election are affirmed, Romans 8–9 and Ephesians 1, for example? He nowhere considers the full sweep of the "golden chain" of Romans 8. For him, Romans 8:28 means not that God works all things together for the good of his people but that he is working good in all things, and the outcome is not guaranteed.[88] But then what becomes of Paul's argument that the people God predestines to be conformed to the image of Christ he also calls, justifies, and glorifies? In Sanders's view, when Paul says that God chose us in Christ beforehand (Eph 1:4), this can only refer to "corporate election." Sanders explains, "According to corporate election it is the group—the body of Christ—that is foreordained from the foundation of the world . . . for salvation," not specific individuals elected by God.[89] But he misses the point that the Ephesian believers were chosen in Christ, not that they chose Christ in an indeterministically free fashion and so became members of an elect body whose members could, if choices had gone the other way, have had more or fewer or different members, or no members at all. How on Sanders's view can God guarantee the salvation of anyone?

Sanders interprets Romans 9–11 as referring solely to God's historical covenant, and so as having a purely historical, temporal reference. As part of the covenant, "God freely chose Isaac and Jacob rather than Ishmael and Esau to be the people through whom he would fulfill his promised redemption."[90] But then the manner of that election (something that Sanders does not dwell on) is clearly indicated by Paul (at least in the case of Jacob and Esau). It was a choice that Jacob did not have to ratify by freely

---

87. Ibid., 130.
88. Ibid., 127; see also 263.
89. Ibid., 102.
90. Ibid., 121.

reciprocating, but a unilateral election of him rather than of his twin brother. And according to Paul the choice was made "that the purpose of God according to election might stand, not of works but of Him who calls" (Rom 9:11 NKJV). Even if we suppose that the passage is restricted in scope in the way Sanders claims, it teaches unilateral election (and reprobation) and that God's gracious election extends to the individuals to whom Paul was writing, vessels of mercy prepared beforehand for glory (Rom 9:29). Sanders's relational God limits himself, or is limited, in the interests of preserving libertarian freedom. He is not "God the Father almighty."

Arminianism

In contrast with open theism, Arminianism attempts to formulate doctrines of divine foreknowledge and predestination. For both the tradition and Arminianism, the number of the elect is unalterably fixed. Yet, as we shall see, the Arminian account of divine foreknowledge is fundamentally different from that of the tradition. God elects those whom he foreknows will, of their own free will, come to Christ. God may provide varying degrees of assistance, depending on the variety of Arminianism in question, but not even the strongest degree of such assistance infringes upon the will's freedom to choose Christ or (at the same moment) freely reject him.

In attempting such formulations of the compatibility of divine foreknowledge and human libertarian freedom, many Arminians currently employ the doctrine of middle knowledge, a tactic which, as we have noted, goes back to Arminius himself. We shall briefly consider such a version of Arminianism in what follows, although it is unnecessary for us to enter the debate about the intelligibility or plausibility of the idea of middle knowledge itself. We shall simply consider the sort of doctrine of grace and predestination that Molinism delivers.[91]

Middle knowledge is the view that besides the knowledge God has of all possibilities—known as his natural knowledge—and

---

91. In the remainder of this section, I shall refer to William Lane Craig, "Middle Knowledge: A Calvinist-Arminian Rapprochement?" in *The Grace of God, the Will of Man*, ed. Clark H. Pinnock (Grand Rapids: Zondervan, 1989).

the knowledge he has of what he freely wills or decrees—known as his free knowledge—God also has knowledge of what possible human creatures, possessed of libertarian freedom, would freely do if placed in various circumstances. Guided by this knowledge, God wills that particular world order which overall suits his purposes. What attracts many to middle knowledge is that it promises a scheme which will preserve both libertarian free will and "perfect providence."

A central feature of middle knowledge is that God deals in "world orders"—or sets of possible worlds.[92] The various possible worlds that God knows by his middle knowledge are not created or willed by him. His knowledge of that possible world which he creates depends on what the free creatures in that world would do were that world to be the actual world. God selects the world which best realizes the ideals that he wants exemplified.[93] This has significant theological implications.

For one thing it reverses the order of explanation of human actions. In the tradition God's decreeing of human actions is sufficient for the occurrence of those actions logically prior to the disclosure of his revealed will, the contents of which and the reaction to which serve to fulfill his decree. Everything is ultimately explained by reference to the divine decree. For Molina, on the other hand, human actions are not explicable in terms of God's prior decree, but his prior decree is explicable in terms of the possible *free* actions, creaturely and divine, which God knows by his middle knowledge, some of which he then creates.

Divine foreknowledge operates in a similar way. Given middle knowledge, divine foreknowledge cannot be God's only knowledge of what he then decrees. Rather, it includes knowledge of

---

92. Ibid., 152.

93. The language of "actualizing" states of affairs, which Craig employs, (e.g., 144) has entered the literature through the work of Alvin Plantinga, *God, Freedom and Evil* (London: George Allen and Unwin, 1975), 39, and *The Nature of Necessity* (Oxford: Clarendon Press, 1974), 169. He prefers it to "create" because "create a state of affairs" is ambiguous as between the creation of the abstraction (such as "the state of affairs of the earth having a moon") which, because it is logically necessary, is not creatable, and creation of what the abstraction denotes, the earth and its moon. Nevertheless, for God to actualize that state of affairs is for him to create the earth and its moon, or (in other biblical language) to decree it (Ps 148:6; Prov 8:29; Jer 5:22; KJV). I shall use the biblical language of "create" for the remainder of this discussion.

what he cannot decree, the exact outcomes of his creatures' free actions. Selecting one of these possible outcomes, God brings it to pass and as a consequence foreknows it. In middle knowledge, the idea of God's two wills is also reversed. God's *absolute will*, which is that no creature should sin,[94] is subordinated to the world order that God chooses to create, a world whose choice is partly (as we noted) determined in the light of God's middle knowledge of the free creaturely choices that will be made in that world in reaction to his *revealed will*. Yet in the tradition God's decreeing of human actions is logically prior to the disclosure of his revealed will to His creatures.

Despite all this the Molinist may appear to endorse the tradition. For example, Molina upheld a doctrine of particular providence. But in what sense? God is concerned with the particular because of the respect he has for the particular choices of libertarian freedom[95] and because he knows by his middle knowledge how they fit into the overall scheme of things, the rest of that particular world order.[96] Yet in the tradition predestination is the destining of a fixed number of people, those chosen by God, to eternal salvation. For the Molinist the predestination of individuals is based on God's foreknowledge of what, if they were created, they would freely do; and his decision to create them is based on whether predestining those individuals (i.e., creating that world in which they freely choose for Christ and so are predestined) is part of that possible world that he chooses to create. "The act of predestination is simply God's instantiating one of the world orders known to him via his middle knowledge."[97] However, the fact that Scripture contains statements of God's knowledge of what would have happened if things had been different (examples are 1 Sam 23:8–14 and Matt 11:21–24) does not establish middle knowledge. It only underscores the fact that God could have decreed what he has not in fact decreed.

The gap between the tradition and Arminianism may appear to close further because according to Molinism predestination is

---

94. Craig, "Middle Knowledge," 152.
95. Ibid., 153. See also 154–55.
96. Ibid., 155.
97. Ibid., 156.

gratuitous in that it is not based on foreseen merit. This is because the choice of those predestined is subordinated to that particular "world order" that God determines. So their being predestined (and not others) is simply a logical consequence for certain individuals of God's choice of world order x (a world which, as it happens, includes them and the good use they'll freely make of God's grace) rather than world order y (a world in which they make a bad use of grace).[98] "Given God's immutable determination to create a certain order, those who God knew would respond to his grace are predestined to be saved."[99] That is, their predestination to salvation is logically subordinate to that world being created.

By contrast we have noted that the tradition upholds the New Testament teaching that personal election, based on God's knowledge of his own will, is fundamental to an understanding of predestination. Predestination is fundamentally concerned with the destining of certain individuals to eternal salvation, those chosen in Christ before the foundation of the world, just those individuals (no more and no less) eternally chosen for that end. But clear New Testament statements regarding predestination, when they are "Molinised," fall within a framework of divine middle knowledge about which these New Testament texts say or imply nothing. Rather, the New Testament argues that the world order decreed by God is for the glory of God and for the ultimate benefit of the predestined: "All things are yours" (1 Cor 3:21–23 HCSB). "All this is because of you" (2 Cor 4:15 HCSB). "All things work together for the good" (Rom 8:28 HCSB). As noted earlier, Thomas Aquinas echoed this New

---

98. Ibid., 158.
99. Ibid. "Molina rejects as Calvinistic and heretical the view of Bañez (Dominigo Bañez ,1527–1604, a Thomistic opponent) that God gratuitously chooses certain persons to be saved and others to be damned and then premoves each elect person's will to produce saving faith while leaving the nonelect in sin, so that the elect are subjects of predestination while the nonelect are subjects of reprobation. At the same time, Molina rejects as Pelagian the view of Lessius (Leonhard Lessius, 1554–1623, a fellow Jesuit) that predestination consists in God's creating certain persons because he knew that they would freely make good use of the grace God would give them and so be saved. Rather, Molina held that God's choosing to create certain persons has nothing to do with how they would respond to his grace; he simply chose to create the world order he wanted to, and no rationale for this choice is to be sought other than the divine will itself. In this sense, predestination is for Molina wholly gratuitous, the result of the divine will, and in no way based on the merits or demerits of creatures" (156).

Testament emphasis. So according to Scripture and tradition, God's reason for choosing that world order is chiefly that just these, and no others, are predestined. There are many possible worlds in which others are chosen and predestined than those who in fact, in the actual world, are chosen. None of these worlds is created.

But according to Craig, God's ultimate ends do not include the salvation of the elect.[100] Craig offers this opinion about Molina's attempt to reconcile divine sovereignty and human freedom:

> He [God] directly causes certain circumstances to come into being and others indirectly by causally determined secondary causes. Free creatures, however, he allows to act as he knew they would when placed in such circumstances, and he concurs with their decisions in producing in being the effects they desire. Some of these effects God desires unconditionally and so wills positively that they occur, but others he does not unconditionally desire, but nevertheless permits them because of his overriding desire to allow creaturely freedom and knowing that even these sinful acts will fit into the overall scheme of things so that God's ultimate ends in human history will be accomplished.[101]

On middle knowledge there cannot be a personal election that is wholly of grace. For according to Molinism the efficacy of grace is not to be found in the inefficacious divine call itself, which issues from the decree of election, but in what men and women will freely do with the divine call that they receive, and how this fits into the overall best world order.[102]

---

100. For evidence for this, see the previous footnote.

101. Ibid., 154–55.

102. "Obviously, then, for Molina grace is not intrinsically efficacious, but only extrinsically efficacious; that is to say, the difference between sufficient grace and efficacious grace lies not in the quality or magnitude of the grace itself, but in the response of the human will to that grace. Sufficient grace for salvation is accorded to all people; for those who assent to its operation this same grace is efficacious in procuring their justification. God desires and has given grace sufficient that all people should be saved. If some believe and others do not, it is not because some received prevenient grace and calling while others did not. Rather, the efficacy of God's grace in our lives is up to us, and

So much for mainline Molinism. Craig believes that Congruism, a variant of Molinism, provides the source of a possible rapprochement between Calvinism and Arminianism.[103] According to Congruism grace consists of sets of divine gifts and aids imparted to certain people and not to others, ordered in such a way that they will in fact be efficacious in eliciting the response desired by God, not by renewing the will but by being perfectly suited to the creature and his or her circumstances. "No grace is intrinsically efficacious; but congruent grace is always in fact efficacious because it is so perfectly suited to the creature's temperament, circumstances, desires, and so forth, as to win his free and affirmative response."[104] But as Craig notes, such grace remains inefficacious; it is "extrinsic grace," for its efficacy ultimately depends on the qualities and powers of the recipient. What is at issue here is not coercion, as Craig believes,[105] but whether grace is efficaciously powerful, not needing the consent of the libertarian free will to make it so. For a Molinist theologian such as Francisco Suarez (1548–1617), who favored Congruism, grace is extrinsically efficacious in the sense that grace is given to those whom God chooses and who by their libertarian free will make it effective, and (as with Molinism proper) its effectiveness depends on the good or other use to which the person freely chooses to put the grace which he has received. "The efficacy of the grace is not to be found in the call itself, but in its coming from a God who possesses infallible middle knowledge,"[106] i.e.,

---

every person, however unconducive his circumstances, is called and moved by God in a measure sufficient for salvation" (Ibid., 157–58).

103. Craig provides this convenient synopsis of Thomism, Congruism, and Molinism. "Thomism: (1) God decides absolutely and gratuitously to predestine S to glory. (2) God then decides to give S a series of intrinsically efficacious graces to cause his free assent to God's offer of salvation. Those not included in (1) are reprobate. Congruism: (1) God decides absolutely and gratuitously to predestine S to glory. (2) On the basis of his middle knowledge, God chooses those graces to which he knows S would freely respond, if he were given them. These graces are therefore efficacious for S. Those not included in (1) are reprobate. Molinism: (1) God decides absolutely and gratuitously to give sufficient grace to every person he creates. (2) On the basis of his middle knowledge, God knows whether S would respond if given sufficient grace. If so, then in creating S, God predestines S to glory and his grace becomes efficacious. If not, then S is not predestined, and God's grace remains merely sufficient" (161).

104. Ibid., 159.

105. Ibid.

106. Ibid., 160.

his knowledge of how men and women will freely respond to the call. Continues Craig:

> For Lutheranism/Calvinism is (with respect to the issue at hand) simply a more consistent Thomism, and Congruism gives the Thomist everything he could desire in terms of God's gratuitous and sovereign election and yet, unlike Thomism, consistently maintains human freedom. With Luther, one could affirm God's infallible foreknowledge of future contingents and, with Calvin, God's sovereign providence over the universe and yet not thereby sacrifice genuine human freedom. Middle knowledge does not entail Congruism, of course, and Arminians are not apt to go so far in affirming the gratuity of election and the efficacy of God's gracious initiatives; but the point remains that by laying a common foundation of a doctrine of middle knowledge, Calvinists and Arminians could reduce the chasm that now separates them to the small divide that serves to distinguish Molina from Suarez, and that would be a monumental and laudable achievement.[107]

What would be sacrificed is the biblical doctrine of gracious personal election that does not depend on God's foreseeing the merits or the faith of the one elected. No Augustinian could agree to such a sacrifice, whatever the conceptual and metaphysical sophistication of the machinery deployed in defending it. So it is not a question of sacrificing "genuine human freedom," as Craig avers, but of sacrificing divine, efficacious grace. It is not clear why Craig believes that Congruistic Molinism makes the divide between Arminians and Calvinists small, for the biblical and Augustinian understanding of God's grace in election and predestination is fatally compromised by it. The divide remains of vital importance—a narrow, deep chasm but one too wide to bridge. As with openness theism, so with Arminianism. Even in those versions, which come closest to the tradition, and despite the employment of the conceptuality of divine middle knowledge, in Arminianism of whatever stripe

---

107. Ibid., 161.

libertarian human freedom remains the controlling, nonnegotiable theological idea.

Modified Calvinism

In his book *God's Greater Glory*[108] Bruce Ware endorses a strong view of God's sovereignty on biblical grounds such as Ephesians 1:11. Entailed by this view is an equally strong view of predestination[109] and of divine providence, divine governing that reaches down to every detail, down as far as it is possible to go. This divine governing embraces evil as well as good, the control of the nations and of history, of good leaders and of evil, Nebuchadnezzar and Pharaoh among them. Ware said that such governing expresses "exhaustive, meticulous divine sovereignty."[110] He is, however, particularly concerned about the need to maintain the asymmetry of God's control over good and evil. God is the author of good, the Father of lights, but not—or not in the same sense—the author of evil. Initially Ware offered the idea of God's permitting evil, allowing what he could prevent—"indirect-permissive" divine agency, as he calls it[111]—as a way forward. Yet he is not content with leaving it in those bald terms because he thinks Scripture reveals more on the issue.[112] He sees it as part of the theologian's role to explain "*just how* God's permission of evil functions in the light of his eternal decree"[113] and believes that "compatibilist middle knowledge" offers such an explanation.

One initial question is why Ware is not more puzzled over his reason for asserting this asymmetry. For surely the problem behind it is more general since it is not simply a question of relating God's agency to evil but to all human agency. If God's relation to evil is puzzling, it is equally puzzling how God can be the source of the goodness of a good human action and in this sense also be the author of the goodness while it is neverthe-

---

108. Bruce A. Ware, *God's Greater Glory: The Exalted God of Scripture and the Christian Faith* (Wheaton, IL: Crossway, 2004).

109. Ibid., 68–69.

110. Ibid., 78, 98.

111. Ibid., 106.

112. Ibid., 100–1.

113. Ibid., 110, emphasis added. Compatibilist Middle Knowledge is "a tool for understanding God's control of evil" (113).

less a human action and not God's action. Quite irrespective of the question of whether Jones is to be praised for his goodness, when Jones does good by, for example, giving to the poor, it is not God who is giving to the poor. Ware touched on this, in denying that people in whom God works good are merely passive and not active on their own account, but he did not press the point.[114] But isn't this equally puzzling?

Not content with simply invoking divine willing permission of evil, Ware avows compatibilist middle knowledge, attempting to combine a compatibilist account of human action—a form of determinism that he strongly endorses—with the appeal to middle knowledge which (as we have seen) was designed by Molina and the others to secure God's perfect providential control over libertarian or indeterministic actions. The idea is this:

> God could know what the agent would choose by knowing fully the circumstances in which the agent would make his choice. That is, because in any one given set of circumstances envisioned by God, the agent in that particular setting, with exactly that particular set of factors present, would make one and only one choice—a choice that would be called for by just those circumstances in that setting—therefore, God could know with certainty [by his middle knowledge] the choice the agent would make by knowing precisely and exhaustively the setting in which the agent would make his choice.[115]

God has all such possibilities eternally in view:

> When God envisions various sets of factors within which an agent will develop a strongest inclination to do one thing or another, the strongest inclination that emerges from these factors is not caused by the factors, nor is it caused by God. Rather, in the light of the *nature of the person*, when certain factors are present, his nature will respond to those factors and seek to do what he, by nature, wants most to do.[116]

---

114. Ibid., 104–5.
115. Ibid., 113–14.
116. Ibid., 122. Emphasis in original.

Is it not possible also for God to know just what impact certain influences will have upon our decisions, so that prior to our choices and actions, God can know the precise choices and actions that we in fact will make and do ? . . . [and] adjust and regulate the influences that come into our lives, so that by controlling the influences he can regulate the choices we will make? Yet when we make those choices, since we choose and act according to our deepest desires and strongest inclinations, we act freely.[117]

This language seems to have a general scope and not to be restricted to God's relation to evil. And doesn't it strongly suggest that God is alongside us, similar to the way in which we are alongside one another in our various relationships? "While his sovereignty assures us that his plans and purposes can never be threatened, his relationality also assures us that he treats us with integrity as persons."[118] Of course, this position differs from openness theism because here God can know in advance the choices we will make, but a classical Arminian affirms this, as well. The major difference from Arminianism is that, in virtue of compatibilism, God can adjust and regulate the influences on our lives, *so ensuring* that we make certain choices. God in his transcendence is assured that his plans and purposes can never be threatened while in his immanence he is alongside us in space and time, influencing us but all the while respecting our integrity. This approach is fairly Congruistic.[119] The irony is that, in the debate with Molinism, while such as Bañez used Congruistic patterns of thought to oppose Molinism and to more closely

---

117. Ibid., 82.

118. Ibid.,147.

119. Space does not permit a discussion of Ware's views on the nature of God's immutability and his relation to space and time (*God's Greater Glory*, chap. 5). Looked at historically his view appears to be a form of Pajonism. Claude Pajon (1626–1685), a professor of theology at Saumur, France, imagined (in the words of B. B. Warfield) that men and women were brought to Christ "not by an almighty, creative action on their souls, by which they are made new creatures, functioning subsequently as such, but purely by suasive operations, adapted in his infallible wisdom to the precise state of mind and heart of those whom he has elected for salvation, and so securing from their own free action, a voluntary coming to Christ and embracing of him for salvation" (*The Plan of Salvation*, [Grand Rapids: Eerdmans, nd.], 91).

approach the tradition, Ware is using those patterns to modify the tradition.

But here's the rub: Ware's appeal to middle knowledge lands him in trouble. First, it seems extremely doubtful that there can be such a thing as compatibilist middle knowledge. As we have noted, Molinism is the view that God prevolitionally knows what A, exercising libertarian freedom, would do if placed in certain circumstances. Ware is clear that he is a compatibilist and emphatically not a libertarian:

> But not only does the Bible's teaching on the nature of human volition need to be *consistent* with its teaching on divine sovereignty, our human volition must be manifested in a manner that is *compatible* with this strong understanding of divine sovereignty. Human freedom, in a word, must be compatibilistic. That is, exhaustive and meticulous divine sovereignty must be compatible with the actual and real manner by which human freedom operates. God's control of all that occurs, including his control of human choice and action, must be compatible with the nature of human freedom, rightly understood.[120]

Yet Ware still refers to his view of a species of middle knowledge. Why does he make that mistake? Perhaps because he thinks that counterfactuality is sufficient for middle knowledge.

> If one proposes a compatibilist view of freedom, however, it seems clear that all of these [viz. instances of God's knowledge of counterfactuals] are examples from Scripture of divine counterfactual *and* middle knowledge, since these are cases of God's knowledge of what would have been that are different from what his decree established ("free knowledge", in Molina). But presumably his decree took into account what we now see as counterfactual possibilities

---

120. Ware, *God's Greater Glory*, 78. Emphases in the original. Note that Ware uses *compatible* in two different senses here, one in which an account of human freedom must be compatible with scriptural teaching about divine sovereignty and the other in which any such account must be "compatibilist" in the philosophical sense in which freedom and responsibility are compatible with determinism. As 85ff make clear, Ware endorses compatibilism in its philosophical sense.

prior to the decree, or else we cannot understand why he would decree just what has obtained instead of the counterfactual possibility. If God considered these other possible states of affairs prior to the decree, then what God possessed is middle knowledge.[121]

This is a misunderstanding. On any account of divine freedom, some possibilities are uncreated or unrealized in virtue of the divine decree to create some world. In creating *this* world, God renders *that* world counterfactual. But it does not follow from this that such counterfactuals signal the presence of standard middle knowledge, as the counterfactuals involving libertarian free acts do. Strictly speaking, there is no "Molinist version" of middle knowledge. Molinism *is* the doctrine of middle knowledge (though of course one can imagine minor variants of it), and intrinsic to middle knowledge/Molinism is the preservation of libertarian freedom. In common with Molinism Ware implies that God knows possibilities by inspecting the natures of possible persons and seeing how they would react differently in the different circumstances in which he could place them. So God first inspects a possible person, Jones, whose nature he knows in every detail, and so comes to know how that person would react in circumstances C1, how he would react in circumstances C2, and so on. And in the light of all this information, God may then create that person in the set of circumstances that overall most pleases him. But this is obviously inconsistent with the tradition (where, as we have seen, God learns nothing) and with other central claims Ware makes about divine sovereignty.

For given Ware's commitment to meticulous, exhaustive divine sovereignty, and especially given his compatibilism, both the nature of the person and his circumstances are equally decreed by God by whose decree everything comes to pass. Strictly speaking, God not only ordains Jones's situation; he also ordains Jones, his character and his particular inclinations in particular circumstances. Of course, what comes to pass is not God's volition; it is Jones's. Nevertheless God brings to pass Jones's volition, thus ensuring that in these circumstances

---

121. Ibid., 116, footnote. Emphasis in original.

Jones will do exactly as God decrees to be done. It is not (as in Molinism proper) as if God has a different kind of relation to the person on account of that person's libertarian freedom than he has to the circumstances in which that person forms his inclinations. On Ware's understanding of the character and scope of God's decree, there can be no genuine middle knowledge in the Molinist sense, only God's natural knowledge of all possibilities (as at one point Ware concedes[122]), and God's free knowledge of what he decrees. God's knowledge of Jones's choice in a given set of circumstances is a subset of his natural knowledge, and his decreeing Jones's choice in these circumstances (if he does decree it) is part of God's free knowledge. So there is no genuine middle knowledge. But, more significantly, invoking compatibilist middle knowledge makes the asymmetry between God's relation to evil and his relation to good no more understandable than it is under the Augustinian and Calvinistic idea of God's willing permission.

Ware's view is unstable because it combines two contradictory positions. On the one hand, he avows meticulous, exhaustive divine control. This clearly puts him in the traditional predestinarian camp. Yet, on the other hand, he avows middle knowledge and distinguishes between God's knowledge as it relates to persons and their natures and how it relates to their circumstances.[123] These two positions are logically incompatible, so something must give. If the distinction between God's relation to persons and their natures and his relation to human circumstances gives by Ware affirming that all of these are uniformly decreed by God, then this places him in the classic predestinarian camp. But if, by contrast, he affirms a difference in principle between God's relation to persons and his relation to their circumstances, this can only be because of the autonomous powers that Ware attributes to people, which means that God's meticulous, exhaustive divine control gives, and this places him firmly in the Molinist camp—in effect, in Arminianism.

---

122. Ibid., 100.
123. Ibid., 121.

Similarly with divine permission, which we touched on earlier—as Ware discusses permission, the difference between Ware's own view and Arminianism becomes one of degree:

> So, in the Arminian model, God's permission of evil is very *general* and *broad*. He creates a world with laws of nature and libertarianly free creatures, and he "permits" that they act as they will. . . . But in the Reformed model, God's permission of evil is *meticulous, specific, and particular*. That is, he does not permit evil in general, but he does permit each and every instance of evil that in fact occurs in human history.[124]

But in the unmodified Reformed understanding, as with Augustine, God's permission is *willing* permission. That is, God is not simply passive in permission, however specific the permission may be; He also wills what he permits. What he permits, he decrees. As Calvin put it, "It would be ridiculous for the Judge only to permit what he wills to be done, and not also to decree it and to command its execution by his ministers."[125] And Augustine, "In a wonderful and ineffable manner nothing is done without God's will, not even that which is against his will. For it would not be done if he did not permit it; yet he does not unwillingly permit it, but willingly."[126]

So Ware is at the crossroads. If "indirect-permissive" divine agency[127] entails that God does not decree and "govern" what He permits, then Ware moves into the Arminian camp. But if it entails that God does decree what He permits, then he is fullbloodedly Augustinian and Calvinistic, and compatibilist middle knowledge is idle.

---

124. Ibid., 109. Emphasis in original.
125. Calvin, *Institutes* 1:18.1.
126. Augustine, *Enchiridion on Faith, Hope and Love*, trans. J. F. Shaw (Chicago: Henry Regnery, 1961), 117.
127. Ware, *God's Greater Glory*, 106.

Philosophy and Understanding

At various points we have noted the part that philosophical theories—libertarian freedom, or middle knowledge, say—may play in developing a "perspective" on the doctrine of God, and we have also noted some of their limitations. In closing, I shall briefly expand some of these remarks into a statement about philosophy's place in the articulation of the Christian doctrine of God.

Those who have confessed the biblical doctrine of predestination as part of their adherence to the scriptural and classical Christian theological spine have all, without exception, regarded aspects of this doctrine as "mysterious" or "ineffable" or "incomprehensible." In using such expressions, they do not mean for one moment that the doctrine of predestination is logically incoherent. And obviously it isn't. Predestinarians feel the force of objections that might be raised to the doctrine, objections such as those considered by Paul in Romans 9, and these objections come to mind precisely because the doctrine is not gibberish. Those who defend it as well as those who attack it have some understanding of what they are attacking or defending. For example, they are able to distinguish the traditional doctrine of predestination from its Pelagian or Arminian deviations. We have *some* understanding of what predestination is, but we lack the sort of knowledge that would free us from all the difficulties that it presents to our minds—difficulties about fairness, or about the way in which the divine decree meshes with human freedom, or about the manner in which God's choice is grounded. These matters are at least presently beyond our full grasp, but they are not completely ungraspable.

We should expect mystery, but it is "targeted" mystery. We can identify the mystery and say why it is so. In the noble tradition of "faith seeking understanding," we should do what we can to understand the mystery insofar as we have warrant to do so in Scripture but not at the expense of what Scripture actually teaches. In a more general sense, some matters are clearly stated in Scripture. In respect of election and predestination, Paul's meaning in Romans 8 and 9 and Ephesians 1 is clear. God has elected countless men and women—not because of any foreseen merit or goodness on their part but of his own grace—and has predestined them to grace and glory through Jesus Christ. Yet much about this election is mysterious. The resurrection of the body is clearly taught, though much about that remains opaque. For example, what is the "spiritual body" of 1 Corinthians 15:44? Justification by faith alone is clearly taught, even though it goes against our natural inclination by which we suppose that justification before God must be the result of what we do. And so on.

This reminds us of an important principle of evangelical Christianity. Predestination is taught in Scripture and is therefore a fit matter for Christians to confess and profit from, but those who confess it should also be bound by the *limits* of Scripture's teaching. Christians must follow not only *all* that Scripture teaches on the matter but also *only* what it teaches. And one important matter that Scripture teaches about election and predestination—particularly on the question of who are elected and who not—is that it is highly mysterious, with roots in God's mind and will, the contents of which he has been pleased not to disclose to us. Paul noted this in the answer that he gave to the objection to God's treatment of Jacob and Esau, "Why then does He still find fault? For who can resist His will?" (Rom 9:19). Paul did not answer: "God finds fault because people wrongly use their libertarian free will." Indeed, he could hardly say this, having just stated that the matter of God's election does not depend on the man who wills or the man who runs but on God who shows mercy (v. 16). Instead, he refers the entire question to God's will, to God's sovereign right, and to the fact that sinful men and women do not have any prior claim on God's mercy. God shows mercy to whom he desires, and he hardens whom he pleases (v. 18).

Paul's doxology at the conclusion of his discussion of these matters (Rom 11:33,36 HCSB) further emphasizes this mystery. "Oh, the depth of the riches both of the wisdom and the knowledge of God! How unsearchable His judgments and untraceable His ways!. . . . For from Him and through Him and to Him are all things. To Him be the glory forever. Amen." This is not the God of "pure will" who is an arbitrary deity and a tyrant. Yet he is a God who in this matter exercises both wisdom and knowledge and mercy in a way that is unsearchable to the human mind. As a consequence, as Calvin noted, we must restrain our curiosity:

> If anyone with carefree assurance breaks into this place ["the sacred precincts of divine wisdom"], he will not succeed in satisfying his curiosity and he will enter a labyrinth from which he can find no exit. For it is not right for man unrestrainedly to search out things that the Lord has willed to be hid in himself, and to unfold from eternity itself the sublimest wisdom, which he would have us revere but not understand that through this also he should fill us with wonder.[128]

All who share Paul's theocentric standpoint come to have this sense of wonder, though it appears that such a standpoint is not one that currently is congenial.

How should we respond in this situation? Thinking generally, we can say this: that someone is definitely on the wrong track when, as a Christian, he or she seeks to develop a philosophical theory, or to offer a way of making certain biblical data consistent, or to answer some contemporary problem or redress some heartache, and in so doing makes claims that are clearly at variance with the plain teaching of Scripture. It is insufficiently Christian to ignore key texts or to "reinterpret" certain clear passages in the interests of developing a consistent system or to meet some contemporary need by a response that may have biblical elements in it but that is driven by a key idea that may be unbiblical, such as the relationship between scientific materialism and the resurrection of the body, or a matter about which the Bible is silent, such as whether human beings possess libertarian freedom.

Of course, if the alleged mystery involves manifest self-contradiction, then we should do what we can to eliminate it because no self-contradiction can be true. The tradition has

---

128. Calvin, *Institutes* 3:21.1.

achieved this, for example, in its confession that God is three in one. The church recognizes that the sense in which God is one must be different from the sense in which he is three. He is three *persons* in one divine *nature*. But what about mysteries which do not obviously involve a self-contradiction and where we have good reason to think that they do not involve one? Here I think the role of Christian theology has been to offer to the church a way of speaking that preserves the mystery.

Readers will have noticed the tendency in Bruce Ware to want to explain God's relation to evil. In explanations we seek to clear up mysteries, not to preserve them. John Sanders repeatedly asserts that an all-decreeing God inevitably "manipulates" the lives and histories of those who are subject to his decree. *Manipulate* can mean "handle skillfully," but it can also mean "handle unfairly." No Augustinian would deny that God's preservation and governing of the universe is incredibly skillful. But does God act unfairly in such activity? In particular, does he infringe or bypass or compromise human freedom? The Bible does not teach this. This fact underlines the danger of using analogies or thought experiments in an effort to understand the nature or the ways of God. The temptation is to "humanize" God, in effect to assert that "if one human person wholly decreed the life of another person this would necessarily be unfair: therefore if God works all things by the counsel of his own will this must be unfair." This reasoning is unsound because it assumes that God inevitably acts like one creature upon another creature. But he is God, *sui generis*. Therefore, the attempt to characterize the divine-human relation by using terms such as *manipulate, brainwash, hypnotize,* or *program* must all necessarily fail.

The fact that we cannot hope to *explain* how God's freedom combines with human freedom obviously produces tension. It is tempting to relieve this tension by giving such priority to God's will that it eliminates human choice or such priority to human choice that the range and manner of God's control over creation is compromised. In *De Concordia* we saw that Anselm wrote against those who so stress the depth and strength of God's grace that human choice is eliminated. John Sanders's view is one contemporary expression of the opposite tendency—a tendency to develop a theology in which the idea of indeterministic freedom (a view not found in Scripture) is so dominant that matters that are clearly found in Scripture, such as the doctrine of predestination, must be drastically modified or simply ignored. We have also seen similar tendencies clearly present in Arminianism, for Molinism, with its invocation of middle knowledge, introduces an idea about which Scripture is silent. The same tendency is (to a lesser extent) also present in Ware's modified Calvinism.

To respect the divine mysteries is peculiarly difficult for systematic theologians and Christian philosophers, for they are accustomed to follow an argument wherever it leads and to aim to maximize explanatory fit and coherence. Yet if Calvin is correct, reverence even in the face of incomprehension must be the basic Christian attitude to the revealed mysteries. [129]

---

129. Thanks to Mark Talbot who read through the penultimate draft with great attention and made numerous helpful suggestions.

CHAPTER 2

Responses to Paul Helm
"Classical Calvinist Doctrine of God"

Response by Roger E. Olson

Like Paul Helm I will begin with a confession. I am seriously put off by his claim that "there is no such thing as the 'Classical Calvinist Doctrine of God.' For this 'doctrine' is none other than the mainstream Christian doctrine of God." Oh, really? This Helmian claim reminds me of the response to a student's question by an Eastern Orthodox priest and theologian visiting my class. The student politely asked if the priest would describe his church's distinctives. The priest replied, "We don't have distinctives; you do." I wonder what the Orthodox priest would say to Helm's claim that the Calvinist doctrine of God is simply the mainstream Christian one. For that matter, what would a Roman Catholic priest or theologian say to it? And what would an Anabaptist theologian say to it? I know what a classical Arminian would say because I am one. Helm's claim is highly problematic if not simply false.

Why select this particular canon of theologians—Augustine, Anselm, Aquinas, and Calvin—and baptize them "the A team" of Christian theology? Another contemporary evangelical theologian who follows a similar line of argument for establishing sound belief is Thomas Oden, and he selects a different "team" that he clearly does not consider "the B team."[1] According to Oden, Helm's "A team" of Christian theologians is just part of the larger great tradition that includes the Eastern Greek church fathers, Arminius and Wesley. Helm's selection of these four theologians as especially authoritative or representative of the traditional Christian doctrine of God seems arbitrary. It appears designed to support his own perspective (which he audaciously denies is any perspective at all!) on the doctrine of God.

For Oden, in contrast to Helm, Arminius's theology (as represented in the Remonstrance) was simply a reappropriation of the ancient Christian consensus about God and salvation.[2] Helm said that "the Arminian account of divine foreknowledge is fundamentally different from that of the tradition." Oden said that Arminian theology is a post-Reformation recovery of the ancient tradition. Clearly then the Arminian Oden and the Calvinist Helm are at loggerheads over identifying the correct canon for determining the "spine of Christian theism" and its deviations. Anyone who knows Oden will agree that he is nothing less than passionate about Christian tradition and identifying its core beliefs. Yet, if Helm is correct, Oden's own theology is deviant because it is in the classical Arminian sense synergistic.

Helm's chapter is primarily about predestination, and in that focus it deviates from the original plan of this book. Bruce Ware and I are the only two of the four authors who were on the original team to write this book. (I won't call it the "A team," but we did know the intent of the project!) The others ultimately declined to participate and were replaced by Paul Helm and John Sanders. When this book was conceived and, so I judge, as it was described to us even in this new format with three new authors, the idea was to delineate four major Christian views of God and God's relationship with the world. Helm's chapter deviates significantly from that original plan and, as I understand it, from the plan as described to this new team. Of course, much of his doctrine of God is revealed in and through his discussion of

---

1. See Oden's three-volume *Systematic Theology* (New York: Harper & Row, 1987, 1989 and 1992). See also his *The Rebirth of Orthodoxy* (New York: HarperCollins, 2003).

2. See Oden's *The Transforming Power of Grace* (Nashville, TN: Abingdon, 1994), 152.)

predestination, but the book was not supposed to be four views of predestination. Helm's deviation from the plan makes it somewhat more difficult to respond without also deviating from the project's description.

As a classical Arminian, I am simply flabbergasted by Helm's characterization of Arminianism as a view that "affirms the power of the human will autonomously to cooperate with God's grace." He compares this with Pelagianism and Semi-Pelagianism and claims that Arminius himself "rejected the Augustinianism of the Reformation on rationalist grounds." According to Helm, furthermore, Wesley later "avowed a more evangelical form of Arminianism." All these claims are simply wrong.[3] How someone of Helm's theological knowledge and stature can claim that Arminians affirm the power of the human will autonomously to cooperate with God's grace is beyond comprehension. A close reading of Arminius and classical Arminian theology shows that Arminianism has always affirmed the absolute necessity of supernatural, prevenient grace for even the first exercise of a good will toward God. The initiative and enablement in salvation are all God's and not at all the human's. There is nothing "autonomous" or Semi-Pelagian (to say nothing of Pelagian) about this grace-enabled human will cooperating with God's grace.

Arminius was not a rationalist and did not reject Augustinianism or Calvinism on rationalist grounds. Nor was his (or any Arminian's) rejection of absolute monergism based on belief in free will as the "controlling, nonnegotiable theological idea" as Helm maintains. Rather, Arminius's and Arminians' rejection of absolute monergism and especially double predestination (to say nothing of supralapsarianism which is what Helm's soteriology amounts to) was based on *their vision of the biblical portrayal of God's character as loving and good*. (I realize that I have just admitted that my Arminian theology is "a vision of the biblical portrayal" and not the biblical revelation itself. Unlike Helm, I cannot claim that any theology is more than man-made; his and mine are both human interpretations colored by our own perspectives. I happen to think mine is closer to the truth than

---

3. I have demonstrated the errors in my book *Arminian Theology: Myths and Realities* (Downers Grove: InterVarsity, 2006).

his, but I would not dare to place it on the same plane as God's revelation itself!)

Also, as I show in my book *Arminian Theology: Myths and Realities,* there was no significant difference between Arminius's and Wesley's theologies. It is simply a myth that Wesley's theology was more "evangelical" than Arminius. They agreed on every significant point including the possibility of entire sanctification or "Christian perfection" as Wesley called it.[4]

Another problem with Helm's treatment of classical Arminian theology lies in his almost exclusive focus on its alleged use of middle knowledge. This section of Helm's chapter, which deals with Molina and William Lane Craig, leaves me scratching my head in bewilderment. Few Arminians agree that Arminius relied on middle knowledge for his account of divine sovereignty and foreknowledge. Craig is free to consider himself an Arminian, but the majority of Arminians do not accept his Molinist account of Arminianism. Contrary to what Helm seems to think, it does not incline away from Calvinism but toward it! This can be seen in Bruce Ware's chapter where he makes use of Molinism and middle knowledge to explain how God uses free will (defined compatibilistically) to control the world and everything in it. The majority of Arminian scholars reject Molinism and middle knowledge used as a strategy to reconcile God's sovereignty and human free will; they see it as ending up with the same problem as classical Calvinism—a morally ambiguous God for whom sin and evil are part of the great plan willed and rendered certain by God.

Why does Helm not deal with classical Arminian sources in his section responding to Arminianism? Is it because he is not well-read in classical Arminianism? Or is it because he wishes to devote the space to refuting Craig's claim to be able to reconcile Arminianism and Calvinism using Molinism? It's hard to tell. But fairness would dictate that there he interact with classical Arminian sources which are just as available to him as Ware's

---

4. For further exposition of classical Arminian theology (including Wesley), I point readers to my book which exposes 10 common myths and supplies the truth about classical Arminianism with copious quotations from well-accepted Arminian sources from Arminius to Oden.

writings and those of open theists such as John Sanders. The collected writings of Arminius are in print as are those of Wesley and more contemporary Arminians such as H. Orton Wiley and Thomas Oden. Choosing to discuss Molina and Craig as the representatives of classical Arminianism is a bit like choosing to discuss Molina and Bruce Ware as the representatives of classical Calvinism. (I intend no insult or injury to my friend Bruce. But he admits that his theology is modified Calvinism and that he uses Molinism/middle knowledge to modify classical Calvinism.)

I believe that Helm should simply bite the bullet, so to speak, and admit that his allegedly unreconstructed Calvinist doctrine of God makes God arbitrary and the author of sin and evil. At least from an Arminian perspective, it also makes it difficult to distinguish between God and the devil. God wants some to go to hell, and the devil wants everyone to go to hell. But the character issue remains a problem. I find it interesting that Helm never mentioned the love of God for the world. He majors in God's attributes of majesty and in God's power and control over everything. But what of God's character? The end result of his delineation of the doctrine of predestination is a morally ambiguous God. For him, "each person is born already destined to life, or to death." And there is no conceivable reason why God destines some to life and others to death. Helm can only appeal to mystery after ruling out every conceivable reason God might have for so unconditionally selecting individuals even before they are born. Surely the only option left is divine arbitrariness because, based on Helm's account, it cannot have anything to do with any decisions or choices persons make that are not rendered certain by God's all-determining decree and power. No wonder Helm doesn't mention God's love; in light of his apparently supralapsarian account of predestination, it could only be, as Wesley put it, such a love as makes the blood run cold.

I cannot help but wonder how Helm can reconcile his claim that the cause of God's "passing over" of some in reprobation lies in their own guilt in light of his strong doctrine of divine providence as all-controlling and all-determining. One must wonder where the first inclination toward evil came from. In light of

Helm's description of providence and in light of his rejection of "autonomous" free will and embrace of compatibilism, it would seem to have come from God. Otherwise, there was at least in the beginning of human history one human act (the rebellious defection from God's command) that was "autonomous." Furthermore, if God saves the elect unconditionally, as Helm more than implies, why does he not save everyone? Wouldn't a good and loving God do that? I detect more than a hint of nominalism in Helm's appeal to God's will as the "highest rule of perfection, and even the law of all laws." In what sense of the words *good* and *loving* could God be considered such while at the same time viewed as unconditionally reprobating some significant portion of humanity who never has any opportunity or ability to obey God and be saved?

Helm's double predestination (if not supralapsarianism and nominalism) creates tremendous difficulties for God's character. His God specializes in domination, control and self-glorification even through the eternal infliction of unimaginable torment on persons who were selected for hell before they were born or did anything good or bad. That they supposedly "deserve it" does nothing to get God off the hook given that his God saves unconditionally. Clearly, he could save everyone. He chooses not to. Why? To appeal to mystery right at that point is unfair. It smacks of obfuscation and evasion. God's character is at stake. Something must be said about that; the good and necessary consequence of Helm's claim of unconditional double predestination is God's morally ambiguous character unless he can say something about God's goodness and love that at least opens up an avenue of thought allowing reconciliation of God's goodness as loving-kindness with this account of his sovereignty.

Response by John Sanders

I have several concerns about Paul Helm's arguments. In relation to his appeals based on tradition and biblical consideration, I must take issue and declare that there are other equally valid views.

Regarding Tradition

Let me say that I appreciate Paul Helm's appeal to tradition because what Christians have taught in the past should be taken seriously. My problem is not with his appeal to tradition but with his use of the term "the tradition" and his identification of his own view with it. Helm presumes that his theological model is the correct view by default, and so if he can show that the other views have problems, then he has proved his case. His first argument is that his position is the correct one because it is the default position of the church. He repeats the terms "the tradition," "the traditional view," and "the spine of the church's teaching" so often that those who do not know the actual tradition of historical theology are likely to believe his claim simply by the number of times he repeats it. It may be asked just what exactly is the tradition? Has there really been a singular tradition on topics such as anthropology, sin, salvation, or ecclesiology? Did not Abelard imply a "no" answer to this question back in the twelfth century in his book *Sic et Non* (*Yes and No*) when he compiled a list of the different views on various doctrines that had been taught by significant figures in the church? Also, when Helm speaks of "the church," he completely omits the Eastern Orthodox as though they are not part of the church. Church tradition is much more diverse than Helm lets on.

Also, Helm repeatedly claims that his view is clearly the traditional view. For instance, he said that the "Classical Calvinist Doctrine of God . . . is none other than the mainstream Christian doctrine of God." This is why he thinks that his view is the "default position" and why "the Arminian account of divine foreknowledge is fundamentally different from that of the tradition." He states that "the other three contributors to this book must be regarded as deviating from the main spine of Christian theism."

Helm gives two items to support his claim. First, he says that theological determinism is what Augustine, Anselm, and Aquinas taught. Second, he says that this view was affirmed by the Council of Orange in 529. Regarding his first argument, though there are a number of experts on Aquinas who disagree that he taught theological determinism, I will not dispute the point. Furthermore, I do not contest that these three thinkers had tremendous influence on subsequent theology. Instead, I call into question Helm's comments that there were "some" who disagreed with theological determinism. He makes it sound as though virtually everyone except for a few rogue pastors and theologians were determinists. This assumption strays far from the facts of history, however, since there never has been a single doctrine of God or view of providence in the church. To speak of "the traditional" view of sovereignty as meticulous providence is to ignore the actual tradition! The understanding of providence put forth by Augustine and others has always been contested by others in the church.

Helm acknowledges that there was debate on the topic. He correctly notes that these folks argued that God used his fore-knowledge to "look ahead" and see which people would respond with faith to his initiatives of grace and then God elects them because he foresees their faith. Historically, foreseen faith was the view overwhelmingly affirmed by the church fathers prior to Augustine.[5] Helm fails to acknowledge how radical an inno-vation was Augustine's view of predestination. The Eastern church fathers did not agree and the Eastern church still thinks Augustine went over the edge on this one.[6] Also, there were many in the Medieval Western church who rejected Augustine's deter-minism; and when one considers that Anabaptists, Wesleyans, Arminians, and Pentecostals also reject theological determin-ism, Helm's claim to "the tradition" is suspect.

Given that the majority of Christians in the world today affirm what the fathers prior to Augustine believed, theological deter-minism can hardly hold claim to "the traditional view." In fact, given the incredible popularity of the simple foreknowledge posi-tion (where God elects on the basis of a foreseen faith response to his grace), I would suggest that this has been the most common

---

5. See John Sanders, *The God Who Risks: A Theology of Providence* (Downers Grove: InterVarsity, 1998), 142–47.

6. See Bishop Maximos Aghiorgoussis, "Orthodox Soteriology," and John Breck, "Divine Initiative: Salvation in Orthodox Theology," both in John Meyendorff and Robert Tobias, eds., *Salvation in Christ: A Lutheran-Orthodox Dialogue* (Minneapolis: Augsburg, 1992) and Kallistos (Timothy) Ware, *The Orthodox Church* (London: Penguin, 1987), 223–30.

view throughout the history of the church. That means that free will theism predates the innovations of Augustine and continues to be the dominant position in the church.

Helm objects to the foreseen faith view because it makes divine election dependent on the faith response of humans and, consequently, is, in his opinion, "recognizably Pelagian." For Helm, all those before Augustine and all those afterwards who affirm simple foreknowledge are Pelagian. This is an unfair characterization considering that none of them affirm what Pelagius is reputed to have actually taught. For Helm, any position but his fails to uphold divine grace. Hence he condemns all free will theism, which includes the Eastern Orthodox, many Roman Catholics, Anabaptists, Arminians, Wesleyans, and Pentecostals as "Pelagian."

Helm's second line of support for his claim that theological determinism is "the traditional view" is that it was affirmed by the Synod of Orange in 529. Several points may be made in response. First, this Synod was not an ecumenical council where all Christian parties were represented, which is one reason the Eastern Orthodox do not recognize it as valid. Second, what was approved at the Synod was a diluted form of Augustinianism.[7] What was unequivocally approved at the meeting was that divine grace precedes any human response of faith and that all who are baptized are saved. Even in the West this Synod did not settle the matter, which is why free will theism has remained a swiftflowing branch of the tradition.

Biblical Considerations

Helm's second line of argument is his claim that theological determinism is clearly taught in the Bible. In this section I will begin with a few general observations and then focus in on Helm's claim that his view is what the Bible clearly teaches. In the biblical section he cites the usual set of texts to which theological determinists appeal such as Romans 9:11 and Ephesians 1. This is just as appropriate as it is for free will theists to appeal to their favorite set of texts. Helm asks why I only address some

---

7. See Justo Gonzalez, *A History of Christian Thought* (Nashville: Abingdon, 1971), 2:59–61.

of the favorite Calvinist texts and not all of them in my book. The reason is that I see no need to reinvent the wheel. Other free will theists such as I. H. Marshall have provided thorough interpretations of such texts, and I only discussed those passages about which I thought I had something new to add. Also, in his book on providence, Helm addresses hardly any of the typical texts cited by free will theists.

Helm does not find the free will theistic explanation of his favorite texts convincing. He thinks that appeals to, for example, corporate election evade the clear meaning of Ephesians 1. But this is precisely how Arminians have felt about the Augustinian-Calvinist explanation of texts such as John 3:16 and 1 Timothy 2:4. As I say in my chapter, for these reasons I do not believe that dialogues between the Hatfields (freewill theists) and the McCoys (theological determinists) will be fruitful.

Concerning Romans 9:11, Helm and I agree that the passage is about God's unconditional election. It is solely up to God who will be classified as the people of God. We disagree, however, when it comes to the content of election. Helm follows a distinguished theological line when he thinks that Paul is talking about God's selection of individuals for salvation. This reading has been common in Protestant thought since the Reformation response to late medieval teaching about merit. Unfortunately, I do not believe that is what Paul was arguing against.

My thinking here has been shaped by what is known as the New Perspective on Paul and the Law and, in particular, by two leading New Testament scholars who represent this position: N. T. Wright and James Dunn.[8] According to this approach, Paul was not arguing about God's selecting particular individuals for heaven. Rather, Paul was continuing with the main argument of the epistle, which was a matter of great contention in the apostolic church (Acts 15): Do Gentiles have to become Jewish before they can be authentically Christian? With this historical background in mind, we can see that Paul was arguing that God has the right to decide to include Gentiles into the people of God solely on the basis of faith in Christ and not by their relationship

8. For my discussion of Wright and Dunn, see John Sanders, *The God Who Risks*, 120–24.

to "badges" which publicly identified the people of God at that time: circumcision, food laws, and observing the Sabbath. These are major issues in many of Paul's letters and a huge matter of disagreement among the early Christian community. Hence, though Romans 9:11 is about God's sovereign right to decide, it is not about whether God selects individuals for heaven. Instead, in its historical context it is about God's decision to include Gentiles into the Christian community solely by faith in Jesus.

Paul is absolutely astonished that the Holy Spirit was moving in this direction since it went counter to much of what he had been raised to believe—especially that Gentiles are obviously not part of the people of God. That is why he expresses his amazement at the end of this section of Romans concerning God's wisdom and unfathomable ways (11:33). Who would have thought God would bring salvation to the Gentiles in this fashion?

Arminians have traditionally raised some theological questions regarding the theological determinist reading of Scripture. First, they ask why God does not save all since it is no skin off his nose. After all, one would think that a God who determines all things and loves everyone could pull it off. In this chapter Helm's answer is to quote Calvin's view that it is a mystery we cannot fathom. It seems it is not really good if all are saved, and it is not really good if all have enough food to eat. In his book on providence, Helm gives an additional answer when he says, "God's own character would not be fully manifest" without evil and redemption.[9] Apparently, God cannot save all people because then God's righteousness would not be fully displayed. If God saved all, then his righteousness would not be fully manifested; and if God damned all, then his love would not be fully displayed. Needless to say, free will theists find this neither biblically faithful nor theologically attractive.

This gets us into the logical problem of evil: if God is almighty and wholly good, then how can evil exist? Free will theists (Olson and Sanders) qualify almightiness by saying that God cannot guarantee what creatures with libertarian freedom will do. Theological determinists (Helm and Ware) qualify divine

---

9. Paul Helm, *The Providence of God* (Downers Grove: InterVarsity, 1994), 214–15.

goodness: somehow God is completely good in spite of the fact that he could guarantee that all humans would be saved (which seems a good thing to do) but chooses not to do so.[10] For Helm, God exercises meticulous providence whereby God micromanages every thought, word, and deed of every human such that there is no aspect of history or current events that God intended to be different than it is. The world is exactly the way God has decreed it should be at any moment. In fact, Helm chides Ware for trying to escape from attributing evil to God's decree. Helm said that all the powers of evil *"are* under the direct control of God." He said, "God does not, then, exercise providential control in a way that leaves two or more possible ways of achieving some goal. Nor does he will the end but leave the means to others. . . . Rather, the providence of God is fine-grained; it extends to the occurrence of individual actions and to each aspect of each action."[11] Hence, though we do not understand why God wants all the rapes and murders in the world, they are part of his blueprint plan that manifests his glory.

Helm sincerely believes that this teaching is found in the Bible. In fact, he thinks it is obvious to anyone with brains enough to read. He claims that theological determinism "can be vividly seen . . . in Genesis" and is "perfectly clear" in the New Testament. Helm said that "matters that are clearly found in Scripture . . . must be drastically modified or simply ignored" by freewill theists. Repeatedly, he stated that "the plain assertions of Scripture are being modified or reinterpreted" by Arminians. He claims that we do not read Scripture properly because freewill theists believe in free will. Hence, we either willingly ignore the perfectly clear teaching of Scripture, or we drastically misread it because of our captivity to the philosophy of free will, or we are simply too stupid to read the Bible properly. I find it astounding that the church fathers prior to Augustine, the Eastern Orthodox, Anabaptists, Arminians, Wesleyans, and Pentecostals are guilty of these sins.

---

10. See Amos Yong, "Divine Omniscience and Future Contingents: Weighing the Presuppositional Issues in the Contemporary Debate," *Evangelical Review of Theology* 26, no. 3 (2002): 255–56.

11. Helm, *The Providence of God*, 104.

Helm's accusations resemble those of my freshmen students who ask why Calvin "drastically modified or simply ignored perfectly clear" texts of Scripture. I disabuse them of such notions by articulating and defending Calvin's reading of their favorite texts. They are amazed that Calvin had seriously considered them. They thought that anyone who simply read the Bible would come to the same free will theistic position since it is what the Bible "clearly" teaches. Of course, free will theists do not find the theological determinist explanations of their favorite texts convincing, but I do hope to get my students to realize that theological determinists are not ignoring the Bible. Once again, the Hatfields and the McCoys arrive at an impasse, and I see no definitive way of resolving the matter.

Helm should know that the question of what the Bible teaches about divine sovereignty has been a key point of contention since the time of Augustine. Christians have long disagreed with one another regarding biblical teaching about doctrines such as baptism and the atonement. In the past certain "clear" passages of Scripture were used to justify a geocentric solar system, deny women any relief from the pain of childbirth, sanction persecution of the Jews, and legitimize slavery of blacks. In fact, until the 1800s the majority of Christians, including well-known conservative pastors and theologians, used the "clear teaching" of the Bible to sanction slavery.[12]

The overwhelming majority of biblical scholars judge that the Bible clearly and plainly teaches that God is not timeless. Yet Helm rejects this and claims that God is timeless. Reformed philosopher Nicholas Wolterstorff takes Helm to task on this point, accusing Helm of overturning the clear teaching of Scripture.[13] Esteemed Old Testament scholars such as Terrence Fretheim and John Goldingay show that the Bible is clear that God sometimes

---

12. See Mark Noll, *America's God: From Jonathan Edwards to Abraham Lincoln* (New York: Oxford University Press, 2002), 388–89, and Kevin Giles, "The Biblical Argument for Slavery: Can the Bible Mislead? A Case Study in Hermeneutics," *Evangelical Quarterly* 66, no. 1 (Jan. 1994): 3–17.

13. Wolterstorff, "Unqualified Divine Temporality," in *God & Time: Four Views*, ed. Gregory Ganssle (Downers Grove: InterVarsity, 2001), 70–72, 188.

changes his mind.[14] Yet Helm claims that this is, in fact, not the case. Rather, God only "appears" to change his mind.[15] The more than 30 texts regarding divine change of mind which seem "perfectly clear" cannot, says Helm, mean what they say. Rather, he claims that those texts are unclear, "weak," and anthropomorphic and that those who disagree with him are "reducing God to human proportions."[16]

To be fair, I do not think Helm is simply ignoring or willingly misinterpreting the plain, clear, teaching of Scripture. Rather, he is using certain texts of Scripture to guide his reading of other texts, and he uses philosophical arguments and tradition to make a case for his view. That is exactly what I do. But it should be clear by now that those who live in a glass house of the clear teaching of Scripture should not throw stones.

Concerning the Other Views

Helm spends a considerable amount of his chapter criticizing the views of the other three authors of this book, and I would like to respond to a few of his comments. To begin, Helm criticizes the view of election known as corporate election because, he says, this is not what Ephesians 1 teaches, and it implies that no single individual is elected for salvation. In my book on providence, I made use of *The New Chosen People: A Corporate View of Election* by the New Testament scholar Ralph Klein.[17] He examines every biblical reference to election and concludes that the vast majority of texts affirm corporate election. Of course, Klein's interpretations are open to question, but whose are not? Apparently, Helm thinks his interpretations are not open to question since his are the "perfectly clear" interpretations. Helm is welcome to disagree with Klein's work but Helm does not offer any exegetical work. Instead, he simply claims that the corporate

---

14. For my discussion see Sanders, *The God Who Risks*, 66–74, and John Goldingay, *Old Testament Theology*, vol. 1 (Downers Grove: InterVarsity, 2003).

15. Helm, *The Providence of God*, 103.

16. Ibid., 50–52. For my discussion of Helm on this issue, see Sanders "On Reducing God to Human Proportions," in *Semper Reformandum*: Studies in Honour of Clark Pinnock, ed. Anthony Cross and Stanley Porter (Paternoster, U.K., and Grand Rapids: Eerdmans, 2003), 111–25.

17. Ralph Klein, *The New Chosen People* (Grand Rapids: Zondervan, 1990).

election view is wrong because it conflicts with his own view of election: unconditional election and irresistible grace.

Next Helm accused me of committing a fallacy. He wrote:

> To say that the traditional view of divine sovereignty is that God always gets precisely what he desires in each and every situation is extremely misleading. As seen in our discussion of the A team, Calvin, and Scripture, what God wills is the total order of things, but this does not imply that he desires, in exactly the same sense, each separately identifiable part of that order. That would be like supposing that each thread of my tartan tie must be tartan, or each daub of a beautiful painting must itself be beautiful.

If a fallacy is here, Helm has failed to expose it. It is correct that theological determinists believe that God does not will all things in precisely the same way. However, it is curious that Helm said, "What God wills is the total order of things." This surely cannot mean that God ordains the general plan and works out the details as he responds to what creatures do since that is the free will theist position. As quoted above, Helm said that "the providence of God is fine-grained; it extends to the occurrence of individual actions and to each aspect of each action." That is, God exercises meticulous control over every detail of creation including every thought and action of every creature. Hence, God does not desire or intend the world to be different in any respect than it is. Since, for Helm, God's will cannot be thwarted in any respect (as it can be in Arminianism), everything that occurs is specifically selected by God to occur. That is what meticulous providence means. Helm said that every daub of paint used in a beautiful painting may not be beautiful, which corresponds to every event that happens in the world may not be good; it is the overall fulfillment of God's plan that is good. However, every bit of red paint in a bucket of red paint is red so everything that happens is precisely what God wanted to happen at that moment.

Helm made three criticisms of open theism that are actually criticisms of any theology that affirms free will. For example, he said if God does not tightly control every detail in the world, then there is no guarantee that God will accomplish his plans. He said that according to open theism, God cannot guarantee that any particular individual would come to faith. This is correct, which is why free will theists speak of God's taking the risk of creating beings with libertarian freedom. However, it is clear from history that God is achieving his aims because lives and communities are being transformed. For free will theists there was no guarantee for God prior to his decision to create this sort of world. But we see after the fact that though sin was not desired by God, God has been successful at redeeming many people. Only a God who exercises meticulous providence can guarantee via irresistible grace that specific individuals will come to faith. Once again, Helm claims that because his view can do something, all other views are false.

Second, Helm said that I am not entitled to say things such as "Christ has brought about our redemption, changing lives and societies," since this entails irresistible grace. Of course, all free will theists from Eastern Orthodox to Pentecostals use this language, but Helm said we are not to use it unless we affirm unconditional election and irresistible grace. For him, any position other than his is salvation by self, not by God.[18] This is simply the age-old Calvinist claim against the Arminians, and I see little hope of the two sides finding agreement.

Third, Helm said that a God who "is limited . . . is not 'God the Father almighty.'" This statement has great rhetorical flourish but does not stand up to examination. As a philosopher, Helm is well aware that one of his A team, Thomas Aquinas, defined *omnipotence* as "the ability to do anything that is not logically contradictory." He also knows that this definition of omnipotence has become the most widely accepted one among Christian philosophers. A central claim of the classic "free will defense" to the problem of evil is that God cannot create beings with libertarian freedom and also exercise deterministic control over them so that they never commit a moral evil because that is logically contradictory. It is logically contradictory to affirm both that humans have libertarian freedom and that they do not have

---

18. Though I specifically addressed Helm on this point in Sanders, *The God Who Risks*, he did not take into account what I said there.

it. Given that at the end of his chapter Helm stated that logical contradictions are inadmissible in theology, I am confident that Helm agrees with Aquinas that God cannot do what is logically impossible. If so, then Helm's God cannot create a metaphysically perfect being. To be metaphysically perfect is to be limitless, and not even God can create a limitless being because to be created entails the limitation of having a beginning. Since even Helm's deity has limitations, it would seem, according to his own criterion, that Helm's God is not "God the Father Almighty."

It is curious that Helm spent so much time on the view of omniscience known as middle knowledge because the vast majority of free will theists throughout history have affirmed, and continue to affirm, the theory known as simple foreknowledge. If any view has a claim to "the traditional view," it is simple foreknowledge in which God somehow "sees" the whole span of history at once.

Helm's main criticism of middle knowledge holds for both the simple foreknowledge and the open theist views as well. Helm takes aim at the *watershed* separating all forms of theological determinism from all forms of free will theism: whether God makes any of his decisions contingent upon the actions of creatures. Theological determinists answer no to this because God's will is not affected by what creatures do or pray for. Free will theists, on the other hand, answer yes because some of God's decisions are contingent upon our actions and prayers. Helm noted: "The divide remains of vital importance; a narrow, deep chasm, but one too wide to bridge." He faults all versions of omniscience held by free will theists because they make some of God's knowledge dependent upon the creatures. That is, the reason God knows that Billy Bob goes home for Christmas instead of going skiing with his friends is because that is what Billy Bob does. If he had done differently, then God would have different knowledge. He correctly stated that according to theological determinism, "God's decreeing of human actions is sufficient for the occurrence of those actions logically prior to the disclosure of his revealed will, the contents of which and the reaction to which serve to fulfill his decree. Everything is ultimately explained by reference to the divine decree." For all forms of free will theism, on the other hand, some of what God decrees is explicable in terms of human free actions. From Helm's perspective, this "reverses the order of explanation of human actions." Of course, free will theists could just as well say that Helm's view is a "reversal" from the older free will tradition which predates Augustine.

Response by Bruce A. Ware

Since Paul Helm's classical Calvinist view is close to my own, I naturally find much affinity with his constructive argumentation. The case he makes from his "A team" representative figures helpfully lays out the contours of the view that all Calvinists have found compelling over the centuries. The doctrines of God's meticulous sovereign control of both the natural world and the realm of moral creatures, the total depravity and total inability of man, the unconditional and deeply loving election of some sinners to salvation, the necessity of efficacious grace for saving faith, and the perseverance of those truly saved owing to the perseverance of God to save to the end those whom he has elected for salvation; these are precious doctrines that have united Calvinists, and I gladly and joyfully align myself with this tradition. Despite some of the ways in which I have found it to be wise and biblically supportable to modify certain aspects of this tradition, the tradition itself represents the most faithful conclusions from the teaching of the whole counsel of God's word as I understand what Scripture says. As such, I gladly affirm the broad strokes and most of the finer details that Helm has described.

What surprised me about Helm's chapter, then, was nothing that he presented constructively in support of the classical Calvinist view, but I was taken aback by his decision to devote nearly half of his chapter to a sort of preemptive critique of the other three views he believed would be represented in this book. Rather than waiting for his opportunity to respond to what his dialogue partners presented in their own chapters, he took from previously published materials what he understood to be the substance of their views and spent nearly half of his allotted space to critique these alternative models of the doctrine of God. As I assess his treatment and critique of these three models, my own judgment is that he fared best in his criticism of open theism, poorly in his assessment of classical Arminianism, and, well, less than the best in his treatment of my model, which I have inelegantly called a "modified" Calvinist model of the doctrine of God.

On the openness model, Helm pointed to some of its central problems, e.g., its conception of libertarian freedom (which is held in all forms of free will theism), its conception of God's general sovereignty (which also is held, in varying ways, in all forms of free will theism), and most notably its denial of exhaustive definite foreknowledge, a denial which makes it impossible to account for so much that the Bible teaches about God and the future. I think Helm is correct that much of what drives this move in open theism, this departure from the classical Arminian tradition from which it has come, is its desire to preserve the integrity of libertarian freedom. Nearly all other of its core values are held univocally with Arminians, but where the openness advocate separates from the classical Arminian is on the question of whether libertarian freedom is compatible with exhaustive definite foreknowledge. Because libertarian freedom is valued so highly, and because the genuineness and integrity of libertarian freedom is seen to be undermined by God's exhaustive knowledge of every future decision and action moral creatures will make, it has seemed to the openness proponent a necessary move simply to deny the latter notion. Helm rightly showed that the openness commitment to libertarian freedom is, at the core, what drives this move, at least as much or more than anything else.

Helm's description and critique of the classical Arminian view was puzzling, to say the least. I will read with interest Roger Olson's response to Helm's discussion, but I suspect that Olson will question the legitimacy of appealing almost exclusively to the Molinist variant of Arminianism as representative of classical Arminianism. In any case, to the extent that it may be questioned that Molinism represents the classical Arminian model, one must question Helm's strong appeal to this tradition in his preemptive criticism of the view Olson would be responsible to describe and defend in this volume.

Helm's critique of my modified Calvinist perspective shows why he was the ideal person to defend the classical Calvinist view. Every suggested modification of the tradition is viewed by Helm with great suspicion. Perhaps he is right to be so suspicious, but it is interesting that Helm stands today in a relatively small company of evangelical Calvinists who have held the classical view with virtually no alteration. On the other hand, the list is significantly longer of those evangelical philosophers and theologians in the Reformed tradition—Bruce Demarest, Millard Erickson, John Feinberg, John Frame, Wayne Grudem, Ronald Nash, David Wells, and others—who have seen the need, to a greater or lesser degree, to modify select aspects of this venerable tradition, all the while keeping its central doctrines and cherished convictions firmly in place. Of course, counting heads on either side doesn't prove anything, ultimately. But it does indicate that quite a few heads, at least, have also thought that some modification might be helpful in rendering our cherished Calvinist tradition clearer and more faithful to what Scripture teaches.

I will not here respond in detail to Helm's critique of my model of the doctrine of God as he has understood this primarily from my book, *God's Greater Glory*.[19] But I will offer a few select responses on the areas I find most important. First, I wish to go on record and state with clarity that I reject outright the Pajonism that Helm muses might be my own view. In a content footnote part way into his critique of the modified Calvinist view, Helm commented that it appears that my view is a form of Pajonism, a view that understands that men and women are brought to Christ, in the words of B. B. Warfield, "not by an almighty, creative action on their souls . . . but purely by suasive operations, adapted in his infallible wisdom to the precise state of mind and heart of those whom he has elected for salvation, and so securing from their own free action, a voluntary coming to Christ and embracing of him for salvation." How could Professor Helm think this is beyond my ability to comprehend! He may

---

19. Wheaton: Crossway, 2004.

not be aware that I have written a defense of the Calvinist doctrines of irresistible grace and effectual calling.[20] There, and in anything touching on this issue in *God's Greater Glory*, I make clear that God must effectually call a sinner, work in his heart with irresistible grace, and regenerate him so that he believes in Christ and is saved. I do not appeal to middle knowledge as a means by which God may bring the elect to salvation! Apart from God's efficacious work in their lives, no sinner will ever choose "from their own free action" to come to Christ for salvation. I fear that Helm read past what I argued and drew conclusions about my view that I fully reject.

Second, I appreciate the fact that Helm finds my appeal to compatibilist middle knowledge unstable. Although I believe that middle knowledge is biblically supportable and although I believe that appeal to middle knowledge along with a view of freedom as freedom of inclination (so, "compatibilist middle knowledge") can help deal with the problem of evil, I fully recognize that the tradition of Calvinism has not chosen to make such a move. I am willing to be convinced otherwise on this, and I appreciate Helm's helpful discussion. If I were persuaded, as Helm suggested, that my position reduces either to the Calvinist predestinarian view in which middle knowledge is superfluous or to the (Arminian) Molinist view in which autonomous human freedom can thwart God's meticulous divine control, then I would gladly drop middle knowledge and remain firmly in my own Calvinist camp, where I belong and where I intend to stay. But at least as of yet, I am not persuaded that these are my only options. It seems to me that the advantage of the notion of compatibilist middle knowledge is precisely that (1) God may use such knowledge in regulating some of what free (compatibilistically free, or free according to a freedom of inclination) moral creatures do—specifically the evil that they do—in a manner that avoids his direct-causative action upon them to bring about their choice and action, while (2) maintaining exhaustive and meticulous control over all that occurs, including what he knows, by middle knowledge, these free creatures surely will do when actualized in the real world

---

20. Cf. my chapter in *Still Sovereign,* ed. Thomas Schreiner and Bruce A. Ware (Grand Rapids: Zondervan, 2000), .

he envisions. The gains here seem worth the effort to consider this model, whether it might explain what Calvinists have long wanted to affirm. Yes, God ordains all that occurs, but no, God is not the author or approver of evil. All this model does is offer some conceptual tools for understanding a small part of how this can be.

Third, I believe that this view of compatibilist middle knowledge truly is middle knowledge and not merely God's knowledge, in real time, of counterfactuals. Among all that God knows by his natural knowledge, including his knowledge of all possibilities, is knowledge of what free creatures *would do* in various settings. Since this is a subset of God's natural knowledge which God possesses prevolitionally (i.e., prior to his free knowledge based on his decision of exactly which possible world to render real or actual in creation), it is properly understood as middle knowledge. Although it is a subset of God's natural knowledge, it is a useful subset! By this subset of middle knowledge, God can imagine any free creature in any setting and know what that moral agent would do, given that particular person's nature along with those particular circumstances and conditions. God's knowledge of these various possible states of affairs and corresponding free decisions and actions provides him with a means of instantiating certain features of reality in which free creatures do what they most want to do, out of their very natures, and in so doing, they fulfill exactly what God wants done—as when Joseph's brothers sold Joseph to Egypt, yet God "sent" Joseph there (Gen 45:4–8). That this view is unstable or, worse, contradictory, simply is not clear to me. At best, I can understand the complaint of some that since middle knowledge, so conceived, is simply a subset of natural knowledge, it isn't anything "specific." But that is like saying that your master bedroom isn't specific since it simply is a subset of your larger house. As I see it, the subset of middle knowledge is a unique, specific, and highly useful portion of God's larger storehouse of natural knowledge; and if it can be shown how it can help understand divine providence a small bit better, then it is worth considering. What I cannot see is the charge that this model is internally incoherent or self-contradictory.

I appreciate the first half of Helm's chapter immensely. He has presented a clear and compelling picture of the Calvinist view, one that I identify with and own as my tradition, as well. Nothing I have written means to undermine this tradition but only to offer adjustments at points where tensions continue to be felt. As a view that intends to represent the whole counsel of God, the "hard sayings" of Scripture along with those more easily accepted, the Calvinist model stands alone. I gladly align myself with this tradition, and I'm grateful for Helm's able defense.

CHAPTER 3

A Modified Calvinist Doctrine of God

BRUCE A. WARE

With great joy I write to commend to readers what I understand of the broad parameters of the doctrine of God. I clearly do not write in a dispassionate and disinterested manner. To do so would betray necessarily that the one writing does not truly know the subject of whom he speaks, namely, God. Without embarrassment and owing to the rich and lavish grace of God, I gladly declare that I fear and love the God of whom I write. My deepest desire is not to "win" what some might consider the implied contest of this four-views book. Rather, through this presentation I long to convey something of why both you and I and all of creation should marvel at the greatness and glory and goodness and grace of the one true and living God, who is Father, Son, and Holy Spirit.

I will present an understanding of the doctrine of God that shares most in common with the Reformed tradition but in certain places makes modifications and alterations of that tradition.[1] The Reformed tradition's understanding of the centrality

---

1. Certainly much about the proposal described and defended here is common to our broad Christian understanding of the God who has spoken and made himself known. But certain central and defining dimensions of this proposed understanding of God align most clearly with the tradition from Augustine through Calvin and Reformed and

of God's preeminent and prevailing sovereignty over all of the created universe he has made, manifest in his ordination of all that occurs and his control over all actions and events in the cosmos, both good and evil, is at the heart of what distinguishes the Reformed tradition from most others. Of course, this commitment to a strong and pervasive sovereignty of God so understood is not by any means all that the Reformed tradition says about God, but it is central to all else that one understands. I affirm this understanding because I believe it to be a faithful representation of God's self-revelation throughout the entirety of Scripture.

There are places, though, in the doctrine of God where I believe that contemporary rethinking on God's nature and actions in the world has led to some helpful and needed modifications of both the Reformed tradition and of the broader classical tradition of which it is a part. In the discussion of the doctrine of God that follows, I will suggest certain adjustments to our understanding of attributes such as the divine eternity and immutability in ways that represent modifications within the Reformed tradition. I also believe that the Scriptures indicate God's possession of what theologians and philosophers have called God's middle knowledge, and it seems clear to me from Scripture that the accounting of middle knowledge within a compatibilist understanding of human freedom helps deal with God's relation to evil in ways that the Reformed tradition has not been inclined to follow. So, while the broad framework and much of the substance of the doctrine of God to be commended here follows closely the Reformed or Calvinist tradition, this proposal also represents something of a modification to this tradition. Since I am as fallible and sinful as any other, I understand that my proposal may fail in the end to accomplish the goal of representing God's self-disclosure faithfully from Scripture. But this is my purpose, and I remain open to correction from others in the body of Christ.

This essay is not my first attempt to put forth these understandings of the doctrine of God that I call a *modified Calvinist conception of God*. Rather, I have had the privilege to write three

---

Puritan writers. Broadly, then, the doctrine of God I believe to be most consistent and thorough in its depiction of biblical teaching is one that shares most in common with this Reformed tradition.

books which provide a more complete presentation of this over-all understanding of God than I can present in this chapter.[2] The following discussion draws heavily from my previous writings in putting together a much more concise depiction of the doctrine of God as I have come to understand it. As we consider these arguments along with the other contributions in this book, may God grant us illumination and wisdom as we endeavor to know God rightly, as he has revealed himself rightly in his Word.

Divine Transcendence and Immanence: The Starting Place

We begin with the question of how best to conceive of a framework for understanding the doctrine of God. In Scripture, which is God's own self-revelation, he portrays himself both as *transcendent*, as existing in the fullness of his infinitely glorious tri-Person unity and apart from the finite spatiotemporal cre-ated reality he freely brought into existence, and also as one who chooses to relate *immanently* as he freely enters into the realm of the creaturely existence that he designed and made. To think of God correctly, then, we must establish our framework for understanding God as containing both of these key elements—both the *transcendent otherness* of God in himself, apart from creation, and also the *immanent nearness* of God with every aspect of the created order.

God's Transcendent Self-Existence

God's transcendence can only be rightly understood, as Scripture makes abundantly clear, in light of the fact that God exists eternally independent of the world, as the One who is fully

---

2. Bruce Ware, *God's Lesser Glory: The Diminished God of Open Theism* (Wheaton: Crossway, 2000); idem., *God's Greater Glory: The Exalted God of Scripture and the Christian Faith* (Wheaton: Crossway, 2004); and idem., *Father, Son, and Holy Spirit: Relationships, Roles, and Relevance* (Wheaton: Crossway, 2005). *God's Lesser Glory* offers a sustained critique of open theism while providing a sketch of a fundamentally Reformed understanding of God's relation to the world in response. *God's Greater Glory* broadly presents an understanding of God's nature and attributes, along with focused attention on God's providential dealings with the world and human creatures he has made, which represents more fully the modified Calvinist understanding I here can only summarize. And, *Father, Son, and Holy Spirit* describes this glorious God's triune existence, develop-ing nuances of the relationships and roles of each of the Trinitarian Persons that extend and elaborate on fundamental commitments of the Reformed tradition.

self-sufficient in his own infinitely perfect self-existence. God exists eternally by his own will and nature, and his existence is of such a quality as to contain intrinsically every quality in infinite measure. The eternal existence of God is the eternal existence of *all perfection, infinitely and intrinsically possessed, within the eternal triune nature of God.* Just as it is unthinkable from a biblical point of view that God could ever not be, so too it is unimaginable that God could ever receive some quality, some value, some knowledge, some power, some ability, or some perfection that he previously lacked. The apostle Paul echoes the Old Testament prophets' understanding of God when he writes:

> "Who has known the mind of the Lord?
> Or who has been his counselor?"
>
> "Who has ever given to God, that God should repay him?"
>
> For from him and through him and to him are all things.
> To him be the glory forever! Amen (Rom 11:34–36 NIV; cf. Isa 40:12–28).

If God were ever in need of food, said the psalmist, he would not inform his creatures, for the world and all it contains is his (Ps 50:7–12). His greatness so surpasses the created realm that the earth itself is the mere footstool for his feet (Isa 66:1). The God of the Bible, the true and living God, is in need of nothing from any created being. Quite the opposite is true—whereas he is not dependent on anything whatsoever, all else is dependent entirely on him. Concerning God's unqualified self-sufficiency, the apostle Paul declares:

> The God who made the world and everything in it is the Lord of heaven and earth and does not live in temples built by hands. And he is not served by human hands, as if he needed anything, because he himself gives all men life and breath and everything else (Acts 17:24–25 NIV).

As the supreme Creator of the world and everything in it and as the sole Giver of everything that is given to all humanity, God, then, possesses within himself all that is, and absolutely nothing can exist independent of him that could contribute in some way to enrich his very being or enlarge his possessions. God is supremely independent of the world, and hence he simply does not need the world he has made. His transcendence is manifest most clearly by his independent and infinite self-sufficiency. He possesses within himself, intrinsically and eternally, every quality in infinite measure. As Karl Barth rightly comments:

> God is not dependent on anything that is not Himself; on anything outside Himself. He is not limited by anything outside Himself, and is not subject to any necessity distinct from Himself. On the contrary, everything that exists is dependent on His will.[3]

God utterly transcends all lesser reality, then, in that he alone exists eternally and of necessity, and his existence encompasses the fullness of all value and perfection entirely within itself. Any and all other existence—goodness, perfection, power, holiness, beauty, or whatever value one might mention—is strictly derivative in nature, as coming to be from the eternal God who alone has all such perfection infinitely and intrinsically. The question of Paul to the Corinthians, "What do you have that you did not receive?" (1 Cor 4:7), is appropriate in regard to all finite beings. The thought that somehow we frail creatures of his making may somehow contribute value to or fill some void within the divine nature is utterly abhorrent to biblical thought. God stands supreme and above all as the one who exists in his fullness, independent of all. And our finite existence bears testimony, not to any human capacity to be anything in itself, much less to some supposed ability to add anything to God, but only to God's gracious will in creating out of nothing all that is and to granting to all his creation each and every quality it possesses.

---

3. Karl Barth, *Church Dogmatics,* ed. G. W. Bromiley and T. F. Torrance (Edinburgh: T. & T. Clark, 1956–75), II/1. 560.

God's Immanent Self-Relatedness

Amazingly, the God of infinite fullness and self-sufficient independence of the world nonetheless has chosen to make this world and to live in relation to the entire world he has made. A.W. Argyle comments:

> The emphasis of the Bible falls upon God's activity, God's initiative, God's approach to man preceding man's approach to God. Both in the Old Testament story and in that of the New, He is an intensely personal God who visits His people, and hears and answers their prayers.[4]

Distinctive of the biblical witness to God as over and against both Near Eastern and Greek conceptions is this fundamental conviction that the one and only true God has involved himself personally at every level of his created order.[5]

Merely to mention some of the major themes of biblical revelation is to illustrate the extent to which the God portrayed in the Bible is a God intimately concerned with and actively involved among his creatures. Take, for example, the prominent emphasis throughout Scripture on God as Creator.[6] The Scriptures proclaim from beginning to end that God, as Ezra declares, has made "heaven, the heaven of heavens, with all their host, the earth and all that is on it, the seas and all that is in them" (Neh 9:6; compare Gen 1:1–31; Pss 89:11; 121:2; 124:8; Isa 42:5; 44:24;

---

4. A.W. Argyle, *God in the New Testament* (London: Hodder and Stroughton, 1965), 11.

5. H. H. Rowley in "The Nature of God," *The Faith of Israel* (London: SCM, 1956) 48–73, has observed that it is not Israel's belief that God exists or that God is one or even that God is powerful, omnipresent, and wise that distinguishes her conception of God from the Gentile world. Rather, it is her conviction that God is personal (57) and moral (61–68), i.e., intimately involved with Israel in a moral relationship, that sets her conception of God apart from all others. On God's personal and active involvement in history, see also Walther Eichrodt, *Theology of the Old Testament*, 2 vols., trans. J. A. Baker (Philadelphia: Westminster, 1961), 1:206–10; T. C. Vriezen, *An Outline of Old Testament Theology*, 2nd ed. (Newton, MA: Charles T. Branford, 1970), 162–64; and J. Schneider and C. Brown, "God, Gods, Emmanuel," *NIDNTT,* 2:66–76.

6. On the doctrine of creation and God as Creator, see, e.g., B. W. Anderson, "Creation," *IDB*, 1:725–32; W. Foerster, "kitizō, ktísis, ktisma, ktistēs," *TDNT*, 3:1000–35; H. H. Esser and I. H. Marshall, "Creation, Foundation, Creature, Maker," *NIDNTT*, 1:376–89; E. Jacob, *Theology of the Old Testament* (New York: Harper & Row, 1958), 136–50; Eichrodt, *Theology of the Old Testament*, 2:96–117; Barth, *Church Dogmatics*, 3/1–4; and Otto Weber, *Foundations of Dogmatics*, 2 vols., trans. D. L. Guder (Grand Rapids: Eerdmans, 1981–83), 1:463–501.

Acts 14:15; Rev 4:11). By his free word, all that is receives its existence (Ps 33:6; Heb 11:3). And that is not all. One learns within the creation account of Genesis 1 and 2 that this God who speaks into existence all that exists created humankind uniquely in his own image (Gen 1:26–27). Man, as male and female, participates from the beginning in relationship and fellowship with God as God grants humankind lordship over the earth (Gen 1:28–30) and as God reveals the conditions of obedience necessary for ongoing personal relations (Gen 2:16–17).[7]

But when one has spoken of the relationship between God and humans only in terms of Creator-creature, one has only scratched the surface of the intimacy and depth of this relationship. The notion of covenant[8] reveals the heart of God with respect to the creatures who willfully turned from him. By means of various covenants, God expressed his desire to relate once again with fallen humanity. Especially significant is the special relationship God established with Abraham (Gen 12:1–3; 15:7–21), a relationship that promised not only the coming to be of a peculiar nation which had privileged communion with God but also the future blessing of all the families of the earth through Abraham's own seed (Gen 12:3). God's concern to relate himself once again in global dimensions is expressed in covenant form to Abraham and, of course, is manifest supremely in God's sending of his own Son to all the world (John 1:29; 3:16) as the fulfillment of this early pledge to Abraham (Gal 3:14).

Beyond this God has acted in history to bring restoration to his fallen and sinful creatures. In Old Testament theology, the high point of God's loving commitment to Israel is demonstrated in the Exodus. At this point in the history of Israel God revealed his covenant name (Exod 6:2–3), a name that forever captures

---

7. Cf. Bruce A. Ware, "Male and Female Complementarity and the Image of God," *Journal for Biblical Manhood and Womanhood* 7, no. 1 (Spring 2002): 14–23, and printed also in Wayne Grudem, ed., *Biblical Foundations for Manhood and Womanhood* (Wheaton: Crossway, 2002), 71–92.

8. See, e.g., G. E. Mendenhall, "Covenant," *IDB*, 1:714–23; J. Behm and G. Quell, "diatithēmi, diathēkē," *TDNT*, 2:104–34; J. Guhrt and O. Becker, "Covenant, Guarantee, Mediator," *NIDNTT*, 1:365–76; E. Jacob, *Theology of the Old Testament* (New York: Harper & Row, 1958), 209–17; G. von Rad, *Old Testament Theology*, 2 vols., trans. D. M. G. Stalker (New York: Harper & Row, 1962–65), 1:129–35; and D. R. Hillers, *Covenant: The History of a Biblical Idea* (Baltimore: Johns Hopkins University Press, 1969).

the special relationship that God causes to exist between himself and Israel.[9] Roland de Vaux suggested that Yahweh, the name of God revealed to Moses in Exodus 3, speaks in a dual sense both of the supreme existence of God and of his specific existence *for* the people of his choosing.[10] The context of Exodus 3 emphasizes God's hearing and seeing the people's distress (Exod 2:23–25; 3:7–9) and his uncompromising commitment to bring them release from bondage (Exod 3:16–22).

The intensity and immensity of God's concern for a fallen humanity is nowhere more visible than it is through the incarnation and cross of Christ. Moltmann is surely right in saying: "God is not greater than he is in this humiliation. God is not more glorious than he is in this self-surrender. God is not more powerful than he is in this helplessness."[11] The God of the Bible seeks relationships with those whom he has freely made, and the cross of Christ serves to implore us never to think lightly of the intensity of this desire within the heart of God.

Though this discussion makes only brief mention of some of the highlights of divine revelation pertaining to the relatedness of God to humanity,[12] the point is clear: the God of the Bible actively seeks intimate relationship with those he has made. His love for the world is unconditional and inexhaustible. Although

9. On the name of God revealed to Moses, see, e.g., D.N. Freedman, "The Name of the God of Moses," *Journal of Biblical Literature* 79 (1960): 151–56; R. Abba, "The Divine Name Yahweh," *Journal of Biblical Literature* 80 (1961): 320–28; R. de Vaux, "The Revelation of the Divine Name YHWH," *Proclamation and Presence: OT Essays in Honour of Gwynne Henton Davies*, ed. J. I. Durham and J. R. Porter (Richmond, VA: John Knox, 1970), 48–75; B. Childs, *The Book of Exodus* (Philadelphia: Westminster, 1974), 60–70; and R. B. Allen, "What Is in a Name?" in *God: What Is He Like?* ed. W. F. Kerr (Wheaton: Tyndale, 1977), 107–27.

10. de Vaux, "Revelation of the Divine Name," 65–75. He writes, "The care of the people is of prime importance: Yahweh sends Moses to lead them out of Egypt and orders Pharaoh to let them go, and it is for their good that he reveals his name. The consequence is implicit: Israel must recognize that Yahweh is for her the only one who exists and the only saviour. This is not a dogmatic definition of an abstract monotheism, but the injunction of a practical monotheism, and henceforth Israel will have no other God but Yahweh" (72).

11. J. Moltmann, *The Crucified God: The Cross of Christ as the Foundation and Criticism of Christian Theology*, trans. R. A. Wilson and J. Bowden (New York: Harper & Row, 1974), 205.

12. Besides the themes mentioned, one could also point to such important features as God's restoration of his people after their captivity, the prophetic witness to God's great holy love for Israel, the promised sending of the Holy Spirit as humans now become the temples in which God dwells, the eschatological promise of everlasting fellowship in the presence of God—all these and more illustrate the intense desire of God, as revealed by him, to relate himself with his creatures.

we willfully turned from him, bringing condemnation on ourselves, he deliberately sought us out at great personal cost (Rom 5:6–8). God's immanent self-relatedness is surely one of the great marvels of his self-disclosure, and in response we can only rightly bow before this gracious God in humble and thankful adoration for such boundless love (2 Cor 9:15).

Relation between Transcendent Self-Existence and Immanent Self-Relatedness

Although God exists eternally independent of all else in the infinite fullness of every perfection, and although he possesses no deficiency or lack which any finite reality could supply, nevertheless, he has freely willed to bring into being a contingent order to which he has voluntarily pledged his intimate and most personal involvement. Barth expressed this point well in contrast to theistic positions which connect God necessarily to a finite order:

> The reason why God gives them [i.e., every aspect of creation] real being and why from eternity they are objects of His knowledge is not that God would not be God without their actual or even possible existence, but because He wills to know them and to permit them to be actuality. As real objects of his will, and therefore already as real objects of His knowledge, they are distinct from Him. He is not conditioned by them. They are conditioned by Him. They have not proceeded from His essence. On the contrary, He has called them and created them out of nothing. He was not obliged to do this. He did not do it to satisfy some need in His own being and life. The eternity and necessity of the divine will do not involve the eternity and necessity of its objects. With whatever necessity God acts in Himself, He is always free in relation to these.[13]

The creation of the world was not necessary to God; as the eternal self-sufficient One, he did not (and could not) choose to make a finite order to add somehow to his inherent and infinite fullness of perfection. And yet he willed to create the world

---

13. Barth, *Church Dogmatics*, II/1. 562.

(Rev 4:11), and in his free willing to create, he also committed his very self in personal relatedness to what was not God, to what he knew would reject him and rebel against his perfect will. Though he needed none of what he made, yet he brought it to be and made it the object of his special care.

If we felt the strain and ultimate inability to comprehend fully each of these two truths central to a proper understanding of God, we now must acknowledge our complete wonder and amazement at an even greater mystery: *The God of the Bible loves and seeks us out with such eagerness and persistence when he himself stands in no need whatever of the objects of his love.* His love, then, is unconditional without qualification. It is, as C. S. Lewis put it, "Bottomlessly selfless by very definition; it has everything to give and nothing to receive."[14] Surely one of the most amazing facets of God's self-revelation is this truth: though God does not need us, he loves us; and though we can do nothing for him, he does everything for us. That God is utterly complete in the fullness of perfection, and that he has brought into being what he need not have made and has pledged to it his deepest personal love—this is undoubtedly at the very heart of the self-revelation of God to his creatures.

Divine Attributes and God's Relationship with His Moral Creatures

Given God's purpose to create a world with which he enters into real relationship, particular questions arise regarding certain attributes of God which have seemed to insulate God from real involvement with the world. This section examines two particular attributes of God which, in the classical tradition, have presented a problem to anyone conceiving of God's real relationship with the world. Both God's relation to time (divine eternity) and God's relation to change (divine immutability) need some reconsideration and reformulation to demonstrate that the God who made us chooses to live in relationship with what he has

---

14. C. S. Lewis, *The Problem of Pain* (New York: Macmillan, 1961), 38.

made. Consider then a sketch of how the doctrines of the divine eternity and immutability may be considered anew.

Divine Eternity and God's Relationship with Creation

One of the perpetual enigmas of Christian theology has been, and continues to be, God's relation to space and time. Particularly, God's relationship to time has been exceedingly difficult to sort out, and the discussion continues with fervor.[15] Two main views have been represented throughout the history of the church.[16] Most, following the lead of Boethius[17] (AD 480–524), have affirmed a view of *divine timelessness* or *atemporal eternity*. Because God created both space and time, and because God exists as infinitely perfect and independent of all finite, creaturely qualities, God's own essence and existence must be apart from these mediums of created life. God, then, is strictly and only nontemporal and nonspatial, in contrast to the creation that is both temporal and spatial. God's relation to the world, then, is through a relation of reason, but no real relation is possible. A minority position, now being pursued with much more intensity even among evangelicals,[18] advocates a view of *divine everlastingness* or *temporal eternity*. In this view, time itself is an eternal reality, and God exists in time eternally. Thus, there is no beginning or ending (literally) to his existence but rather he exists in every moment of everlasting time. God has existed, then, in every moment of the infinite past, he does exist in the present, and he will exist in every moment of the infinite future. God alone, then, is infinitely everlasting.

---

15. See, e.g., Gregory E. Ganssle, ed., *God and Time: Four Views* (Downers Grove: InterVarsity, 2001). The four views are written, respectively, by Paul Helm (chap. 2, "Divine Timeless Eternity"), Alan G. Padgett (chap. 3, "Eternity as Relative Timelessness"), William Lane Craig (chap. 4, "Timelessness and Omnitemporality"), and Nicholas Wolterstorff (chap. 5, "Unqualified Divine Temporality").

16. For a helpful discussion of these prominent positions on God and time, see Ronald H. Nash, *The Concept of God* (Grand Rapids: Zondervan, 1983), 73–83.

17. Boethius, *The Consolation of Philosophy*, trans. V. E. Watts (Harmondsworth, U.K.: Penguin, 1969).

18. See, e.g., John S. Feinberg, *No One Like Him: The Doctrine of God* (Wheaton: Crossway, 2001), 375–436, for a stimulating and innovative proposal, interacting in careful detail with the history of this doctrine, and arguing for a temporalist view of divine eternity.

When considering the relative merits of each position, it is worth asking the question whether one must decide between the two. In what follows, I propose that we seriously consider adopting something of a synthesis of these two positions. Must God be viewed exclusively as timeless or exclusively as temporal? Are there good reasons to consider a model of God's relation to time in which both, in different senses, are true?

In the classical tradition, "eternity" signifies God's nontemporal existence; God exists necessarily apart from time altogether, so his eternity is "timeless eternity." But consider the difference in what is communicated by the attribute of God's "omnipresence." Here, rather than discussing God as existing necessarily apart from space, or as fully and only nonspatial in his existence, this doctrine regularly has to do with God's "everywhere" presence throughout the entirety of the universe. Psalm 139:7–10 is often cited as a key supporting passage. It begins,, "Where shall I go from your Spirit? Or where shall I flee from your presence?" God's omnipresence is most often, then, about the real and universal presence of God throughout the created order.

But of course, we know that God brought the created order into existence, so God's own existence precedes or, better, stands apart from the spatial creation he made. In a sense, then, we hold in regard to God's relation to space both (1) that God is nonspatial in himself apart from the spatial created order that he has made, and (2) that God is everywhere present so that his existence and every quality of his life are present fully at every point of created space. It seems, then, that with regard to God's relation to space, we have given expression to both truths: God is nonspatial in himself (*in se*) apart from creation, and God is everywhere spatially present in relation to creation (*in re*)—and without conflict or contradiction.

But not so with time. Consider for example Louis Berkhof's definitions of God's eternity and God's immensity (i.e., omnipresence), especially in relation to the issues we are discussing. First, eternity:

His [God's] eternity may be defined as *that perfection of God whereby He is elevated above all temporal limits and all succession of moments, and possesses the whole of His existence in one indivisible present.*[19]

But Berkhof's definition of *immensity* reads:

It [divine immensity] may be defined as *that perfection of the Divine Being by which He transcends all spatial limitations, and yet is present in every point of space with His whole Being.*[20]

And he continues with this interesting and helpful comment:

It [definition of divine immensity] has a negative and a positive side, denying all limitations of space to the Divine Being, and asserting that God is above space and fills every part of it *with His whole Being.*[21]

Berkhof is happy to discuss two senses of God's relation to space. God both "transcends all spatial limitations," and he "is present in every point of space with His whole Being." That is, God is both nonspatial in himself (*in se*) apart from creation, and God is everywhere spatially present in relation to creation (*in re*). But, interestingly, with regard to time, Berkhof says just one thing: God strictly is "elevated above all temporal limits and all succession of moments." He exists in "one indivisible present" but not in moments of time.

I suggest that we follow the same procedure in understanding God's relation to time as Berkhof and most others have of God's relation to space. That is, we can understand God's relation to time as comprising both his atemporal existence in himself (*in se*) apart from creation, and his "omnitemporal" existence in relation to the created order he has made (*in re*). If so, both doctrines are made parallel in nature, and what they say is powerful indeed. Put together, they would articulate the dual understandings, first,

19. Louis Berkhof, *Systematic Theology* (London: Banner of Truth Trust, 1939, 1958), 60.
20. Ibid.
21. Ibid.

that "prior" to the creation of the world, God existed in himself, apart from any spatiotemporal reality, in the fullness of his infinite and glorious existence, as transcending both space and time, being essentially (i.e., in his essence or nature) both nonspatial and nontemporal. But second, when he created the heavens and earth, he brought into being their twofold dimensions of spatiality and temporality. Since God chose to become immanent with the creation he had made, he chose, then, to "enter" fully into both the spatial and the temporal dimensions of creation. In so doing, the same God who in himself is intrinsically and eternally both nonspatial and atemporal chose to "fill" all of the space and time he created. Amazingly, then, at creation God became both omnipresent and omnitemporal while remaining, in himself and apart from creation, fully nonspatial and timelessly eternal.

Hence, in becoming omnipresent and omnitemporal, God did not change in any respect who he eternally is apart from creation. He only adds, as it were, the qualities of his being also immanently related to his creation, in all of its points of space and in all of its moments of time. In a manner not dissimilar to the doctrine of the incarnation, where the eternal Son took on (added) to himself the nature of a man while in no respect diminishing his eternal and immutable deity, so too here, the nonspatial and timelessly eternal God who created a spatial and temporal universe chose to "take on" or inhabit fully its dimensions of space and time and so become both everywhere present (omnipresent) and everytime present (omnitemporal).[22] God can be understood, then, as both transcendent in his eternal nonspatial and atemporal existence independent of everything created, and immanent in his omnipresent and omnitemporal inhabiting of everything created. Spatially and temporally, God is both apart from us and near us, other than us and with us, separate from us and close at hand. What glory there is in both sides of these truths.

---

22. John Frame in *The Doctrine of God* (Phillipsburg, PA: P&R, 2002), 557–59, argues for a position similar to the one advanced here, and Frame uses the language of spatial omnipresence and temporal omnipresence for the dual sense in which God is "present" in all of space and in all of time. In relation to the analogy of the incarnation to God's relation to created space and time, Frame wrote, "In Christ, God entered, not a world that is otherwise strange to him, but a world in which he had been dwelling all along."

Divine Immutability and God's Relationship to Creation

Through much of the history of the church, God has also been understood as absolutely immutable in every respect. After all, it was often reasoned, if God can change, then that changeability must indicate a change for the better or a change for the worse. But if for the better, then he was not God before; and if for the worse, then he no longer can rightly be conceived as God.[23] Other arguments for God's absolute immutability appealed to God's simplicity (change requires a compounded nature in which part, not all, is altered), eternity (change requires temporal succession to mark what a thing was before the change compared to what it now is), and immortality (things that change can cease to exist).[24] So, to ensure that God's perfection is secure and that his transcendent excellence is beyond question, God was widely presented as absolutely incapable of change whatsoever.[25]

As one considers Scripture's teaching on God's relation to change, it is clear that a number of passages indicate the changelessness of God's essential nature (Ps 102:25–27; Mal 3:6; Jas 1:17). One might refer to this quality, then, as God's "ontological immutability," since his very being is eternally who he is as God. But Scripture also affirms God's changelessness of word and promise. For example, in Malachi 3:6 God's nature and his covenant pledge link together in such a way that the changelessness of God's promise is based on the changelessness of God's nature. The prophet wrote, "For I the LORD do not change; therefore you, O children of Jacob, are not consumed." Because of the constancy of God's character and nature, his people can be assured that even though God will come as a refiner's fire and destroy all those who persist in their shameful defiance of him (Mal 3:1–5

23. See, e.g., Gregory of Nyssa, "Letter to Eustathia, Ambrosia, and Basilissa," in *NPNF*, 2, 5, where Gregory writes that God is "incapable of changing to worse or changing to better, because the first is not His nature, the second He does not admit of." Similar statements can be found in Athanasius, Arnobius, Augustine, and others.

24. More detail on the history of the doctrine of divine immutability can be found in my doctoral dissertation on the subject. See Bruce Ware, "An Evangelical Reexamination of the Doctrine of the Immutability of God," Pasadena, CA: Fuller Theological Seminary, PhD dissertation, 1984.

25. I have argued elsewhere for a view that I will only summarize briefly here. See Bruce Ware, "An Evangelical Reformulation of the Doctrine of the Immutability of God," *Journal of the Evangelical Theological Society* 29, no. 4 (December 1986): 431–46; and idem., *God's Lesser Glory*, 86–98.

ESV), nonetheless, since God has pledged his salvation and restoration to his people, they will not be consumed with the rest. We might refer to the changelessness of God's Word, promise, and pledge, then, as God's "ethical immutability."

Having affirmed God's ontological and ethical immutability, we have not said all that the Bible says about the relation of God to change. If we listen attentively to God as revealed in Scripture, it is clear that he changes in some very important respects. May I suggest that all of us who have been saved by God's marvelous grace celebrate the fact that while we once faced the severe "wrath of God" revealed from heaven against our "ungodliness and unrighteousness" (Rom 1:18; cf. Eph 2:3), yet now in Christ by faith "we have peace with God through our Lord Jesus Christ" (Rom 5:1). God's disposition toward us in our unforgiven sin is one of judgment, wrath, and condemnation; but in Christ his disposition toward us is one of peace, acceptance, and fatherly love.

This is just an example of what might be called the "relational mutability" of God, a change not of his essential nature, nor of his word or promise, but of his attitude and disposition toward his moral creatures in ways that are commensurate to changes that happen in them. So, when we change, say, from rebellion to repentance, God changes commensurately, as described above. Likewise, when we turn from him in disobedience and rebellion, God's attitude and disposition toward us changes from one of acceptance to one of disappointment and even anger.

Furthermore, it seems clear that God's relational mutability is in many cases simply an expression of his ethical immutability. That is, because God is faithful to his promise, when the moral situation of his creatures changes, his faithfulness to his own pledge and promise requires that he change in appropriate ways in relation to them. Consider, for example, God's "change of mind" regarding his threatened judgment of Nineveh in the days of Jonah. As you remember, following a period of exceeding reluctance, Jonah eventually traveled to Nineveh and proclaimed God's message, "Yet forty days, and Nineveh shall be overthrown" (Jonah 3:4). When the people of Nineveh repented, believed God, fasted, prayed, and turned from their sin, God "relented of the disaster that he had said he would do to them" (Jonah 3:10). Open theists, of course, endeavor to make much of cases like this, as if God learned something new and so literally changed his mind.[26] In this particular case, if God learned that the Ninevites would repent at the preaching of Jonah, this would be odd, since Jonah seemed already to suspect strongly that repentance would occur, and hence he refused to obey God's command to preach impending judgment to this people. Rather than presuming Jonah to have more insight than God, we come to a far better understanding when we consider the ethical immutability and the relational mutability of God in this situation. Because God had established from the beginning that those who repent and turn from their sin will be forgiven, he sent Jonah to Nineveh to preach the message he knew, and Jonah also knew, would elicit the repentance that he sought from them. In light of their change of heart, God "relented" from what he had said. I take his action to mean that because God is ethically immutable, when the Ninevites repented at the preaching of Jonah, God honored his long-standing word and so changed in his relationship with them. Rather than bringing them the threatened judgment, he brought them merciful forgiveness. In this, God kept the word of his promise ("If you repent, I will forgive your sin") that required that he change when they changed. Hence, God's ethical immutability formed the basis here for God's relational mutability as expressed in Jonah 3:10.

So as we marvel at God's constancy, stability, and immutability, we should also marvel at his chosen path of variability, relational adaptability, and mutability. What a God, and what an unspeakable privilege to be in relationship with him.

Biblical Support for God's Providential Governance

Readers of Scripture are constantly encouraged, in account after account, to think of God as in control of what takes place

---

26. See, e.g., Gregory A. Boyd, *God of the Possible: A Biblical Introduction to the Open View of God* (Grand Rapids: Baker, 2000), 55–56; and John Sanders, *The God Who Risks: A Theology of Providence* (Downers Grove: InterVarsity, 1998), 64–69.

in this world. And this control extends to the large (Acts 2:23; 4:27–28) and the small (Prov 16:33), both to all that is good (Ezek 36:24–28) and all that is evil (Isa 10:5–15), and it encompasses occurrences in nature (Ps 147:15–18) as well as the free choices and actions of people (Prov 21:1). While never minimizing either the genuineness of human choosing or the moral responsibility attached to human choice, Scripture presents God as exercising ultimate and exacting control over just what happens.[27]

Ephesians 1:11 expresses one of the most sweeping summary statements of God's sovereign control over all things.

"In him [Christ] we have obtained an inheritance, being predestined according to the purpose of him who *works all things according to the counsel of his will*" (NKJV, italics added).[28] The last portion of this text indicates that God exerts his sovereign control over absolutely everything. God's will encompasses all things that occur in the universe, and this divine will is efficacious such that God works all things in fulfillment of his purpose.

If we wonder whether "all things" in 1:11 really refers to absolutely everything, we need only look back to 1:10 where "all things" are united in Christ, things "which are in heaven and which are on earth." Yes indeed, "all things" means absolutely everything. And because our predestination to receive the inheritance is included in the purpose of God which is fulfilled as all things are accomplished according to what God has willed,

---

27. For an insightful and scripturally saturated discussion of God's sovereign control of all things, see John Frame, in "God's Control: Its Efficacy and Universality," *The Doctrine of God*, 47–79.

28. Notice that this statement occurs in the opening section of Ephesians (1:3–14) where Paul extols God for the many blessings that have been brought to us by the Father through his Son. What begins this list of blessings for Paul are the dual truths that God has chosen us in Christ before the foundation of the world (1:4) and that he predestined us to be adopted through Jesus Christ for himself, out of his love, according to his will, and to the praise of his glorious grace (1:5–6). It is nothing short of astonishing that when Paul brings to mind reasons God should be praised, election and predestination are the first and second items he exclaims. How is this instructive? Simply that for Paul, apart from the sovereign will of God in choosing us to be saved, and in predestining us to become his children, our salvation would never have happened. But, because God has so ordained, we are assured that God will bring about what he has planned. See my chapter, "Divine Election to Salvation: Unconditional, Individual, and Infralapsarian," in Chad Brand, ed., *Perspectives on Election* (Nashville: Broadman & Holman, 2007).

we can be sure that all those in Christ will surely and certainly receive this inheritance.

Those who hold to a universal and efficacious understanding of God's sovereignty are sometimes accused of falsely generalizing from selected instances of God's control to argue for his universal control.[29] In these words, however, the generalizing comes from the apostle Paul himself. The greatest security Paul can offer his readers of the certainty of God's fulfilling all that he has promised is this: God "works all things according to the counsel of his will" (Eph 1:11b). Nothing is left out, and all things occur as God has willed. If this is what Scripture teaches, then we need to bow to it and work out our understanding of human volition and moral responsibility in ways that accord with this central truth.

Spectrum texts also offer overwhelming support for the comprehensive and universal sovereign rulership of God.

One of the most compelling of all biblical themes demonstrating God's comprehensive sovereign control is the teaching found in a number of spectrum texts. [30] These are passages which indicate in sweeping language that God controls both sides of the spectrum of life's occurrences, both those actions and events considered pleasant and good and those considered harmful and evil. Consider the force of these five passages: [31]

> "Now see that I, even I, am He, and there is no God besides Me; I *kill* and I *make alive*; I *wound* and I *heal*, nor is there any who can deliver from My hand" (Deut 32:39 NKJV).

> "The LORD *kills* and *makes alive*; He *brings down* to the grave and *brings up*. The LORD *makes poor* and *makes rich*; He *brings low* and *lifts up* (1 Sam 2:6 NKJV).

> Consider the work of God: for who can make straight what *He has made crooked*? In the day of *prosperity* be joyful, but

---

29. Boyd, *God of the Possible*, 25, 29.

30. I discussed these texts by this name previously, in Ware, *God's Lesser Glory*, 150, 204–7.

31. I have added italics to each of these texts to highlight God's active control and sovereignty.

in the day of *adversity* consider: Surely *God has appointed the one as well as the other*, so that man will find out nothing that will come after him (Eccl 7:13–14 NKJV).

I am the LORD, and there is no other; there is no God but Me. I will *strengthen* you, though you do not know Me, so that all may know from the rising of the sun to its setting that there is no one but Me. I am the LORD, and there is no other. I *form light* and *create darkness*, I *make success* and *create disaster*; I, the LORD, *do* all these things (Isa 45:5–7 HCSB).

Who is there who speaks and it comes to pass, Unless the Lord has commanded it? Is it not from the mouth of the Most High That both good and ill go forth? (Lam 3:37–38 NKJV).

Most Christians would affirm without hesitation that God has control over the good that happens; after all, James 1:17 tells us that "every perfect gift" is from the Father of lights. So it is not surprising or troubling to read in these passages that God makes alive, God heals, God raises up, God makes riches, God exalts, God brings about days of prosperity, God makes straight, God forms light, God makes well-being, and God brings about what is good. But what is amazing and instructive about these texts is that they attribute to God, in the same breath, human realities on the opposite side of the spectrum. Not only does God make alive, but God kills; not only does God heal, but God wounds. Indeed, God is said to make poor, to bring low, to make crooked, to bring about adversity, to create darkness, to create disaster, and to bring about what is bad.

In fact, to deny God's control of both sides of the spectrum is to deny the very "Godness" of God and to remove from him his own stated basis for claiming to be the one and only true and living God. Perhaps Isaiah 45:5–7 is especially clear. Notice the buildup in 45:5–6 preceding God's claims to control all in 45:7: "*I am the Lord, and there is no other; there is no God but Me.* (italics added). Following this repeated emphasis on "I alone am

God!" comes God's own declaration of what he as God is like: "*I form light and create darkness, I make success and create disaster; I, the LORD, do all these things.*"

Three features of this text underscore the intentional and deliberate force of the language used. First, the verb *bara* ("create"), a term used uniformly throughout the Old Testament only with God as its subject,[32] is used in relation to "darkness" and "calamity" and not for "light" and "well-being." That is, the strongest verb indicating God's control is connected with the negative, not positive, divine actions. Second, the term translated as "disaster" is the Hebrew word *ra* and is most often translated "evil." There is no stronger Hebrew term than this one for all that is ruinous and calamitous and wicked, both in relation to human life and as seen from God's own perspective.[33] That the text would declare, "I, God, create evil / wickedness / disaster" is nothing short of astonishing. And third, God does not do just *some* of these things, but God does *all* (*kol* in Hebrew) of these things. The buildup in Isaiah 45:5–6 ("I am the LORD, and there is no other, besides me there is no God") is matched, then, by the conclusion here ("I am the Lord, who does all these things"). Clearly God wants us to understand that his own deity, his own "Godness," manifests itself through his power and authority to control all that occurs, both good and evil.

Additional texts speak of God's control of the nations of this world.

Many other Bible passages speak of the nations' rise and fall, their successes and defeats, their boundaries, their wars—in short, what they do and cannot do. Psalm 33:8–11 provides a sample of Scripture's teaching concerning God's governance of the nations:

> Let the whole earth tremble before the LORD;
> let all the inhabitants of the world stand in awe of Him.
> For He spoke, and it came into being;
> He commanded, and it came into existence.
> The LORD frustrates the counsel of the nations;

---

32. Thomas E. McComiskey, "bārā," in *TDOT*, 1:127–28.
33. G. Herbert Livingston, "rā'rā'," in *TDOT*, 2:854–57.

> He thwarts the plans of the peoples.
> The counsel of the LORD stands forever,
>   the plans of His heart from generation to generation.
>   (HCSB)

The contrast could not be plainer. While God speaks and what he says certainly comes to pass, and while his counsel stands forever, unshakable and permanent, the nations' plans are frustrated by the Lord and all of their counsel comes to nothing. Psalm 2:4 gives us a glimpse of how seriously God takes the nations' collective striving against him: "He who sits in the heavens shall laugh; The Lord shall hold them in derision" (NKJV). So much for free will creatures causing God to be frustrated and keeping him from being able to accomplish his will! And Isaiah 40:15 provides some rich metaphors for understanding just how puny and trivial the nations' power and wisdom is in comparison with God's: "Look, the nations are like a drop in a bucket; they are considered as a speck of dust on the scales; He lifts up the islands like fine dust" (HCSB) The prophet continues in 40:17, "All the nations are as nothing before Him; they are considered by Him as nothingness and emptiness" (HCSB).

How much power and wisdom do the nations have that could in any way rival God or add to the infinite fullness of his omnipotence and omnisapience? In comparison to God, the nations' masses of knowledge, wisdom, and power are "as nothing before him . . . nothingness and emptiness." The God of the Bible, the true and living God, simply cannot fail to accomplish his will, and the nations are subject fully to him, not him to them.

The great Nebuchadnezzar, king of the mighty Babylon, has given expression to one of the greatest tributes to God's universal and uncontested sovereignty found in all of Scripture. After humbling the king for his pride and arrogance, God once again brought his reason back to him, and he was moved to praise and honor of God, saying:

> For His dominion is an everlasting dominion, and His kingdom is from generation to generation. All the inhabitants of the earth are counted as nothing, and He does what

He wants with the army of heaven and the inhabitants of the earth. There is no one who can hold back His hand or say to Him, "What have You done?" (Dan 4:34b–35 HCSB).

With language reminiscent to Isaiah 40:17, Nebuchadnezzar speaks of the inhabitants of the whole earth, before God, as "counted as nothing." That is, the inhabitants of the earth can simply do nothing to thwart, jeopardize, or sabotage God's will or to keep God from doing what he has planned. It is in this sense, then, that they are "counted as nothing." Despite what the nations plot or plan or devise or scheme, God does exactly as he wills with the hosts (army) of heaven and the creatures of earth, so that the fulfillment of his will is universal in scope. And Nebuchadnezzar ends with this astonishing conclusion: "There is no one who can hold back His hand or say to Him, 'What have You done'"? No one can keep God's hand from doing what God chooses and wills, and no one can rightly charge God with wrongdoing or call into question the wisdom and rightness of his actions. God's power, his will, his authority, his wisdom, his knowledge all render any check to the power of his hand or any affront to the rightness of his plan strictly impossible.

Freedom under Comprehensive and Universal Sovereignty

Since God is sovereign over all that occurs in human history, we must seek, then, to understand the nature of human freedom in a way that accords with that divine sovereignty. And, since the Scriptures that teach us about God's sovereignty also teach us about the nature of human volition, we anticipate understandings of both that are consistent with one another. Whether we can understand fully how they fit together is another question. But that both teachings of Scripture are true and that both are consistent when taken together is our expectation from the outset.

But not only does the Bible's teaching on the nature of human volition need to be *consistent* with its teaching on divine sovereignty, because the doctrine of sovereignty just surveyed reveals God's comprehensive and universal control of all that occurs, our human volition must be manifest in a manner that is *compatible* with this strong understanding of divine sovereignty. Human freedom, in a word, must be compatibilistic. That is, comprehensive and universal divine sovereignty must be compatible with the actual and real manner by which human freedom operates. What, then, is human freedom, and how is it compatible with divine sovereignty?

Freedom as a Freedom of Inclination

Probably the single most important biblical conception relating to the question of human freedom is the notion that we human beings perform our choices and actions out of what we desire in our hearts. What we want most and what our natures incline us most to do combine to create the pool out of which the stream of our choices and actions flow. Using a different metaphor, consider Jesus' words:

> A good tree doesn't produce bad fruit; on the other hand, a bad tree doesn't produce good fruit. For each tree is known by its own fruit. Figs aren't gathered from thornbushes, or grapes picked from a bramble bush. A good man produces good out of the good storeroom of his heart. An evil man produces evil out of the evil storeroom, for his mouth speaks from the overflow of the heart (Luke 6:43–45 HCSB).

Our wills function, according to Jesus, as agents of our hearts. Out of the abundance of our hearts, we choose to speak what we will. If our hearts are filled with love for fishing or golf or computers or cars, of those loves we will speak. There is a necessary connection between character and conduct, heart and hands, desires and decisions. Our choices and actions and words and plans betray what we are on the inside. A good tree bears good fruit, and a bad tree bears bad fruit. Our wills give expression to the nature and character of our hearts.

Given this, what then constitutes our freedom as individuals? If, as Arminians propose, our freedom consists in the power of contrary choice, then unlike what Jesus has taught us, regardless of our hearts and characters, we are always free to choose good or evil. But Jesus indicated just the opposite—that a good tree cannot bear bad fruit, and a bad tree cannot bear good fruit. In other words, our volition expresses the precise kind and quality of the characters we have. So our freedom cannot consist in the power of contrary choice, but rather it consists in the power to choose according to what we are most inclined to do. We are free when we choose and act and behave in accordance with our strongest desires since those desires are the expressions of our hearts and characters. We are free when we choose to do what we want. Freedom, then, is not freedom of contrary choice but freedom to choose and act in accordance with what I most want. It is, as Jonathan Edwards called it, our "freedom of inclination." We are free when we act in accordance with what we are most strongly inclined to do.

Compatibility of Divine Sovereignty and Human Freedom

Can a strong sense of divine sovereignty be compatible with human freedom? To begin, it is clear that many factors influence our choices, yet we remain free so long as no influences are themselves coercive. When we choose what we most want (i.e., when we exercise freedom of inclination), we make our choice in the presence, as it were, of innumerable factors that influence, to one degree or another, what actually becomes our highest desire. Furthermore, God surely knows just what impact these influences have upon our decisions, so that prior to our choices and actions, God can know the precise choices and actions that we will do. God may know that certain influences will result in our acting in one particular way, but with a different set of influences we will be inclined to choose and act in a different way. Therefore, by knowing the sorts of influences that incline our wills or give us the strongest desires, he can know in advance what choices we will make.

As a result, God is able to know not only what impact a certain set of influences will have upon our decisions, but as God he also is able to adjust and regulate the influences that come into our lives, so that by controlling the influences he can regulate the choices we will make. Yet when we make those choices, since we choose and act according to our deepest desires and strongest inclinations, we act freely. Therefore, the picture is complete: God's sovereign control of human choice and action is fully compatible with our freedom in choosing and acting in accordance with our strongest inclinations and deepest desires.

There are many biblical examples of this compatibility. Numerous passages describe situations in which human beings do precisely what they most want to do, and they are both free and responsible for their actions, while at the same time, those actions humans freely choose to do, in turn, accomplish precisely what God has ordained and determined that they do. We could easily fill a whole book discussing examples from Scripture of the compatibility of divine sovereign regulation of human choices with the human freedom and moral responsibility in making those very choices.[34] One striking example is in chapter 10 of the book of Isaiah.

As this section begins, God describes Assyria as "the rod of My anger; the staff in their hands is My wrath" (Isa 10:5 HCSB). The point is immediately clear that Assyria is carrying out God's will and performing God's work. They are, that is, God's very rod and staff by which God is accomplishing his will. And so it is. In the following verses God declares, "*I will send him* against a godless nation; *I will command him* [to go] against a people destined for My rage, to take spoils, to plunder, and to trample them down like clay in the streets" (Isa 10:6 HCSB, italics added). Our preliminary hypothesis has now been confirmed. God sends Assyria to do this work of his, he commands Assyria to carry out his will. Assyria, then, is God's tool (rod and staff) that performs precisely what God commissions (sends and commands) him to do.

And just what is this work that God commissions? It is divine judgment against God's own people, Israel. God had warned Israel that should she disobey his word and turn from following him, he would bring judgment upon her. In part, this judgment would come in the form of other nations defeating Israel, taking

---

34. At least one book already has been filled on this subject. For an excellent discussion of many Old Testament passages and passages from John illustrating compatibilism, see D. A. Carson, *Divine Sovereignty and Moral Responsibility: Biblical Perspectives in Tension* (Grand Rapids: Baker, 1981).

her away in exile and plundering her cities and lands (see Deut 28:25–26, 36–37, 47–50, 63–65). Of course, such a warning is totally ineffectual unless God can control what nations do! For God to come true on his word that he will send other nations against her to plunder her and take her children into exile, God must be able to control the nations so that when Israel disobeys, he can actually fulfill what he has said. Isaiah 10 provides us with one picture of just how God, indeed, is able to carry out the warning he gave to Israel. He controls Assyria so much that the devastation that he brings upon Israel is, most importantly, *God's work* of judgment even though Assyria is the tool executing the judgment.

Some might conclude that Assyria cannot, then, be acting freely. But this clearly is not the case. We read in Isaiah 10:7, "But this is not what he [Assyria] intends; this is not what he plans. It is his intent to destroy and to cut off many nations" (HCSB). Notice particularly the phrase, "It is his intent to destroy." In other words, Assyria is doing exactly what he wants to do when he plunders and annihilates God's people, Israel. Assyria has no clue that he is being used as a tool of God to perform the will of God—hence, the opening phrase of 10:7, "But this is not what he intends." Rather, Assyria simply is doing exactly as he most wants, out of the deepest desires of his heart, and so Assyria acts freely. And for this, Assyria bears full moral responsibility and will be the object of God's just judgment (Isa 10:12,16).

Therefore, God's prior determination to raise up and use Assyria is fully compatible with Assyria's own freedom of will to do what he wants from the depths of his heart to do. And that desire at the same time fulfils exactly what God has ordained that he do. Comprehensive and universal divine sovereignty is fully compatible with human freedom that consists of people doing what they most desire to do.

God's Asymmetrical Control of Good and Evil

In light of the nature and extent of God's sovereign control, obvious moral questions arise that necessitate further exploration. Because God's nature is good and not evil and yet God has complete and absolute control over both good and evil, we must carefully consider God's relation to both good and evil, respectively. More specifically, it is incumbent upon us to view God's relationship to good and evil in asymmetrical terms. We must consider that when God controls *good*, he is controlling what *extends from his own nature*; yet when he controls *evil*, he controls what is *antithetical to his own nature*.

God's Relation to Good

In the case of good, first, God's own nature "breathes" goodness and exhibits goodness. No goodness external to God exists apart from God, for God is the giver of every good gift and every perfect gift (Jas 1:17 NKJV). In this sense, no goodness exists that is not God's goodness, since no goodness can originate anywhere other than in and by the very nature of God. Therefore, God's control over goodness must be through the mechanism of his own natural bestowing, out of his very nature, of the goodness that is produced. If no goodness can be produced apart from God's bestowing of it (see also Ps 34:8–10; 1 Cor 4:7; Acts 17:25), then all the goodness that occurs in the created order, including all goodness produced through human choices and actions, must flow from the very nature of God, as an extension of his own work and character.

Perhaps we should speak, then, of God's relation to goodness as through a kind of direct and immediate divine agency in which there is a necessary correspondence between the character and agency of God and the goodness that is produced in the world. We might call this kind of divine agency "direct-causative" divine action since it is strictly impossible for any goodness to come to expression apart from God's direct causation and as the outgrowth of his own infinitely good nature. Goodness, then, is controlled by God as he controls the manifestation and expression of his own nature, causing all the various expressions of goodness to be brought into our world, whether goodness in nature or goodness manifest through human (secondary) agency.

It stands to reason, then, because all goodness produced in the world results from the direct-causative agency of God, including even (and especially) that goodness that comes to be through human choice and action, that God should rightly receive *all* the glory for the good that is done. This understanding makes sense, for example, of Jesus' statement in Matt 5:16: "In the same way, let your light shine before men, so that they may see *your good works and give glory* to your Father in heaven" (HCSB, italics added). Or consider God's work of regeneration and conversion in the life of a sinner. Before God did his saving work in our hearts, we were slaves of sin (John 8:34; Rom 6:17a), blinded to the light of the gospel (Acts 26:18; 2 Cor 4:4), spiritually dead (Eph 2:1–3), and unable to do anything that pleased God (Rom 8:6–8). But God, by his love and grace (Eph 2:4–9), made light shine in our hearts (2 Cor 4:6) and awakening them (Acts 16:14) so that we now see the beauty and glory of Christ, having turned in love to the Light that we formerly hated (John 3:19–21). What divine agency, then, shall we say brought about our regeneration and conversion? Clearly God's own character of love, grace, mercy, and truth shone within us and caused us to believe and be saved. Therefore, the control that God exhibits in conversion must be through his direct-causative divine agency, by which aspects of his own nature are given expression in and through our lives as we embrace what is of him and make it our own. And as such, no boasting may be done before God for our salvation since all the good done originates from and is granted by God (1 Cor 1:30–31; Eph 2:8–9).[35]

And yet this direct-causative divine agency by which God's character is manifest in and through our lives is not a passive

---

35. One could add that all progress and fruitfulness in the Christian life must be by this same direct-causative divine agency. Consider Jesus' teaching in John 15 that unless the branch abides in the vine it cannot bear fruit, but when it abides and so draws from of the vine the life that flows in and through the branch, it bears much fruit. Jesus applies this to the lives of his followers, saying, "I am the vine; you are the branches. The one who remains in Me and I in him produces much fruit, because you can do nothing without Me" (John 15:5 HCSB). Jesus' agency, directly at work in and through us, bears his fruit through our lives. Hence, life lived in reliance on the power and risen life of Christ manifests in fruitfulness the character qualities of Christ. Or, in parallel language, if we walk in the Spirit, we will bear the fruit of the Spirit—those character qualities of the Spirit of Jesus lived out in our lives (Gal 5:16,22–23).

matter. Consider Paul's admonition to "work out your own salvation with fear and trembling. For it is God who is working in you, [enabling you] both to will and to act for His good purpose" (Phil 2:12b–13 HCSB). While it is God's work in us that causes both our willing and our working God's purpose, nonetheless this occurs only as we lay hold of the mandate to trust and obey and serve God with all of our heart. This is no independent work of ours separate from the work of God in us, but as John Murray has put it, "*because* God works we work."[36] The work that God does, then, in the life of a believer to produce fruitfulness and growth is by his direct-causative agency in and through us, flowing from out of his very character of wisdom, truth, goodness, holiness, and love. And because it is altogether his work, to him belongs all the glory, honor, and praise (Eph 1:6,12,14).

God's Relation to Evil

The case of evil presents a very different situation. Since evil can never extend from the nature of God in the way that good does and must, evil quite clearly stands against God and is antithetical to his very character. And yet as we saw earlier, the spectrum texts of Scripture do not blush to present God's control over evil in terms that are equal to his control of good. While evil never flows from the nature of God, it is in all cases controlled by the agency of God. So how shall we speak of the divine agency that controls evil?

Since God's control of evil does not extend from his own nature, it cannot be direct in the way his control of good is direct. That is, God cannot will directly and immediately to cause evil, since all that God wills to do himself (immediately) is good (Gen 1:31), and it is impossible for him to do evil of any kind. But, if God does not directly cause evil and yet evil happens under his exacting control, must it not be the case that he permits the evil to occur that he could, in any and every instance, prevent?[37]

We referred above to the mechanism by which God controls good as his direct-causative divine agency, so here we can refer to

---

36. John Murray, *Redemption—Accomplished and Applied* (Grand Rapids: Eerdmans, 1955), 149 (emphasis in original).

37. See Paul Helm, *The Providence of God*, in Contours of Christian Theology, series ed. Gerald Bray (Downers Grove: InterVarsity, 1994) for a helpful discussion of the divine permission in the Reformed sense as permission of what God could prevent.

God's control of evil as his "indirect-permissive" divine agency. While this indirect-permissive control of evil is no less exact or meticulous or comprehensive as his direct-causative control of good, nonetheless it is of a different kind. In God's control of evil through indirect-permissive agency, God's own character and nature are separated from the evil that is done. This stands in stark contrast to the union of his character and nature to all good that he accomplishes with the control he exerts over good through his direct-causative agency. So, while God controls both good and evil and his control of both is equal in force and measure, this control is also strikingly different in quality and in manner.

Is the notion of God "permitting" actions and events to occur a biblical idea? Consider these texts, where it seems clear that the biblical writers recognize and invoke this concept and way of speaking:[38]

> He [Laban] has cheated me [Jacob] and changed my wages 10 times. But *God has not let him harm me* (Gen 31:7 HCSB).

> "Whoever strikes a person so that he dies must be put to death. But if he didn't intend any harm, and yet *God caused it to happen by his hand,* I will appoint a place for you where he may flee" (Exod 21:12–13 HCSB).

> The demons [in the Garasene demoniac] begged Him, "Send us to the pigs, so we may enter them." And *He gave them permission.* Then the unclean spirits came out and entered the pigs, and the herd of about 2,000 rushed down the steep bank into the sea and drowned there (Mark 5:12–13 HCSB).

> In past generations *He allowed all the nations to go their own way* (Acts 14:16 HCSB).

---

38. I have added italics to each reference.

When they [Paul and Silas] came to Mysia, they tried to go into Bithynia, but *the Spirit of Jesus did not allow them* (Acts 16:7 HCSB).

I don't want to see you now just in passing, for I hope to spend some time with you, *if the Lord allows* (1 Cor 16:7 HCSB).

And we will do this *if God permits* (Heb 6:3 HCSB).

The language of divine permission is biblical, and the writers of Scripture evidently see no conflict between this language and conception and its other strong teaching on divine sovereignty. And, while some of these texts indicate permission from God for good things to occur, some specify God's permission of evil. Exodus 21:12–13 is especially instructive, where God "caused it to happen" when, obviously, as omnipotent, God could have prevented this event. Divine permission, then, is a legitimate category, and it has the advantage of indicating a way in which God retains full control of evil while not actively and directly causing it to occur. God is able to permit only those occurrences of evil that he knows will serve and never thwart or hinder his purposes. He is able to do this because, for any evil that may occur, it is always in God's power to prevent that specific evil even from happening.

One might say that this is also true for the God of Arminianism; this God, likewise, is omnipotent, and he also possesses the power to keep anything from happening that he would choose to prevent. Yet there is a significant difference between what might be thought of as the actual "functional power" of God in the world for the God of Arminianism and for the God of Reformed theology. The Arminian God has created the world with a sort of personal pledge that he will not violate the libertarian freedom of his moral creatures, except in the direst circumstances. Furthermore, he pledges also not to interrupt the normal processes of natural law and the forces of nature unless he deems it absolutely crucial so to do. Why? Simply because if he grants libertarian freedom and natural law but then constantly micromanages just *which* libertarian choices and *which* outworkings of natural law he will permit, such actions trivialize the value of having given both libertarian freedom and natural law in the first place. No, the integrity of the whole design of God by which he chose to make the world this way and not another requires that since he gave libertarian freedom, he will let it be used, and since he created natural laws, he will let the forces of nature operate without interference. Of course, he reserves the right to interfere in the most extreme of emergencies, but in the vast majority of cases, he chooses to permit both moral creatures and laws of nature to operate uninterrupted by God, even when those moral creatures or natural forces end up inflicting enormous gratuitous evil upon people. So in light of God's design for creation to operate by generally uninterrupted libertarian freedom and natural law, he is not functionally able to prevent the vast majority of evil from occurring.

How different this is from the Reformed understanding of God and his created design for the world! Here, God has full and absolute functional power to prevent any and every instance of evil that might occur, whether it is evil done by human volition or by laws of nature. Because God has determined to exercise meticulous sovereign rulership over the world, when it comes to regulating evil, God specifically permits only those instances of evil to occur that by his infinite wisdom and in light of his ultimate purposes he judges will advance and not hinder his designed ends for the world. Whereas in the Arminian (and open theist) understanding God accepts a world filled with innumerable instances of gratuitous or pointless evil, in the Reformed conception there is never, at any time or in any circumstance, such pointless evil. Rather, God regulates exactly the evil that occurs, since for any and every instance of evil, he specifically permits according to his wisdom and ultimate purposes what he could otherwise have prevented.

In the Arminian model, then, God's permission of evil is general and broad. He creates a world with laws of nature and libertarianly free creatures, and he "permits" that they act as they will. He permits them to carry out both natural evil and moral evil, but this permission is of the whole category of evil in general, not any specific instance of evil in particular. But in the Reformed model, God's permission of evil is meticulous, specific, and particular. He does not permit evil in general, but he does permit each and every instance of evil that occurs in human history. His permission is specific, in that for any instance of evil, both natural and moral, he possesses the power and absolute authority to prevent whatever action or event might conflict with the fulfillment of his purposes. So while both Arminian and Reformed models may appeal to God's "permission" of evil, the Arminian model supports God's general permission of the *class* of evil, and the Reformed model supports God's specific permission of *any and every particular instance* of evil. In the Arminian model God cannot functionally prevent evil without preventing the whole possibility of evil, in turn, by eliminating natural law and libertarian freedom altogether. But in the Reformed model, God can prevent any specific instance of evil that might be, ensuring that no evil is gratuitous and that only those instances of evil occur that advance, not hinder, God's ultimate aims.

Compatibilist Middle Knowledge and Divine Providence

One of the most perplexing questions that those in the Reformed tradition have endeavored to address is just how God's permission of evil functions in light of his eternal decree by which he ordains all that will come to be. That is, if God determines all that occurs, in what meaningful sense does God *permit* some things to occur (especially, evil) while he actively brings other things to pass? Put differently, using the language suggested above, if God decrees or determines all that will come to pass in human history, how can the distinction be meaningfully maintained between God's direct-causative agency and his indirect-permissive agency?

One promising answer to this question may result if a modified version of Molina's notion of middle knowledge[39] is incorpo-

---

39. Luis de Molina, *On Divine Foreknowledge*, Part IV of the *Concordia*, trans. Alfred J. Freddoso (Ithaca, NY: Cornell University Press, 1988). For contemporary defenses of the middle knowledge view, see especially William Lane Craig, *The Only Wise God: The Compatibility of Divine Foreknowledge and Human Freedom* (Grand Rapids: Baker,

rated, here, within a fundamentally Reformed and compatibilist model of divine providence.[40] Luis de Molina, a Jesuit theologian in the post-Reformation period, argued that God has three logical moments of knowledge prior to creating the universe. God not only possesses knowledge of what *could* be, i.e., knowledge of all bare possibilities and logical necessities (what Molina calls "natural knowledge") and knowledge of what *will* be, i.e., knowledge of all future actualities, or exact and detailed knowledge of the way the world, when created, will be (what Molina calls "free knowledge"). Significantly, God also possesses knowledge of what *would* be if circumstances were different from what they in fact will be in the actual world, i.e., knowledge of those possible states of affairs which would have become actual had circumstances other than those in the real world obtained (what Molina calls "middle knowledge").

According to this theory, sometimes referred to as Molinism, God knows all possible states of affairs, and he also knows what free creatures would do in various possible sets of circumstances. Although God does not and cannot control what free creatures do in any set of circumstances (they retain libertarian freedom in Molinism), he is able to control certain aspects of the circumstances themselves, and by this he can regulate which choices and actions *actually* obtain from among all those that are possible. Accordingly, by middle knowledge God exerts massively more providential regulative influence over the world than is the case if God possesses only simple foreknowledge, yet he does so in a manner in which libertarian freedom is retained for God's moral creatures.

Despite the appeal of Molinism, there are at least two significant problems with it as seen from a Reformed perspective.[41] First, it is not at all clear *how* God can know by middle knowledge

1984); and Thomas Flint, *Divine Providence: The Molinist Account* (Ithaca, NY: Cornell University Press, 1998).

40. Terrance L. Tiessen, *Providence and Prayer: How Does God Work in the World?* (Downers Grove: InterVarsity, 2000), 289–336.

41. Both classic Arminians and open theists would agree with the first of these two problems with Molinism, but they would deny that the second is a problem (since they affirm libertarian freedom) and they would object instead to Molinism being too deterministic in its overall framework and outcome.

just what choices free creatures would make in various sets of possible circumstances. The problem is this: since freedom in the libertarian sense is defined as the ability *all things being just what they are* to choose differently, it is impossible to know what decision will be made simply by controlling the circumstances within which it is made; all conditions being just what they are, one can choose otherwise. Control of the conditions exerts no regulative power over the actual choice made within those conditions. Therefore, it is impossible to know what decision *would* be made just by knowing the conditions within which it is made.

Second, Molinism's insistence on libertarian freedom is itself problematic. In brief,[42] libertarian freedom reduces human choosing to arbitrariness since no explanation can be given for why an agent would choose one way over another, all things being just what they are when he chooses. Further, the strong view of divine sovereignty taught in Scripture simply is incompatible with libertarian freedom. Therefore the very notion that humans have the power of contrary choice (as understood in the libertarian model of freedom) simply must be rejected. Hence, the Molinist model as it stands cannot and should not be adopted by Reformed thinkers.

But notice that both of these objections are fundamentally objections to libertarian freedom. The second objection is an explicit one. But the first objection, at root, points out the impossibility of God's knowing by middle knowledge what a free creature would do, if the type of freedom the creature has is libertarian freedom. It is clear, then, that the main problem the Molinist model faces, as traditionally conceived by Molina, is its insistence on libertarian freedom. But can middle knowledge be conceived, instead, with compatibilist freedom?

I believe not only that it can but that such a conception can be a tool for understanding God's control of evil that accords with biblical teaching and illuminates biblical texts. In what follows, then, I shall first explain how middle knowledge works with

---

42. For fuller discussion of these problems, see Ware, *God's Greater Glory*, 85–92; and John M. Frame, *No Other Name: A Response to Open Theism* (Phillipsburg, NJ: P&R, 2001), 122–31.

compatibilist freedom, and second, I will develop briefly the help this may be in understanding God's relation to evil.

Middle Knowledge and Compatibilist Freedom

Consider more specifically how middle knowledge might work if we assumed that human beings possessed compatibilist freedom—the freedom of inclination—rather than libertarian freedom. Recall that the freedom of inclination proposes that we are free when we choose according to our strongest inclination or deepest desire. In short, we are free when we do what we most want to do. This means that the circumstances and factors that influence our decisions result eventually in our having, at the moment of choice, *one* desire or inclination that stands above all others. The fact that we have *one* desire that is our *highest desire* explains why we make the *one choice* that we do, in that particular setting. Put differently, the set of factors in which the agent makes a choice constitutes a set of individually necessary and *jointly sufficient* conditions[43] for forming within the agent a strongest inclination or highest desire by which to make the one choice that is in accordance with that highest desire. And, the agent's freedom is then expressed when he chooses according to that highest desire.

What is different about this understanding of middle knowledge is that since freedom means that we always do what we most want and since what we "most want" is shaped by the set of factors and circumstances interacting with one's nature eventually giving rise to one desire that stands above all others, therefore God can know the circumstances giving rise to our highest desires; and by knowing these, he can know the choice that we would make, given those particular circumstances. What the Molinist

---

43. Necessary conditions are those which must be present for the effect to occur; sufficient conditions are those which, whether necessary or not, when present require that the effect occurs. As an example, consider the individually necessary and jointly sufficient conditions of combustion. Each of the following is necessary for combustion to occur: oxygen, fuel, friction/heat. But the presence of either merely one or two of these necessary conditions will not produce combustion. Rather, all three have to be present for combustion to occur; and when all three are present, combustion will occur. Therefore, we can say that oxygen, fuel, and friction/heat are the individually necessary (i.e., each must be present) and jointly sufficient (i.e., when all three are present, the effect occurs) conditions for combustion.

version of middle knowledge lacks—viz., a necessary connection between knowledge of the circumstances within which an agent makes a choice and knowledge of just what choice the agent would make—is here remedied by the replacement of libertarian freedom with compatibilist freedom. So, as a result, middle knowledge is explicable, and it "works" when compatibilist freedom is employed in a way it does not with libertarian freedom. Now the question is whether the notion of middle knowledge is biblical and how Scripture may indicate its use in understanding more clearly God's control of the world, particularly his control of evil.

Compatibilist Middle Knowledge and God's Relation to Evil

First, we should establish what others have shown also, viz., that Scripture indicates that God possesses middle knowledge[44] and that he makes important use of this middle knowledge. Consider a few scriptural examples of God's middle knowledge:

> When Pharaoh let the people go, God did not lead them along the road to the land of the Philistines, even though it was nearby; for God said, "The people will change their minds and return to Egypt if they face war" (Exod 13:17 HCSB).

> Then Saul summoned all the troops to go to war at Keilah and besiege David and his men. When David learned that Saul was plotting evil against him, he said to Abiathar the priest, "Bring the ephod." Then David said, "Lᴏʀᴅ God of

---

44. See, e.g., William Lane Craig, "The Middle-Knowledge View," in James K. Beilby and Paul R. Eddy, eds., *Divine Foreknowledge: Four Views* (Downers Grove: InterVarsity, 2001), 123–25. Craig comments that the passages he cites clearly support God's knowledge of counterfactuals (i.e., knowledge of states of affairs that are contrary to fact but could have obtained were circumstances different), but whether they are specifically examples of middle knowledge is difficult to know. If one proposes a compatibilist view of freedom, however, it seems clear that all of these are examples from Scripture of divine counterfactual and middle knowledge, since these are cases of God's knowledge of what would have been that are different from what his decree established ("free knowledge," in Molina). But presumably his decree took into account what we now see as counterfactual possibilities prior to the decree, or else we cannot understand why he would decree just what has obtained instead of the counterfactual possibility. If God considered these other possible states of affairs prior to the decree, then what God possessed is middle knowledge.

Israel, Your servant has heard that Saul intends to come to Keilah and destroy the town because of me. Will the citizens of Keilah hand me over to him? Will Saul come down as Your servant has heard? LORD God of Israel, please tell Your servant."

The LORD answered, "He will come down."

Then David asked, "Will the citizens of Keilah hand me and my men over to Saul?"

"They will," the LORD responded.

So David and his men, numbering about 600, left Keilah at once and moved from place to place. When it was reported to Saul that David had escaped from Keilah, he called off the expedition. David then stayed in the wilderness strongholds and in the hill country of the Wilderness of Ziph. Saul searched for him every day, but God did not hand David over to him (1 Sam 23:8–14 HCSB).

I did not send these prophets, yet they ran [with a message]. I did not speak to them, yet they prophesied. If they had really stood in My council, they would have enabled My people to hear My words and would have turned them back from their evil ways and their evil deeds (Jer 23:21–22 HCSB).

"Woe to you, Chorazin! Woe to you, Bethsaida! For if the miracles that were done in you had been done in Tyre and Sidon, they would have repented in sackcloth and ashes long ago! But I tell you, it will be more tolerable for Tyre and Sidon on the day of judgment than for you. And you, Capernaum, will you be exalted to heaven? You will go down to Hades. For if the miracles that were done in you had been done in Sodom, it would have remained until today. But I tell you, it will be more tolerable for the land of Sodom on the day of judgment than for you" (Matt 11:21–24 HCSB).

None of the rulers of this age knew it, for if they had known it, they would not have crucified the Lord of glory (1 Cor 2:8 HCSB).

Each of these examples from Scripture is helpful in establishing both that God in fact has middle knowledge (in other words, knowledge of what would have occurred, contrary to what did in fact occur) and in giving some indication of what use his middle knowledge may be to him in regulating the affairs of the world.

First, notice that middle knowledge is not restricted to God's dealing with evil. For example, Exodus 13:17 indicates that God used his middle knowledge of what Israel would have done had they traveled "along the road to the land of the Philistines" in order to prevent them from returning to Egypt. Similarly, the complicated account cited from 1 Samuel 23 indicates that when God told David that Saul *will* come down and that the men of Keilah *will* surrender him into the hand of Saul, we know that the statement actually means, "If you stay here, these things *will* happen" (it was an implicitly conditional divine prediction). We know this because David left and God spared his life! So, because David left and lived on, we now know from these statements from God that Saul *would have* come down and the men of Keilah *would have* surrendered him into Saul's hand, had David stayed. It is clear, then, that God provided David with middle knowledge of what would happen in order to bring about something positive.

Second, God's middle knowledge is so sure and certain that he even invokes it as the basis by which he discriminates varying degrees of punishment that will be meted out in the final judgment. Consider again Matthew 11:21–24. Christ indicates that the judgment upon Chorazin, Bethsaida, and Capernaum will be more severe than even the judgment upon the sinful cities of Tyre, Sidon, and Sodom! Why? What greater offenses have Chorazin, Bethsaida, and Capernaum committed? These cities in Jesus' day, hearing his preaching and witnessing his miracles, have not repented. Yet, he says, if the same miracles had been performed in the ancient cities of Tyre, Sidon, and Sodom, they *would have* repented. So the relative evaluation of greater offense and greater punishment for these contemporary cities is based on what would have been true had circumstances been different. This observation should give anyone pause who thinks that middle knowledge is a useless aspect of God's knowledge, even if it is true.

Third and last, Jeremiah 23:21–22, Matthew 11:21–24, and 1 Corinthians 2:8 indicate God's middle knowledge of what God himself could have provided to others that would have kept them from some evil that they in fact did commit. Yet God chose not to provide what he could have, presumably because he chose that the evil not be precluded or eliminated. That is, while God has middle knowledge, it is clear that he is not obligated to use it to spare others from the evil that will come upon them or the evil that they will commit. All three of these passages are sobering, as one contemplates seriously what they indicate. In Jeremiah 23, God could have sent prophets to his disobedient people, and had he done so, the people "would have" turned from their evil. But he did not. In Matthew 11, God could have performed miracles of the sort Jesus did at Tyre, Sidon, and Sodom; and had he done this, they "would have" repented and remained. But he did not. In 1 Corinthians 2, God could have given the rulers of Paul's age an understanding of God's wisdom in Christ, and had he done this, "they would not have crucified the Lord of glory." But he did not.

This last example from 1 Corinthians 2 has a particular significance since it relates to the unfolding of God's predestined plan of salvation in Christ. Recall Peter's words in Acts 4: "For, in fact, in this city both Herod and Pontius Pilate, with the Gentiles and the peoples of Israel, assembled together against Your holy Servant Jesus, whom You anointed, to do whatever Your hand and Your plan had predestined to take place" (vv 27–28). When one places 1 Corinthians 2:8 alongside Acts 4:27–28, one realizes that part of the fulfillment of what God's "plan had predestined to take place" involved his middle knowledge of what the "rulers of this age" (which would include, surely, both Herod and Pontius Pilate) should know or not know. God knew what these rulers would do with knowledge of God's wisdom in Christ and what they would do if they remained ignorant of that knowledge. So it appears that middle knowledge figured into the fulfillment of what God had "predestined" to occur through these rulers (and others, of course). Here, then, God's middle knowledge assists in the formation of God's predestined decree, by granting him knowledge of what would be true in one situation or in another, so that God is able to select for his decree the particular situation (that of the rulers of Paul's age not understanding God's wisdom in Christ) that will advance, not hinder, the fulfillment of God's plan.

Second, we turn now to consider more carefully just what use God's middle knowledge may have particularly in God's regulation of evil. As argued above, God's relation to good is through his direct-causative agency, since any good that is produced must flow from the only source there is of any and every good, viz., God's own nature. But God's relation to evil must of necessity be markedly different. As noted earlier, although God controls both good and evil (Isa 45:7), God is good and not evil (Ps 5:4). Therefore evil cannot flow from God in the way good does, but rather, evil stands diametrically opposed and antithetical to God's nature. God's control of evil for this reason cannot be direct or immediately causative as it is with good. Instead, God's relation to evil must be *indirect*, i.e., never in any respect expressive of his nature yet controlled altogether by his wisdom, authority, and power. And God's relation to evil must be *permissive*, i.e., produced altogether by portions of his sinful creation and never in any respect immediately by him yet regulated in every instance so to allow or disallow any and every instance of evil that occurs, as his wisdom, authority, and power direct.

Given this, middle knowledge would seem to have a special importance for God's regulation of evil. By controlling human sinful choices and actions in this manner, it never is the case that God either does evil directly (as he often does good directly), nor is it the case that he causes a person to do evil. When God envisions various sets of factors within which an agent will develop a strongest inclination to do one thing or another, the strongest inclination that emerges from these factors is not caused by the factors, nor is it caused by God. Rather, in light of the *nature of the person*, when certain factors are present, his nature will respond to those factors and seek to do what he, by nature, wants most to do. In short, the cause of the strongest inclination and the resultant choice is the nature of the person in response to factors presented to it.

By analogy, consider for a moment two persons, one with a serious smoking habit and the other without. Imagine the two walking together outdoors, away from the sight and smell of cigarettes. It may well be the case that in this setting there would not be anything present at that moment that would give rise in the heart of either person to a strongest inclination to smoke a cigarette. But if the two of them walked past an outdoor café where some people were smoking, just the sight and smell might elicit from the nature of the smoker a strongest inclination to light up a cigarette, whereas that same sight and smell might elicit from the nature of the nonsmoker a strongest inclination to walk quickly past the café and away from the smoke. In other words, what explains the choices each made is *how their natures responded to the factors presented to them*. Those factors do not cause the choices made, for notice that the factors were identical for the smoker and nonsmoker, yet the choices made by each were opposite in kind from one another. Nor would controlling the factors cause the choices made, because whether someone had "planted" smokers at that outdoor café or not would not affect the opposite choices of each in response. Rather, the causes of the respective choices were the two different natures of the respective individuals, each in response to the factors presented them, resulting in choices reflective of the natures of each person. The fact is, we act according to our natures, and what various factors in differing situations do is to elicit in each case the strongest inclination that our natures want in light of what factors are present.

Perhaps we should think of God regulating the factors of a situation, then, as "occasioning" a particular choice to be made, rather than causing a particular choice to be made. Because God knows the natures of each person perfectly, he knows how those natures will respond to particular sets of factors presented to them. Thus, without causing a person to do evil, he nonetheless controls the evil they do. He controls whether evil is done, what evil is done, and in any and every case he could prevent the evil from being done. But in no case does he cause the evil to be done. In this way God maintains meticulous control over evil while his moral creatures alone are the agents who do evil, and they alone bear moral responsibility for the evil they freely do.

With this big-picture view in mind, please consider now an example or two from Scripture where incorporating an understanding of middle knowledge contributes rich explanatory power to what seems to be taking place. First, let me remind the reader of one text already cited above. Recall Exodus 13:17: "When Pharaoh let the people go, God did not lead them along the road to the land of the Philistines, even though it was nearby; for God said, 'The people will change their minds and return to Egypt if they face war'" (HCSB).

Here we have a clear and indisputable case where Scripture reveals that God used middle knowledge of what Israel would do under other circumstances in order to regulate what they would in fact choose to do. Judging from what we read here, God knew that the people of Israel would act according to their strongest inclination. And he knew that factors in various settings would affect both the strongest inclinations they would have, and through these, what choices they would make. God could envision taking them by the way of the land of the Philistines, and he knew, by middle knowledge, that this situation would lead to their natures developing a strongest desire to return to Egypt. Now, of course God could act in this case in a direct-causative manner and simply give them a stronger desire to keep following him despite traveling through the land of the Philistines. But in God's wisdom, he chose instead to adjust the setting and by this ensure that the strongest inclinations that would develop within their hearts would be to continue following him and not to return to Egypt. But one thing is clear from this account, and that is that God respects the integrity of their choices, realizing that they truly do carry out what they most want. Therefore, he regulates their choices by presenting them with a situation in which the free choices they make accord with his will for them. God's sovereign control and their free moral agency are compatible, and in this case the compatibility occurs through God's use of middle knowledge.

Conclusion

God truly is glorious. In the infinite fullness of his transcendent self-existence and through the intimate presence of his immanent self-relatedness, he displays both his greatness and his goodness, his majesty, and his mercy. And how grateful we are that this glorious God, perfect in every way, is the God who also rules perfectly over heaven and earth. In the end, when every knee bows and every tongue confesses the lordship of Jesus the Christ, it will be evident to all that God has done all things well. Our only rightful response can be to live in trust and love and hope because of the greatness of God's character and the exactness of his work. Indeed, to God alone belongs all glory, both now and forevermore.

CHAPTER 4

Responses to Bruce A. Ware
"A Modified Calvinist Doctrine of God"

Response by Paul Helm

As I consider Bruce Ware's essay, the points of particular interest to me are the modifications, alterations, and adjustments Ware proposes to the classical Reformed and traditional Christian doctrine of God. I will specifically examine three areas: God's immanence, immutability and change, and compatibilist middle knowledge, which, to my surprise, Ware still commits himself to.

Divine Immanence

Like all theists Ware affirms both the transcendence and the immanence of God. God is apart from his creation, independent, and self-sufficient. He is also at work within his creation as he conserves and governs all his creatures and all their actions.

In an effort to make clear God's relationships with what he has made and to show that God is not insulated from involvement with the world, Ware proposes that God (transcendent) is timelessly eternal and that God (immanent) is in time. In this he partly follows, though he does not explicitly endorse, the proposal of William Lane Craig that God is timeless *sans* creation but in time at the first moment of the creation onwards.[1] Ware applies this proposal in parallel fashion to God's omnipresence, which he takes to be "the real and universal presence of God throughout the created order," possessing a life which is "present fully at every point of created space." As it is with space, so it is with time:

> 'Prior' to the creation of the world, God existed in himself, apart from any spatiotemporal reality, in the fullness of his infinite and glorious existence . . . when he created the heavens and earth, he brought into being their two-fold dimensions of spatiality and temporality. . . .God chose "to . . . 'enter' fully into both the spatial and the temporal dimensions of creation. . . . Hence, in becoming omnipresent and omnitemporal, God did not change in any respect who he eternally is apart from creation.

Nonetheless, it becomes possible for him to enter into a real relation with his creation, a relation in which he changes. But this is not quite the Craigian view, for according to Ware "at creation God became both omnipresent and omnitemporal while remaining in himself and apart from creation fully nonspatial and timelessly eternal."

But whatever the payoff of this view, it won't stand up. If God is wholly spatially present in the universe in the manner proposed by Ware, then he is spatial. However diffuse a form we may suppose such immanence to take, he has a spatial form or dimensions. It won't do to say that God is transcendently nonspatial and immanently spatial because that raises vital questions for divine unity, not to mention divine simplicity. The analogy with the incarnation is not apt, for Christ is two natured, but the immanence of God is not a nature of God alongside his transcendence. If God has a spatial form or dimensions, then he is spatial. He may, in creating, become immanent within his creation in the Warian fashion, but then he must cease to be nonspatial just as (in Craig's view) in creating, the timelessly eternal God becomes sempiternal and so ceases to be timeless. Ware makes

---

1. William Lane Craig, *Time and Eternity* (Wheaton: Crossway, 2001), chap. 6.

matters worse by supposing that God "chose" to fill space and time, as if he could have created space and time and chosen not to fill them, or have chosen to fill space but not time, creating "no-go" areas for himself. Is it possible that one could flee from God's presence or never be in his presence to begin with?

Let us state the problem as a dilemma: In becoming spatial, was God's spatial self related to his nonspatial, transcendent self? If so, how was it related? Spatially related? Then how, if X is spatial and spatially related to Y, can Y fail to be spatial? The view is reductionistic; God becomes nothing but spatial. Alternatively, was God's spatial self nonspatially related to his nonspatial self? Then how, if X is nonspatial and nonspatially related to Y, can Y be spatial? Again, the view is reductionism: God becomes nothing but nonspatial. Having abandoned divine simplicity Ware endangers divine unity. When God knows temporally, does he also know eternally?

I wonder whether behind Ware's proposal is a way of thinking about or visualizing God's boundlessness that is in fact deeply at odds with the tradition. It is as if Ware thinks like this: God's transcendence is like a fine, ethereal gas, spread out through the infinities of spacelessness. At the first moment of creation, God is faced with a decision: Shall I enter the universe? He decides to and enters. But necessarily he cannot be fitted into the universe, and some of him is left outside. What is left outside is God's transcendence; what enters is his immanence. But of course this is incoherent. Nothing can be spread out in spacelessness.

Finally, it is not at all clear what the problem is to which Ware's ingenious (though flawed) suggestion is the answer. God's immutability and atemporality are said to "insulate" God from real involvement with the world. But this is extremely puzzling. For if God's immutability and atemporality insulate him from real involvement with the world, they presumably insulate him from creating the world in the first place. But Ware does not claim this much, asserting merely that the eternal and immutable God may create the world, but in relating to the world he has created, he himself needs to be in space and time. But why?

Immutability and Change

What is behind Ware's talk of "real relationships" is his desire for a concept of a God who is thoroughly sovereign in the traditional sense but who really changes in important respects, as he thinks Scripture teaches. Although God is absolutely immutable in himself, in his nontemporal and nonspatial "face," in his spaceful and temporal "face" he really changes; he really responds to our prayers, grieves over our sins, is surprised by our actions, and the like. This desire for significant real change in God takes Ware once more some way toward the position of some Arminians who posit divine temporality in order to account for divine responsiveness to libertarianly free choices.[2] But once one such change in God's temporal "face" is introduced, it is impossible to stop it multiplying. For the subject of such changes (unless one is adopting a sort of bitheism) is God, and if the eternal God in his temporal face changes, then God changes.

But the puzzle here is, why does Ware, as a Calvinist, see the need for such an account of divine change? While affirming God's metaphysical and ethical immutability, he claims that God has "relational mutability." This is quite a shift away from the historic position; the move is unnecessary. Ware says, "God's disposition toward us in our unforgiven sin is one of judgment, wrath, and condemnation, but in Christ his disposition toward us is one of peace, acceptance and fatherly love." God is "relationally mutable" he changes.

Note that Augustine does not see things in quite the way that Ware does.

> When a righteous man begins to be a friend of God, he himself is changed; but far be it from us to say, that God loves any one in time with as it were a new love, which was not in Him before, with whom things gone by have not passed away and things future have been already done. Therefore He loved all His saints before the foundation of the world,

---

2. This is, by the way, a fairly modern Arminian view. Time was when Arminianism stood by the idea of divine eternality and saw it, as did Boethius of old, as one way of reconciling divine foreknowledge with human libertarian freedom, since if God is timelessly eternal, he cannot foreknow or predestine.

as He predestinated them; but when they are converted and find him, then they are said to begin to be loved by Him, that what is said may be said in that way in which it can be comprehended by human affections. So also, when He is said to be wroth with the unrighteous, and gentle with the good, they are changed, not He: just as the light is troublesome to weak eyes, pleasant to those that are strong; namely, by their change, not its own.[3]

Calvin endorses this view.[4] In fact, what Augustine and Calvin affirm is that it is unnecessary to think of God's eternal disposition to his people changing from hatred to love, as, paradoxically, Ware himself goes on to show. Changes in time are the result of eternally changeless dispositions. Ware puts it this way: "God is faithful to his promise . . . when the moral situation of his creatures changes, his faithfulness to his own pledge and promise requires that he change in appropriate ways in relation to them." But this is not required. What is required is that the conditionality of God's faithful promise be understood. Ware is on firmer ground when he says, "Because God had established from the beginning that those who repent and turn from their sin will be forgiven, he sent Jonah to Nineveh to preach the very message he knew, and Jonah also knew, would elicit the repentance that he sought from them." So the data Ware uses in fact point in the other direction from that in which he wishes to go. When Nineveh repented, God did not change, Jonah did. This is not a case of the Lord's saying, "If the Ninevites repent, then I will change my mind," but, "I eternally decree to threaten judgment upon Nineveh and to grant them forgiveness upon their penitence." No change is therefore needed on God's part, and no need for an ethical immutability weaker than that ontological immutability that makes it impossible for God to lie (Heb 6:18). The one unchanging God is a blessing to some and a curse to others. When men and women are saved by grace, they change; they move from being "children of wrath" to enjoying his peace

---

3. Augustine, *On the Trinity*, trans. A. W. Haddan (Edinburgh: T. and T. Clark, 1873), 164.

4. John Calvin, *Commentary on 2 Corinthians 5:19*. See also the second half of *Institutes* 2.16.2.

and grace. Ware does not need to say, "God's disposition toward us in our unforgiven sin is one of judgment, wrath, and condemnation; but in Christ his disposition toward us is one of peace, acceptance, and fatherly love."

Furthermore, the Pauline and Augustinian doctrine of grace rules out such ideas. Ware says, "So, when we change, say, from rebellion to repentance, God changes commensurately." But why and how do people change in these ways? By the love and grace of God in Christ working in them. What is the origin of that love and grace? They are loved eternally in Christ, chosen in him from before the foundation of the world, eternal life promised "before the ages began" (Titus 1:2). That love is free. We could conceive of that love being other than it is. But it is, nevertheless, eternal love. Where is the room, in Ware's scheme, for God's eternally prevenient grace operating in the effectual call of his people?

What is worrisome is that Ware's idea that God really changes his mind requires him to substitute the language of God knowing for the language of God decreeing. Ware says that God knew that Jonah's preaching would elicit the Ninevites' repentance. But as a Calvinist Ware must hold that God ordained their repentance, even that he granted it. Why does he not say so? And if God knew, merely, and changed when they changed, did he come to know? If so, when? Ware chides the open theists for their view that God learns. But is his merely ethically immutable God any different?

Compatibilist Middle Knowledge

It is a feature of Ware's view of human action that compatibilism is intrinsic to it. I have argued in my reply to Sanders that such unqualified endorsement of philosophical doctrines is dangerous and unnecessary for the Christian thinker. Compatibilist middle knowledge, like free will theism, embeds a philosophical idea into the understanding of Christian doctrine in a manner that is highly unusual and surely gives hostages to fortune. Like Jonathan Edwards, Ware goes so far as to claim that libertarianism is logically incoherent [5] and therefore that compatibilism is logically necessary. Where does Scripture claim as much?

His appeal to Scripture as the ground of compatibilism does not work for at least two reasons. One is that the texts he cites (e.g., Luke 6:43–45) do not prove that "we are free when we choose and act and behave in accordance with our strongest desires." Jesus' teaching here is about action types, not action tokens: the good person produces good, but this fact does not entail that the goodness of a good person determines what particular good actions that person willingly performs, only what types of action. Such teaching is perfectly consistent with the power of contrary choice. The second is that Ware's moral psychology is tautological and not consistent with Paul's teaching in Romans 7. He says, "We are free when we choose and act and behave in accordance with our strongest desires, since those desires are the expressions of our hearts and characters." Paul teaches that we often do what we do not want to do and that we are responsible for so acting. We may, as Ware claims, be free when we do what we want to do, but it does not follow that what we want to do on some occasion is what we most want to do on that occasion, as Paul shows, and as the phenomenon of weakness will bear independent testimony.

From endorsing compatibilism Ware moves to compatibilist middle knowledge as a way of understanding God's relationship to evil. I have argued in my contribution that there is no such thing as compatibilist middle knowledge. It is important to underline this argument in the face of Ware's renewed endorsement of it. He wishes to go beyond the mere idea of God's permission of evil to show *how* God's permission of evil functions in the light of his eternal decree. Ware notes that Scripture employs counterfactuals, stating what might have been but has not in fact been, as in the incidents of David at Keilah, and of Christ's pronouncing of woe to Chorazin and Bethsaida, cited by Ware. But he mistakenly thinks that God's knowledge of such possibilities amounts to "the very notion of middle knowledge," and that Molinism is

---

5. Bruce Ware, *God's Greater Glory* (Wheaton: Crossway, 2004): "Human freedom, in a word, must be compatibilistic" (78).

but one "version" of such divine middle knowledge, the version that embodies libertarian choices.

This is a mistake on a matter of historical fact and theologically confusing as a result. To be consistent with his Calvinistic commitment to the divine decree of all things, Ware has to say that the counterfactual possibilities of Scripture represent sets of possibilities that God might have *decreed* but none of which he has, in his wisdom, in fact decreed. If so, God's "middle knowledge" does not come into it. That is a Jesuit device designed to accommodate libertarian freedom—no more and no less. So wherever Ware appeals to the items of compatibilist middle knowledge consistently with his Calvinism, he ought to be appealing to the divine decree. To use one of his examples, Jeremiah 23, the fact that God could have sent prophets to his disobedient people has nothing to do with God possessing middle knowledge but everything to do with God's having in his mind an array of possibilities each of which he could equally well have willed. He could have decreed that prophets go to his disobedient people and by their means his people turn from their evil. But he did not so decree. The Lord did not simply *know* what his people would do in the circumstance where prophets were sent to them; he knew this fact because he knew something about himself—that he could *decree* preaching of such a character which, together with his work in the hearers' hearts and minds, would have been sufficient for his people to turn from their evil. He could have decreed such preaching, but he did not.

The puzzle is that Ware seems to be dimly aware of this. Let us suppose for a moment that God does possess genuine middle knowledge, the sort that the Molinists appeal to. From where does he obtain it? According to Ware, it is "knowledge of what God himself could have provided;" that is, (I presume) knowledge of what he himself could have decreed but chose not to. "Middle knowledge" in these circumstances is simply a misnomer for God's natural knowledge, the knowledge he has of all possibilities.

In the case of much evil, God's decree is what he willingly permits. But not all evil—some he brings about through secondary agency, as Ware graphically illustrates from Isaiah 10. Of course in both good and evil, God "respects the integrity of [human] choices," which is just to say that it is his creatures who make the actual choices, not God; his people choose not to go into the land of the Philistines; it is not God making that choice for them. I type this page; it is not God typing the page for me, and so on. But all that happens does so (according to the Calvinism that Ware espouses) in accordance with the divine decree. So according to Scripture, despite Ware's protestations to the contrary, God's relation to evil is not simply permissive; "I will send him against a godless nation; I will command him [to go] against a people destined for My rage, to take spoils, to plunder, and to trample them down like clay in the streets" (Isa 10:6 HCSB). This is particularly so where the evil action is employed punitively.

There is no such thing as compatibilist middle knowledge, and I submit that Calvinists can get no farther in understanding the Lord's relation to evil than by using the age-old distinction between primary and secondary causation and, in some cases, by invoking divine willing permission.

Response by Roger E. Olson

I am grateful to my friend Bruce Ware for demonstrating in his chapter the significant common ground we share in the doctrine of God. As a classical Arminian, I agree wholeheartedly and enthusiastically with the basic concepts he expounds about God's nature and relationship with the world. This may come as a surprise to many readers including both Calvinists and Arminians. (I do not say "both Reformed and Arminians" because I consider classical Arminian theology a type of Reformed theology.[6]) It may also come as a surprise to Bruce! I was myself somewhat surprised to discover the breadth and depth of our agreement by reading his chapter. I found I could say a hearty "Amen!" in many cases.

Arminians agree with Bruce's vision of God as both unqualifiedly good and loving toward the world. According to Bruce

---

6. See my book *Arminian Theology: Myths and Realities* (Downers Grove: InterVarsity, 2006).

(in contrast to some Calvinists), "(God's) love . . . is unconditional without qualification." In the first part of his chapter Bruce's description of God's character, nature, and relationship with creatures evokes nothing but full agreement; indeed, it is inspiring and soul stirring even to an Arminian. It may surprise Bruce to know that classical Arminians can also affirm with him God's "strong and pervasive sovereignty." The agreement dwindles somewhat as he expounds his meaning of this phrase in the second half of his chapter. Nevertheless, contrary to what many Calvinists (and perhaps others) believe, classical Arminians have never denied God's sovereignty.

Classical Arminians also agree with Bruce's affirmation of God as both transcendent and immanent. To his statement that "the eternal existence of God is the eternal existence of *all perfection, infinitely and intrinsically possessed, within the eternal triune nature of God,*" Arminius and all of his faithful followers would say, "Amen." No less agreement appears when Bruce turns to God's divine immanence and relatedness to creatures. Arminians are in total agreement with the affirmation that "the God of the Bible actively seeks intimate relationship with those he has made. His love for the world is unconditional and inexhaustible."

The only problem is that we are not sure how that belief is consistent with Bruce's claims about God's meticulous providential control of evil in the rest of his chapter. This is especially true about the apparent consequences of those claims that Bruce does not explicitly draw out of them. If God's love for the whole world is unconditional and inexhaustible, why would he render certain the eternal suffering of some significant portion of humanity in hell? Bruce does not explicitly say that he does, but that seems to be the good and necessary consequence of his doctrine of providence and predestination.

As a classical Arminian, I have no particular qualm about Bruce's delineation of God's attributes of eternity or immutability. These ideas are by no means inconsistent with classical Arminian theology even if not every Arminian has viewed them this way. The nineteenth-century Arminians such as Richard

Watson, Thomas Summers, William Burton Pope, and John Miley posited similar attributes of God. God's ethical immutability is clearly affirmed by classical Arminianism and what Bruce calls God's "relational mutability" rings true to Arminian sensibilities. The only question Arminians would pose to Bruce about his description of relational mutability is whether it is entirely consistent with his strong vision of God's sovereignty. How can an all-determining God be affected by anything creatures do since God is rendering their actions certain even if only indirectly? Is this not God affecting himself? Of course, God can indeed affect himself and even cause himself to change in some ways, so if that is what Bruce means, instead of what he seems to say, there is no problem. Arminians agree completely with Bruce's statement that "as we marvel at God's constancy, stability, and immutability, we should also marvel at his chosen path of variability, relational adaptability, and mutability. What a God, and what an unspeakable privilege to be in relationship with him."

Arminians begin to disagree with Bruce's section entitled "God's Providential Governance." He says, "While never minimizing either the genuineness of human choosing or the moral responsibility attached to human choice, Scripture presents God as exercising ultimate and exacting control over just what happens." Most Arminians will believe that in the rest of his chapter Bruce does inadvertently and unintentionally minimize the genuineness of human choosing and the moral responsibility attached to human choice. Furthermore, they will judge that his description of "God's ultimate and exacting control over just what happens" contradicts his earlier affirmations of God's unconditional love and creaturely moral responsibility. And, most seriously, classical Arminians will decide that his doctrines of providence and predestination do, indeed, make God the author of sin and evil even if against his own wishes.

The problem lies in Bruce's description of the divine will as all-encompassing and efficacious. It is not that Arminians disagree with God's sovereignty as control of everything that happens. Classical Arminians agree wholeheartedly that nothing whatever can happen without God's agreement. Like most

Calvinists known to this writer, Bruce fails to understand and correctly describe the classical Arminian concept of God's sovereignty. His description of it sounds more like deism than Arminianism; Arminius and all of his faithful followers, including current ones (e.g., Jack Cottrell), agree that God is intimately involved in everything that happens; absolutely nothing can happen that God does not decide to permit and God does not take a "hands-off" approach to dealing with his creatures. There is nothing in Arminian theology that forbids divine intervention in nature or history (including human freedom) unless that would require that God will or cause (including render certain) evil. Like most Calvinists, Bruce overlooks the Arminian doctrine of prevenient grace in which God is actively persuading his human creatures to the good and enabling them to do it.

Arminians agree that "all things occur as God has willed." However, they distinguish between God's antecedent will and God's consequent will in order to avoid the implication that God is the author of sin and evil. Antecedent to moral choices made by free persons, God wills that no one perish. Consequent to the moral evil and lack of repentance God allows in his creatures, God wills that some perish. Why? Because the only alternative even for him would be to force some persons into heaven against their wills. This would violate the nature of personal, loving relationships. In other words, for Arminians God's will is not always efficacious. Sometimes it is consequent and reluctant. If God's will were always efficacious, as Bruce and most Calvinists affirm, how would God not be the author of sin and evil?

Arminians will raise questions about Bruce's statements about God's plan and will when, for example, he says that "the fulfillment of his will is universal in scope." Is he talking about God's perfect and ideal plan and will? Or his consequent will in view of human defection from his perfect antecedent will? Does not this statement and many others Bruce makes necessarily imply that God is the author of sin and evil? Are sin and evil encompassed in God's will? Arminian theology answers both yes and no. Sin and evil are not encompassed in God's antecedent will but only in God's consequent will. God reluctantly allows them without planning them or wanting them in his world. This view implies a divine self-limitation. Perhaps it is the most significant difference between Bruce's vision of God and the Arminian one. The latter sees God as self-limiting for the sake of the genuineness of his relationship with human persons. God does not always get his way. That is because he reluctantly chooses for it to be so. Bruce's account of God's plan and will seems to imply that God wants whatever is happening to happen and that there is no reluctance on God's part in permitting sin and evil. Does this include the fall of humanity in the garden, the Holocaust, and the eternal suffering of some significant portion of humanity in hell? If so, what kind of God is that? As Wesley said of the claim by some Calvinists that this is compatible with God's love, it is such a love as to make one's blood run cold.

Some Arminians embrace the compatibilist understanding of free will so expertly described by Bruce. The majority, I judge, do not. That is because it is inconsistent with libertarian freedom and libertarian freedom is necessary for persons to be morally responsible for their actions and for personal relationships to be real and meaningful. I would like to register an Arminian complaint about Bruce's claim that "if, as Arminians propose, our freedom consists in the power of contrary choice, then quite unlike what Jesus has taught us, regardless of our hearts and characters, we are always free to choose good or evil." This statement completely ignores the Arminian affirmation of total depravity and the Arminian belief in the necessity of prevenient grace for choosing the good. According to classical Arminian theology, no fallen person of Adam's race can ever choose the good without supernatural assistance from God. The larger question here, however, is whether compatibilist freedom makes sense. Bruce says that "our freedom cannot consist in the power of contrary choice [ability to otherwise than we do], but rather it consists in the power to choose according to what we are most inclined to do." We are controlled by our motives; and our motives, it seems, flow from our natures. Thus, free will is compatible with determinism as all our decisions and actions are determined by natures and motives.

Why do most Arminians reject this account of free will in favor of the power of contrary choice or libertarian free will as ability to do otherwise? First, let's be clear that Arminians do not believe we are always free to do otherwise; our free will is situated, limited, and, in the case of good and evil, enabled by God's grace to choose the good. Second, free will as power of contrary choice seems necessary for moral responsibility. If you sit on a jury and have to decide the guilt or innocence of a person who committed a crime but could not have done otherwise how would you decide? Most jurors would judge the person not guilty insofar as he or she could not do otherwise than he or she did. If people's decisions and actions are determined by anything such that they could not do otherwise than they do, wherein lies their moral accountability or guilt? Even more significantly, however, the Arminian asks, if people always act out of their strongest inclinations that are determined by their natures, where do the moral qualities of their natures and inclinations come from? To put it bluntly, from where (or whom) did the first inclination to evil come? Given the strong account of God's meticulous providence provided by Bruce and most Calvinists the answer can only be "from God." If he or they were to say "from the creature," that would open up an enormous hole in their account of God's sovereignty and imply that creatures were able to act or decide independently of God's control. But if they say "from God," then God is the author of sin and evil, which is something Bruce and most Calvinists do not want to say.

The problem becomes even more intense when Bruce turns to combining his compatibilist account of human freedom with God's middle knowledge. This account more than implies that God uses his knowledge of what a "free" creature will necessarily do in a particular set of circumstances to render certain everything in history exhaustively. (Bruce does not use the language of "rendering certain," but I judge it to be equivalent to what he says about God's active and willing permission of everything including evil.) If I understand Bruce's account of providence correctly, then, he argues that whatever happens, including moral evil, lack of repentance, and eternal suffering in hell, is rendered certain by God. This is not by "direct-causative agency" but by "indirect-permissive agency." But, given his understanding of God's use of middle knowledge in arranging and controlling all creaturely decisions and actions, how does the latter *functionally* differ from the former? To claim that God is not the author of sin and evil or morally responsible for them because he does not directly cause them but only renders them certain using middle knowledge and control over human choices in order to make history perfectly fulfill his plan sounds like a verbal subterfuge to Arminian ears.

Like most Calvinists, then, Bruce appeals to a kind of divine permission in contrast to divine causative agency to fit evil into God's sovereign plan and purpose. I judge this to be an "efficacious permission" (a term used by some Calvinists) even if Bruce does not specifically call it that. In other words, for Bruce, God efficaciously permits evil without being stained by it. That is, he renders it certain using his knowledge of what free creatures will do in any given set of circumstances and placing them there. This is more than implied when Bruce says that "God's middle knowledge assists in the formation of God's predestined decree, by granting him knowledge of what would be true in one situation or in another, so that God is able to select for his decree the particular situation . . . that will advance, not hinder, the fulfillment of God's plan." In the middle of that sentence, Bruce explicitly mentions "the rulers of Paul's age not understanding God's wisdom in Christ." That is more than to imply that the sin of crucifying Jesus Christ was rendered certain by God. Two crucial questions arise. First, if sinners cannot do otherwise, how are they responsible? Second, if God renders sin certain how is he not stained by it?

The distinction between God's direct-causative agency and indirect-permissive agency seems scholastic and artificial once one recognizes that the latter is efficacious—which it must be given Bruce's account of God's use of middle knowledge to render every human decision and action certain. How does his strategy get God off the hook, so to speak, for authorship of sin and evil? Sure, God does not directly cause them, but he renders them certain. (Notice that the "them" includes the eternal suffering of the wicked.) If God controls everything in this meticulous manner that renders everything certain, including evil and eternal suffering, why doesn't he save everyone? He could. When Arminians read or hear this kind of account of God's sovereignty, they immediately think that, in spite of Calvinists' good intentions, this God is at best morally ambiguous. He is certainly manipulative, and his manipulation of creatures extends to their being condemned to hell for eternity. Yes, Bruce would no doubt, like most Calvinists, argue stringently that God is not guilty because creatures who go to hell deserve their fate. But Arminians wonder how this can be since they could not do otherwise? Their fate is sealed, so to speak, by God's control of their "free" choices through use of middle knowledge. And to appeal to their natural desires does not get God off the hook because he could have put them in circumstances where they would have chosen differently. It also does not explain why these particular persons have natures and desires so directly contrary to their Creator's. How did that come about?

The Arminian disagreement with Bruce will focus on one of his final claims: "God maintains meticulous control over evil while his moral creatures alone are the agents who do evil and they alone bear moral responsibility for the evil they freely do." Arminians agree with this statement on its face, but given the context in which it appears, they cannot agree with it because here "meticulous control" means efficacious permission rendering the evil actions of creatures certain. Even more, it means positive manipulation of creatures so that they will do evil actions (not repenting, for example) and suffer eternally for them.

After all is said and done, the classical Arminian will have to judge that Bruce's account of the doctrine of God is not really "modified Calvinism." Or at least it is not sufficiently modified to avoid the Achilles' heel of classical Calvinism—implying that God is the author of sin and evil and thus rendering God morally ambiguous at best.

Response by John Sanders

There is much in Bruce Ware's discussion with which I agree. We agree that God is both transcendent and immanent and also that God does not create a world out of neediness, but rather out of grace. Ware's emphasis on God's work in human history is admirable, and his quotation of Moltmann to the effect that God's real glory is manifested in his humiliation is wonderful. Other areas of agreement lie in our affirmation that since creation God experiences temporal duration and that God is weakly rather than strongly immutable. That is, we both believe that though the divine nature does not change, God can be and is affected by his creatures. These are important points of agreement, and I am glad to share in these beliefs with Ware.

There are, of course, differences between the way Ware and I parse out some of these beliefs, and there are several key issues about which we disagree. On several occasions Ware has stated these differences clearly and helpfully. In the remainder of my response I will follow the flow of his chapter and raise some questions for further reflection.

To begin, I heartily affirm Ware's discussion of God's transcendence and immanence and the fact that God does not need us as far as God's ontological existence is concerned. Also, we agree that the triune godhead eternally possesses all perfection, infinitely and intrinsically. Ware's explanation of this point is well done. For me, several questions arise about which I am not sure of Ware's meanings, and so there may or may not be real differences between us on these points. To begin, he claims that "Scripture makes abundantly clear" and that the "biblical point of view" teaches these highly philosophical assertions about the divine perfections. Though I agree with Ware on these perfections, I do not believe they can simply be read off the pages of the Bible as though these are the precise meanings the biblical writers had in mind. He says that "God exists eternally by his own will and nature." This may be correct, but I can think of no biblical text that expressly affirms such an abstract concept. On several occasions in his essay, Ware makes such remarks and then claims that this is the biblical view. Though Ware and I agree, for example, that God created the universe out of nothing, neither Genesis nor any other biblical text explicitly teaches this. It would be better for Ware to say that he arrives at these conclusions via both biblical and philosophical reasoning.

Second, Ware says that "it is unimaginable that God could ever receive some quality, some value, [or] some knowledge." If by this Ware means that the divine nature is never improved by what creatures give to God, then free will theists agree. It would seem that this is his meaning since he later says that God is affected by what creatures do. However, the inclusion of the word "knowledge" in his statement raises a question. If Ware had spoken of the divine wisdom rather than knowledge this question would not arise. When he says that God cannot receive knowledge, Ware could mean that none of the divine knowledge can be dependent upon what creatures do. This is, in fact, the position of great thinkers such as Aquinas and Calvin. This is precisely the reason they rejected the traditional way that the free will tradition explained God's foreknowledge of what creatures with free will do. According to "simple foreknowledge" God, so to speak, "looks ahead" and "sees" what we are going to do in the future, and God does this without causing us to do what we do. That is, God's knowledge of what we will do is determined by what we do. God would have different knowledge if we chose differently. For example, God foreknows that Billy Bob will wear a blue shirt to church next Sunday; but if Billy Bob had decided to wear a yellow shirt, then God's foreknowledge would have been different.

Theological determinists reject simple foreknowledge because it makes *some* of the divine knowledge dependent upon what creatures freely decide to do. For free will theists, divine knowledge of what we will freely do is not under God's control. All free will theistic understandings of divine omniscience (simple foreknowledge, dynamic omniscience, or middle knowledge) include this aspect of dependence, which is one reason Paul Helm rejects them. According to the usual way the theory of middle knowledge is explained, the so-called counterfactuals of creaturely freedom are not under God's control. According to middle knowledge, God knows what any creature would freely do if any of the circumstances of the situation were altered. For example, God knows that Sally Mae would help a fellow student study for an exam under one set of circumstances but that she would refuse to help that same student under a different set of circumstances. The rub is that God's knowledge of what Sally Mae would do in these different circumstances is dependent upon the sort of character Sally Mae possesses. If she were slightly different, then God would have slightly different knowledge. Again, what God knows about what creatures with libertarian freedom will or would do is not under God's control according to free will theists; and since Ware rejects libertarian freedom, it seems that by his statement that God cannot receive knowledge from creatures he rules out all forms of free will theism.

A third and and related issue is that Ware seems to believe that some of the emotions God has are dependent upon or conditioned by what creatures do. This would mean that God's independence from the world cannot be absolute as it is for Helm because God is, in some respects, affected by what creatures do. Relational mutability is logically inconsistent with unqualified divine independence.

This brings us to the fourth consideration. Ware's affirmation of relational mutability corresponds with the revisions he makes in the traditional doctrine of divine timelessness. He rightly says, "Both God's relation to time (divine eternity) and God's relation to change (divine immutability) need some reconsideration and reformulation to demonstrate that God chooses to live in relationship with what he has made." The revisions Ware and some other Calvinists make to these doctrines warm the heart of free will theists, for we think they are moves in the right direction. If I understand him correctly, Ware means that prior to creation God was atemporal or timeless but after creation God is temporal, experiencing duration.

Time and change are related because if, for example, God changes from a state of bliss to being grieved over human sin, then there was a moment when God experienced one emotion followed by another moment in which God experienced a different emotion. This is why Augustine, Aquinas, Calvin, and

Helm affirm both divine atemporality and strong immutability (God cannot change in any respect). It is logically inconsistent to affirm divine atemporality and that God changes in some respects because a timeless being cannot change, for change involves time. Though Ware is here breaking away from a strong theological heritage, he is not saying that God's nature, character, or his attitudes toward creatures undergo changes. God is constant, but God is also adaptable. I wholeheartedly concur when Ware writes: "As we marvel at God's constancy, stability, and immutability, we should also marvel at his chosen path of variability, relational adaptability, and mutability."

Ware then applies this approach to the story of Jonah. He says that God has always operated with the principle that those who repent of their sin will be forgiven. God's attitude toward the people of Nineveh is one of wrath intending destruction for their sins. When Jonah announced this judgment, the people repented and so God honored his principle and relented from his threatened judgment. Says Ware, "God honored his long-standing word and so changed in his relationship with them."

In this passage Ware criticizes and rejects the way open theists explain God's "relenting" from his announced judgment. I have two brief comments on this. The first is that some open theists explain the text the same way Ware does. Gregory Boyd, for example, argues that prior to creation God decided how he would respond to any possible situation that might arise. Hence, God eternally established the principle that if he announced judgment on sin and then the people repented, then God would forgive them. Not all open theists take this route, but at least one prominent open theist uses the same road as Ware. Second, Ware accuses open theists of "presuming Jonah to have more insight than God." This is a terrible caricature of our position. Even those open theists who do not follow Boyd's eternally "preplanned response" idea believe that God operates with eternal wisdom, justice, and love. They believe that God establishes principles such as the one Ware specifies: If you repent, then I will forgive. We believe that God was genuinely going to destroy the people but responds to their repentance by changing his mind from what he had originally said. This change of mind is not flippant but grounded in what Ware calls God's "ethical immutability."

Open theists do not believe that God eternally knew exactly how the people of Nineveh would respond to his announced judgment. Ware believes that God did eternally know how they would respond, and this belief returns us to a fundamental difference between theological determinism and all forms of free will theism. According to theological determinism, God knows the future actions of creatures because God determines them. God foreknows because he foreordains everything. Free will theists, on the other hand, believe that God's knowledge of what free creatures do is determined by the creatures, not God. This reasoning brings us back to the discussion above regarding whether any of God's knowledge is conditioned by or dependent upon what creatures do. Theological determinists answer no while free will theists answer yes.

At this juncture a fundamental incongruity appears between Ware's affirmation of relational mutability and his affirmation of meticulous providence. In his section on providence, Ware states that God determines everything that occurs, including all human actions whether good or evil. God meticulously controls everything such that only what he has foreordained comes to pass. God's will is never thwarted in the least detail because God micromanages creation. God foreknows what will happen because God writes the script. Helm argues this position as well; but whereas Helm rejects any idea of God's being conditioned by creatures, Ware seems to affirm it by his relational mutability.[7] For Ware, God seems to be genuinely affected by creatures.

The free will tradition has always maintained that, for some things, God is affected or conditioned by creatures. This is why free will theists affirm doctrines such as conditional election and that our prayers can genuinely affect God. It seems to me that Helm, unlike Ware, is logically consistent on this point. After all, what sense does it make to say that everything happens, includ-

---

7. Louis Berkhof objects to any sort of conditionality in God. He claims that if infralapsarians affirm conditionality in God, then they are Arminians and no longer Calvinists. See his *Systematic Theology*, 3rd ed. (Grand Rapids: Eerdmans, 1946), 118–25.

ing all human actions, exactly the way God ordains it to be and then also affirm that God is grieved by some things that happen? We grieve because something does not go the way we wanted. If a loved one dies or strays from the good, we are saddened. But why would God be saddened when absolutely everything is working out precisely as he intended? Why would anyone be grieved if his blueprint was being carried out to perfection? Ware is inconsistent to affirm both meticulous providence (theological determinism) and that God is grieved. Augustine and Calvin both understood this, which is one of the reasons they denied that God is ever grieved.

Ware says that God knows precisely how we will respond if we are placed in various circumstances, so God providentially enacts circumstances that lead us to perform the act that he knew and specifically ordained we do. If so, then how can God be grieved? If God does not intend the world to be any different than it is at any particular moment, then the course of events is precisely what God ordained it should be. If you get exactly what you want, why would you be sad? Helm's position is logically consistent because theological determinism entails strong immutability, and a being that is strongly immutable does not experience time. If God exercises meticulous providence, then God is strongly immutable and if strongly immutable then atemporal. Consequently Ware's revisions of Calvinism do not work. These modifications seek to make God responsive and sound as though God enters into dynamic give-and-take relations with us. Ware's revisions comport better with evangelical piety but at the cost of logical consistency.

At this point I will discuss Ware's understanding of divine providence and human freedom. For Ware, God is able to attain meticulous control over human actions without rendering humans puppets by means of compatibilistic freedom. Compatibilism seeks to combine divine determinism with human responsibility. Compatilistic freedom means that though our desires are determined by forces we cannot control, we act freely so long as we act on our strongest desire. For example, remote causes determine Billy Bob's desires. He cannot change what his strongest desires are. If remote causes have determined that his strongest desire upon entering an ice cream store is for chocolate ice cream, then he will choose chocolate, and he cannot choose butter pecan. Billy Bob is free in the sense that he, and nobody else, acts on his strongest desire to choose chocolate. Though his desires are determined, he is free because he is doing what he wants to do. He does not want any other flavor, and he is free to choose only chocolate.

Compatibilistic freedom is logically consistent with meticulous providential control. It explains how God can guarantee that absolutely everything that happens is specifically ordained by God to happen and how God's blueprint is carried out in exhaustive detail such that God does not desire the world to be any different than it is at any particular moment. All that God has to do is to ensure that our desires are determined in the way he wants. For example, if God intends for Billy Bob to fix the flat tire on his neighbor's car, all God has to do is to ensure that remote causal factors produce that desire in Billy Bob. Since he can only act on this strongest desire, he will, in fact, change the tire. If God wants Billy Bob not to fix the flat tire, God arranges the remote causes such that Billy Bob's strongest desire will be to ignore his neighbor's plight. God does not directly cause Billy Bob's actions; rather, God determines his desires, and it is his desires that are the immediate or direct cause of his actions. Billy Bob is the one choosing to act on his desire, and no one is coercing him because he wants to act on his desire. In this way, God is able to guarantee that everything that happens in human history is exactly what God ordained should happen even though God is not the direct cause of all that happens. There is, to my knowledge, no refutation of compatibilistic freedom, but clearly, free will theists do not find it satisfactory as an explanation of human decision making or for getting God off the hook for evil.

Let me finish my discussion of Ware's view of human freedom with two brief comments. First, Ware needs to nuance his understanding of how libertarian freedom works.[8] Proponents

---

8. For works supporting libertarian freedom that carefully qualify it, see Peter Van Inwagen, *An Essay on Free Will* (New York: Oxford University Press, 1983); Austin Farrer, *The Freedom of the Will* (London: Adam and Charles Black, 1958); Robert Kane, *The*

of libertarian freedom do not claim that each and every decision we make is free in this sense. Also, proponents believe that as our characters deepen, we act more in accord with them. But characters, for most of us, are in process rather than being fully formed, which is why we speak of someone "acting out of character" or "she's not herself today." Generally speaking, a "good" person does not produce bad fruit on a consistent basis. If they did, we would not classify them as good. But we all have heard of genuinely good people who slip up from time to time.

My second minor point concerns the verse Ware uses to support compatibilistic freedom. He references Isaiah 10:5–19 where Assyria is portrayed as God's servant, freely doing exactly what God wanted them to do. Several times in the Old Testament God uses nations to carry out his wrath. However, in a couple of these instances, God rebukes a nation such as Babylon for use of excessive violence against Israel. God tells the nation that though he sent it to punish Israel, the foreign power went beyond his intent and so now God must punish it as well. If the nations are under God's meticulous control, then they do no more and no less than what God's blueprint for history foreordains. If this is true, then why does God get angry at them for doing precisely what God ordained they do? It seems ridiculous to think God is angry with his own blueprint.

This leads into my next major point on Ware's discussion of God's relation to evil. Ware writes: "God specifically permits only those instances of evil to occur that by his infinite wisdom and in light of his ultimate purposes he judges will advance and not hinder his designed ends for the world." He says that God specifically ordains any and every evil that happens in the world so that any and every evil has a purpose or a specific reason it occurs. Most of the time we will not know what that specific reason is unless God discloses it to us, but we can rest assured that there is no "pointless evil" because "God regulates exactly the evil that occurs." Hence, if Sally Mae is sexually abused, we can be assured that God has a specific reason it is best for this to occur to her.

Significance of Free Will (New York: Oxford University Press, 1998); and Robert Kane, ed., *The Oxford Handbook of Free Will* (New York: Oxford University Press, 2002), chaps. 15–18.

However, in this section Ware is at pains to distance God from responsibility for evil. He seeks to accomplish this by means of compatibilistic freedom and the notion of divine permission. According to compatibilistic freedom God determines the remote causes that form human desires into precisely what God wants them to be at any particular point in time. Though God determines which desires we have at any particular moment, we are the ones who act on those desires; and we do so in "freedom" because you are free so long as you act on what you want to do. To this Ware adds these comments:

> God is able to permit only those occurrences of evil that he knows will serve his purposes and never thwart or hinder those purposes. . . . Thus, without causing a person to do evil, he nonetheless controls the evil they do. He controls whether evil is done, what evil is done, and in any and every case he could prevent the evil from being done. . . . In this way God maintains meticulous control over evil while his moral creatures alone are the agents who do evil, and they alone bear moral responsibility for the evil they freely do.

We can raise a number of questions about this theodicy. To begin, one can ask whether the idea of divine permission really conveys what Ware asserts. Calvin ridicules "those who, in place of God's providence, substitute bare permission—as if God sat in a watchtower awaiting chance events, and his judgment thus depended upon human will."[9] Calvin is here criticizing the free will tradition for rejecting the idea of meticulous providence. Ware, however, does not think of God sitting in a watchtower because he believes God actively ordains absolutely everything that comes to pass. So God "permits" in a rather unusual sense. Remember, if none of God's knowledge is dependent upon creatures, then God foreknows because he foreordains. If so, then God's knowledge of evil acts is not dependent upon creatures but upon God's own determining power. Consequently, there is not enough separation between God and the evil act to alleviate

---

9. Calvin, *Institutes* 1.18.1. G. C. Berkouwer follows Calvin in rejecting "permission" since it makes God a balcony observer, a mere reactor. See his *The Providence of God,* trans. Lewis B. Smedes (Grand Rapids: Eerdmans, 1952), 137–41.

divine responsibility for evil. This reasoning leads to the next point.

The main purpose of this section of Ware's chapter is to claim that God is not responsible for evil in the same sense that God is responsible for good. Yet it may be asked why, if the world is exactly the way God determines it to be and if everything serves his purpose, we label things evil? According to meticulous providence would it not be correct to say that what we call "evil" is actually for the good if we only could see it from the "big picture" of God's blueprint? It seems to me Ware would be better off using the "greater good" defense which many Calvinists have employed. In this view the evil that occurs is never pointless because it serves to fulfill a specific plan of God. Hence, whatever we suffer is for the greater good (God's blueprint). Ware correctly explains the difference between his approach to the problem of evil and that of free will theism. Free will theists use the free will defense in which God creates beings with libertarian freedom and so cannot guarantee that they will do only good. That is, they are not tightly under God's control and so may commit evils that God never intended. Ware correctly notes that the free will defense is not available to theological determinists because, according to it, everything is under God's meticulous control.

Theological determinists such as Ware and Helm believe that God providentially controls each and every action of humans including each aspect of each action.[10] God has an exhaustive blueprint for all things such that everything happens precisely the way God ordained it should happen. Though we call certain events accidents or tragedies, since they seem to be evil from our vantage point, from God's perspective they are really necessary for achieving the greater good. There is no pointless evil. The free will theist position is quite different, for it is one thing to say that God, for reasons we don't fully understand, *allows* autonomous agents to do tragic and terrible things. It is quite another thing to say that God deliberately plans and *intends* for all these evil things to happen, so that in no single respect would God want the world to be any different than it actually is. A consistent

---

10. See, for instance, Paul Helm, *The Providence of God* (Downers Grove: InterVarsity, 1994), 104.

theological determinist would say that God does not grieve over the rape of a little girl, for it is exactly what God determined to happen. For free will theists, God does not intend or ordain such evils. Rather, he grieves over them and seeks to redeem them.

I will conclude my response with two brief comments. Ware cites a number of the usual biblical texts used by proponents of theological determinism to support his position. Ware is within his rights to cite the sorts of texts he believes support his theological position. Free will theists do the same.[11] This has resulted in a long-standing feud between these two theological schools of thought, and I know of no definitive way to settle these differences in biblical interpretation.[12]

Ware makes use of the theory of omniscience known as middle knowledge in order to maintain the distinction "between God's direct-causative agency and his indirect-permissive agency." In his chapter in this book, Helm has already criticized this move. Early Calvinists rejected middle knowledge because the knowledge of what humans with libertarian freedom do is not under God's control. If one affirms compatibilistic freedom, then I agree with Helm that middle knowledge is superfluous, an unnecessary appendage.

---

11. I have given my explanation of several of the key texts (e.g., Isa 45:7) typically used by theological determinists in John Sanders, *The God Who Risks: A Theology of Providence* (Downers Grove: InterVarsity, 1998), 81–87. The work of Fredrik Lindstrom is particularly important because his is a careful, detailed exegetical study on the Old Testament texts used by Ware. See his *God and the Origin of Evil: A Textual Analysis of Alleged Monistic Evidence in the Old Testament*, trans. Frederick H. Cryer (Sweden: CWK Gleerup, 1983).

12. For elaboration on the impasse, see John Sanders, "How Do We Decide What God Is Like?" in *And God Saw That It Was Good: Essays on Creation and God in Honor of Terence E. Fretheim*, ed. Fred Gaiser, Word & World Supplement Series, vol. 5 (April 2006): 154–62.

CHAPTER 5

The Classical Free Will Theist Model of God

ROGER E. OLSON

Free will theism[1] is not a bounded category; it admits of many variations. Therefore it is important to establish its meaning up front. Free will theism is, at the very least, a denial that God is the all-determining reality. But it is more than a negative notion; it is the affirmation that God gifts human beings (and possibly other creatures) with a degree of free will such that God and they may enter into genuinely loving relationships. According to Christian free will theists, God cares so much about personal, loving relationships that he does not control or dominate everything creatures do. Instead, God limits his power and control in order to allow humans (and perhaps some other creatures) limited, situated freedom of decision and action. In free will theism, God is in charge (because he is God and therefore the omnipo-

---

1. According to Christian philosopher David Basinger, he was the first to use the term "free will theism" in this sense (as used in this chapter). See *The Case for Freewill Theism: A Philosophical Assessment* (Downers Grove: InterVarsity, 1996). This chapter's exposition of free will theism is influenced by Basinger's but also by other Christian philosophers and theologians such as William Hasker, Vincent Brummer, Jack Cottrell, Adrio König and Richard Swinburne. Contrary to Basinger's usage here the words *free* and *will* are separated into two words; Basinger and some others refer to "freewill theism." This is purely a matter of style and not at all of substance.

tent Creator of all) but not fully in control (because he chooses to relinquish some control to others).

Classical free will theism is that form of this model found implicitly if not explicitly in the ancient Greek church fathers, most of the medieval Christian philosophers and theologians, the radical Reformers (Anabaptists), Arminius and the Remonstrants, John Wesley and the Methodists, and many other Christians throughout history. It is sometimes simply called "Arminianism" because of its embrace by the seventeenth-century Dutch Protestant theologian Jacob Arminius and his followers. However, many other Christian thinkers besides Arminius have embraced and promoted this model of God and his relationship with creatures in history.

The burden of this chapter will be to unpack this form of free will theism called "classical." It will be distinguished from other newer forms of free will theism with which it shares the denial of God as the all-determining reality and affirmation of God's limitation in relationship with freedom-endowed creatures such as human beings. Those other newer forms of free will theism include especially open theism and process theology (which are not identical).

A Complicated Gift

All forms of free will theism believe in libertarian free will as a possession of God and a gift of God to creatures. It is a complicated gift; it is a mixed blessing. But it is one most humans would prefer not to give back. Classical free will theism describes free will as incompatible with determinism; the free will it affirms both in God and in creatures (as gift) is thus "noncompatibilist free will." Understanding this concept is crucial as many divine determinists (such as classical Calvinists) speak of free will but only in the compatibilist sense. That is, they believe free will and determinism are compatible with each other.[2]

2. Some readers already educated in this subject may wonder about so-called middle knowledge. That would be God's knowledge of what any free creature would do in any given set of circumstances in any possible world. Some scholars such as William Lane Craig consider it compatible with free will theism; I agree with those who do not and consider that William Hasker has presented a definitive critique of it in *God, Time, and*

Absolutely crucial to all forms of free will theism is the belief that persons only exercise free choice or liberty of decision and action when they could do otherwise than they do. A person who cannot do X instead of Y cannot be exercising free will when doing Y even if he or she wants to do Y. According to many divine determinists, all that is required for free will decision and action is doing what one wants to do even if one could not do otherwise. Free will theists reject this notion of free will as philosophical, speculative, and counterintuitive. It is also inextricably tied to a deterministic worldview and thus undermines responsibility for sin and evil except on the part of the person determining them.

Let's be clear. For readers who have not encountered these concepts and categories before, it is absolutely crucial that we here and now describe this difference lucidly. Free will theism is that theology that denies compatibilist free will and instead affirms noncompatibilist free will. Noncompatibilist free will is part of God's nature; God can do otherwise than he does. He is not a robot or mechanism or computer; he is a person who deliberates with wisdom and makes choices. He could choose otherwise than he does. To illustrate, according to free will theists God did not have to create the world; creation is an expression of the goodness and freedom of God. But God could have been good without the world ever coming into existence. Nothing within God or external to God caused him to create the world. Something inclined him to do it, and he chose to do it, which is different from having to do it. God shared something of this liberty of decision and action with his human creatures. (Presumably he also shared it with angelic creatures; whether animals have liberty is debatable.[3])

Knowledge (Ithaca and London: Cornell University Press, 1989). In general, advocates and defenders of middle knowledge consider libertarian free will compatible with determinism which is why I (and many other classical free will theists) reject it from free will theism. More often than not it is used to defend divine determinism, often under the disguise of being a form of free will theism.

3. No doubt some divine determinists believe God possesses libertarian free will, but this falls into conflict with the argument most divine determinists use to demolish free will among creatures, which is that it is an incoherent concept because it assumes ability to go against one's strongest motives (via deliberation and action) and that it assumes the possibility of an uncaused effect. When libertarian free will is criticized in this manner as irrational and incoherent, it cannot be attributed to God any more than to human beings.

Just as God created the world, even though he could have not created the world, so humans have free will to do this or that. They do not have free will to do anything; they are finite and therefore their range of liberty is limited. Free will does not mean being able to flap one's wings and fly or turn oneself into a dog or jump over a mountain. Christian free will theists affirm that creaturely free will is limited by many factors: God, sin, the environment, and others. Every exercise of creaturely free will is situated within a context that conditions and limits it. Furthermore, according to Christian free will theists, God provides impulses that draw humans' free will in certain directions, but God also allows them to resist his drawings up to a point. Occasionally God suspends free will with a dramatic intervention that virtually forces a person to decide or act in some way. But in general God steps back and allows human beings a limited range of choices. They make those choices freely insofar as they could do otherwise than they do.[4]

Compatibilists (divine determinists) believe that God works through secondary causes to render his creatures' choices certain. (Some divine determinists withdraw secondary causes and view God as the immediate cause of all that happens, including human decisions and actions.) Human beings make choices, but what they choose is determined by God. They cannot choose otherwise than they do. So in what sense are they free? Compatibilists define free will as doing what you want to do; it is noncoerced decision and action. If a person wants to order a pizza and eat it and does that, he or she is free unless coerced. If the decision and action are coerced, then freedom is lacking. But even if the person could not do otherwise because compelled by divine power, however hidden and indirect it may be, he or she may still do it freely insofar as it is desired.

So two main models of divine-creature relationship stand opposed to each other: compatibilist and noncompatibilist. The

---

But that makes the creation of the world necessary even for God which cuts across the grain of Christian orthodoxy by importing the world into God's being.

4. Free will theists debate among themselves whether and to what extent God may intervene to suspend free choices and actions by creatures. Most Christian classical free will theists believe God can and sometimes does exercise such power but never in matters of sin and salvation.

former is usually designated divine determinism and the latter is generally called free will theism. The best known form of the former is Calvinism; the best known form of the latter is Arminianism (at least among Protestants). However, many Lutherans, like Martin Luther himself, are divine determinists especially in the area of salvation. They would not like being called Calvinists. Similarly, many Anabaptists (e.g., Mennonites) are free will theists and would not like being called Arminians because their tradition predates Arminianism by almost a century. A distinction must be made and maintained between classical free will theism and newer varieties of free will theism such as open theism and process theology. Explicating that distinction will be an important burden of this chapter. Also important will be delineating reasons for classical free will theism. Finally, this chapter will seek throughout to dispel myths about classical free will theism.

Misconceptions about Free Will Theism

Before proceeding it is helpful to distinguish between freedom and free will. Many critics of free will theism object that it provides only a shallow and perhaps modern (Enlightenment-inspired) account of freedom. Adherents of Augustinian-Reformed theology especially like to cast this aspersion at free will theism. According to them this theology reduces freedom to individualistic liberty of decision and action thus denying the more profound biblical idea of freedom as life as God intends it to be. In other words, so the criticism often goes, in biblical revelation true freedom is life abundant and free—the life provided by God's grace wherein a person is conformed to the divine design for humanity shown in Jesus Christ. Freedom is being all you were meant to be by the grace of God. It is restoration of the image of God and more. The illustration of a train on its tracks is sometimes used by these critics. A train is truly free when it runs on its tracks; if it "chooses" to jump off the tracks in order to exercise freedom, it loses freedom and is destroyed. So humans are only free when they conform to God's design.

Ultimately freedom is eschatological; it arrives in the resurrection with glorification in the restored image of God.

Classical free will theism (and probably also open theism) gladly affirms this account of true freedom. The reductionist criticism misses its mark entirely. Free will theists do not reduce freedom to liberty of decision and action. Rather, they agree with the (mostly) Reformed critics that true freedom is eschatological and until the eschaton it is found only in increasing grace-enabled conformity to the image of God and to Christlikeness. However, free will theists believe that part of the path to freedom lies in voluntary decision and action and that voluntary (and thus responsible) decision and action require ability to do otherwise. Free will as liberty of decision and action, then, is not true freedom but an instrument for its achievement. A homely illustration might help. A prisoner of war learns that his own troops are camped only a few miles away. In their midst lies true freedom from captivity. But the only way to get there is by choosing to make a break for it and escape the POW camp. His exercise of free choice to escape is not true freedom; it is merely a step in that direction. Or he could choose not to risk capture and punishment by exercising voluntary choice not to make a run for it. In that case he is doomed to captivity and will not discover freedom.

The point should be clear; the criticism misses the mark. Free will theists do not confuse free will with freedom even if the terms are sometimes used interchangeably. Freedom is the goal and may be experienced in part on the way to the goal. Free will is only a tool or instrument in either achieving the goal or not achieving it. The Bible's emphasis is on freedom, not free will. But free will is everywhere presupposed in the Bible as a gift of God. And without it freedom is a gift imposed on some and withheld from others by an arbitrary and seemingly tyrannical God.

A few other misconceptions of free will theism must be dispelled. It is not humanistic as some critics maintain. A common accusation is that free will theism is "man centered" and inspired by humanism. Far from being that, however, in truth free will theism is God centered and inspired by biblical revelation. Were the church fathers Irenaeus, Tertullian, Origen, and Athanasius humanists? Were their theologies human centered rather than God-centered just because they believed in free will as liberty of decision and action? They could not have been inspired by the Enlightenment; they lived long before the beginning of the modern age. The same can be said of the medieval theologians and the Catholic reformer Erasmus as well as the Anabaptists such as Balthasar Hubmaier and Menno Simons who all lived and affirmed free will theism before modern humanism arose in the seventeenth century. They all derived their beliefs in liberty of decision and action from the Bible rather than from philosophy. There were deterministic philosophies such as Stoicism around them; they rejected those because they believed in the goodness of God and the responsible sinfulness of human persons.

In what sense is free will theism God-centered? Its main concern is with the character of God. Critics who charge it with being humanistic or "man centered" rather than God centered often assume their own particular view of God-centeredness as focus on God's glory as power, domination, and control. Classical Christian free will theism arises not so much from a desire to elevate free will as from a desire to do justice to God's character as loving-kindness—not only toward a portion of humanity (or even creation) but toward all (John 3:16–17). Libertarian free will is not an idol erected to exalt humanity; it is rather a necessary protection of God's goodness. Without it God would be virtually indistinguishable from the devil. That is the way free will theists view the matter. Apart from libertarian free will, persons' destinies would be determined entirely and solely by God. Insofar as one believes in hell as eternal damnation (however precisely conceived) one would then have to attribute the reality of eternally suffering persons to God's sovereign and seemingly arbitrary decision—arbitrary because it cannot have anything to do with freely chosen character. In summary, then, the accusation that free will theism is not God centered simply misses the mark; it is God centered in that it is wholly constituted and determined by desire to preserve the goodness of God as well as the sovereignty of God.[5]

Another misconception is that free will theism undermines God's sovereignty. That is simply not the case. Free will theism affirms God's sovereignty. Is sovereignty the same as control? Not in human affairs. No human sovereign controls every turn and twist or thought of his or her subjects. Rather, a sovereign is in charge of a territory. So God is in charge of the world including free creatures who sometimes thwart his perfect will. God allows that to happen by an act of self-restriction; he could control creatures meticulously, but he chooses not to for the sake of genuinely loving, reciprocal relationships. A relationship controlled is an artificial relationship. A sin or a salvation determined is likewise artificial because it is impersonal. All classical free will theists agree that God is omnipotent; God has the power to do anything consistent with his character.

They also agree (whether they have said so explicitly or not) that God limits his power in relation to creation and especially in relation to human persons. This is a kenosis (self-limitation or self-emptying of God). Not that God gives up any of his divine nature; that is inconceivable. Rather, God restricts the exercise of his power in order to give human persons the ability and responsibility to respond freely and responsibly to his overtures of love. By no means does this undermine God's sovereignty. God determines the ultimate outcome of history and oversees its course; he intervenes miraculously and supernaturally to stabilize it and keep it moving toward his foreseen and intended goal, the consummation. Which individuals and perhaps nations are redeemed and which are lost along the way toward that goal is not determined unilaterally by God but cooperatively by God and people because God decides it will be so.

Another misunderstanding (and too often misrepresentation) of free will theism is that it undercuts or diminishes God's glory. Again, one assumes a particular notion of God's glory that not all Christians share. For free will theists, God's glory is not might but goodness. Yes, God is almighty, but his glory

5. See Jerry L. Walls, "The Free Will Defense, Calvinism, Wesley, and the Goodness of God," *Christian Scholar's Review* 13, no. 1 (1973), 19–33.

is his loving-kindness, faithfulness, wisdom, mercy, and grace. Free will theists turn the tables on those who say their view of the God-creature relationship diminishes God's glory. How can God's glory be diminished if God predetermines everything and renders everything certain? If God is the all-determining reality, does not everything serve God's glory? Why would God foreordain and raise up (or throw down) anything unless that brings him glory? Most Reformed theologians believe that God's self-glorification is God's primary purpose and that everything is predetermined by God for his own glory. But, if that is true, how can anything at all diminish God's glory? If it exists, it is foreordained and determined by God for his glory. To say it diminishes God's glory is to contradict one's own theology.

Free will theism is a theology of God's glory. God's glory means God's goodness. God is glorious precisely in giving humans limited freedom of decision and action and responding mercifully and graciously to their failures. A God who does not have to respond, who takes no risks and suffers no setbacks is less glorious than one who deals with other beings in personal relationships that involve risk, pain, redemption, and restoration. The glory of God, according to free will theists, lies precisely in his being able to deal creatively, faithfully, lovingly, and restoratively with a wayward world. His glory lies in his remaining himself in and through it all.

Classical free will theists believe that God foreknows the entire course of the future as well as its end; God is omniscient in the biblical and traditional sense. Every true proposition is known exhaustively and infallibly by God. But classical free will theists do not believe this reality robs the future of contingency or freedom. God simply knows the future because it will happen; his knowing future free decisions and actions of creatures does not determine them. Rather that they will happen determines God's knowing them because God has decided to open himself up to being affected by the world. But, according to classical free will theists (as opposed to process theologians and open theists), God does not learn anything. The Bible does not condemn fortune-telling because the future cannot be known; it condemns it because foreknowledge belongs to God alone.

Classical free will theists know this is a problem for some critics. Calvinists and open theists unite to argue that absolute divine foreknowledge conflicts with libertarian freedom of future decisions and actions. Insofar as the future is free and not yet determined there is nothing to know. Calvinists say, therefore, since God knows the future God must determine it. Open theists say, since the future is not yet (exhaustively) determined even God must not know it (exhaustively). Classical free will theists claim these responses confuse the orders of knowing and being; to be real is one thing and to be known as real is something else. Just because God "sees" the future does not mean it is determined. Simple foreknowledge is simply future vision. It is mysterious to humans, but it is a divine power and prerogative attested in Scripture.[6]

A final false accusation against classical free will theism is that it is based on philosophy or experience rather than on divine revelation. Free will theists of all types point to experience to support their belief in libertarian free will. That we act freely at least some of the time is a matter of intuition. Determinism is counterintuitive. Deliberation, choice, and responsibility for action all point to and support libertarian free will as power of voluntary decision and action. That people could do otherwise than they do is fundamental to society's systems of criminal justice. Why be outraged over or angered by the actions of others if they are determined? If a person could not do otherwise than he or she does, why rise up in righteous indignation against them? Why not just say, "What will be will be," or, "That was bound to happen"?

However, just because free will theism uses intuition and reason to support itself does not mean it is based entirely or exhaustively on them. Classical Christian free will theists base their belief in libertarian freedom not on intuition or reason but on divine revelation. While there may not be any *locus classi-*

---

6. For those who wonder whether a philosophical argument for the coherence of belief in foreknowledge of future contingent events can be made, I recommend Alvin C. Plantinga, *God, Freedom, and Evil* (Grand Rapids: Eerdmans, 1974), 65–73.

cus or proof text in Scripture about libertarian free will, it is a presupposition everywhere in Scripture. Every time Scripture says God repents or relents or changes his mind in response to human decisions or actions libertarian free will is taken for granted as divine determinism is denied. Of course, we could dismiss these passages as anthropomorphisms (describing God in human terms), but what would they be anthropomorphisms of? In other words, what characteristic of God would changing his mind point to? For what is it a metaphor? Is it only describing a feeling in human beings when they contemplate God's actions? The same thing could be said about every humanlike action of God, and in the end very little could be known of God. Free will theists suggest that at least some of these biblical references to God's change of heart and mind and God's grief over wayward humanity must be taken seriously as they are part of the warp and woof of divine revelation.

Biblical Evidence

The personal God of the Bible who enters into real relationships with people in which God suffers (as in his relationship with Hosea) presupposes that God is not the all-determining reality. Otherwise it is all a charade, and God does not really have interpersonal relationship outside of himself or suffer anything. Apart from libertarian free will and with divine determinism, God becomes an uncarved block or a force or a principle rather than the passionate, responsive God of the Bible.[7] Thus, classical free will theism finds its root and support in the Bible and not in philosophy or experience even though these can be used to support it. Both critics and defenders of free will theism look in vain for proof texts for it; there is no chapter or verse that, taken alone, demonstrates conclusively that persons have libertarian free will. That should not surprise anyone. If it is the case that the biblical writers all simply assumed libertarian free will (as

---

7. For a Reformed theological expression of this point, see Adrio König, *Here Am I: A Believer's Reflection on God* (Grand Rapids: Eerdmans, 1982). The point is a major theme of the book and wrapped into the warp and woof of its argument against divine determinism.

most of Judaism certainly has over the centuries), why would they ever feel the need to affirm it? The religious and cultural milieu within which they lived and wrote generally assumed that persons have the power of voluntary decision and action; apparently that was self-evident to most people. One exception within the Roman Empire was the Stoics, but the biblical writers nowhere evidence concern with them.

Everywhere the Bible calls for spiritual or moral delibera-tion, decision, and action, it assumes free will. The early church fathers read the Bible this way. They also assumed it and occa-sionally affirmed it against philosophers such as the Stoics. Virtually no defender of divine determinism claims that the early church fathers before Augustine denied libertarian free will; it is simply a given among patristic scholars that especially all of the Greek church fathers rejected determinism in favor of the Hebraic view of persons as possessing free will. Demanding bibli-cal "proof" of free will is something like demanding proof that George Washington believed in a free market economy rather than in communism. Even if he never wrote on the subject, we may safely assume he believed in capitalism because that was the accepted economic system of the day; communism did not even arise as an alternative to capitalism until decades after Washington's death.

The surest biblical "proof" of libertarian freedom of will lies in the attempt to square divine determinism with God's good-ness in the face of sin, evil, and hell. If God is the all-determining reality and human persons do not have free will, what doctrine of God must follow? Throw into the mix eternal suffering in hell for some people, and the problem becomes intense. Without lib-ertarian free will human decisions and actions would be divinely determined. Of course, a divine determinist might opt for a mixed view and claim that some human decisions and actions such as sin and evil are determined by something other than God such as nature and nurture. But one has to press right to the point: from what source did the very first inclination to evil arise? If a person who denies libertarian free will says "not from God," he or she is under pressure to say whence it came. If it arose from within the heart or mind of a creature was it determined to arise there, or was it freely chosen? If determined to arise there, what force or power determined it? How did it come into being? If it was freely chosen, then libertarian free will is at least partly affirmed.

The point is that deniers of free will theism must explain the existence of sin and evil in the world; divine determinism ultimately has to trace it back to God. In some way, directly or indirectly, God willed it and rendered it certain. But how does that escape making God the author of sin and evil? Most Christian divine determinists (e.g., classical Calvinists and many Lutherans) flinch at this point. They cannot bring themselves to say that God is the author of sin and evil. But if these are not part of creation itself (in which case God would still be responsible for them as he is the Creator of everything), how did they enter it or arise within it? Ultimately, divine determinism, the only viable alternative to belief in free will within a theistic worldview, cannot get God off the hook. If God is the all-determining reality and people do not have libertarian free will, God is the Creator or author of sin and evil including the very first inclination to evil within a creature's mind or heart.

Some divine determinists wish to say that some creatures such as Satan, angels, and humans had free will before they fell into sin but lost it after that. The early church father Augustine apparently believed this. For him the human condition before the fall of Adam and Eve was *posse non peccare*—possible not to sin. After the fall the human condition became *non posse non peccare*—not possible not to sin. This is an attempt to get God off the hook for the first inclination to evil (and its consequences in sinful actions). Many Calvinists embrace this idea. But another similar problem arises insofar as a person believes in the eternal suffering of the wicked. Even if they are wicked due to the first parents' misuse of free will, if God saves people unconditionally and not in response to their free acceptance of his mercy and grace (which they could reject and often do), why does he not save everyone?

If God is good and saves without regard to people's freely developed character or free (undetermined) choices, why does he allow some to go into eternal perdition and select others to take into eternal blessedness? How is that consistent with goodness? How is it consistent with love? John Wesley referred to that "love" as "such as to make the blood run cold." How can words like love and goodness be meaningful in a system that includes divine determinism? If there is no sense in which a human person would ever be considered good if he or she unconditionally condemns other persons to, for example, lifelong existence in a concentration camp, how can "goodness" be attributed to God if that is what he does and worse—because in hell there is no death to end the misery?

The argument is simple. The rock of free will theism does not need to be a Scripture passage or a string of Scripture passages; it is the revealed goodness of God throughout Scripture and especially in Jesus Christ. Where is God ultimately and perfectly (if not completely) revealed? Where else but in the character of Jesus Christ? If God is revealed as good and if the word *good* means something (and is not merely an equivocal sound from the throat that conveys no meaning analogous to something in human existence), then free will must exist. It is the precondition for understanding and explaining hell in light of God's goodness. People determine themselves for hell by their free choices and especially by their rejection of God's offer of salvation (whether through the explicit preaching of the gospel or through the light of God present in every culture and in conscience). If not, then God determines them for hell. There really can be no alternative.

Someone might wonder at this point about Satan. Doesn't he send people to hell? Satan alone cannot send anyone to hell, and the Bible nowhere says he does; the one who should be feared because he can destroy both body and soul in hell is God. But if God does that arbitrarily and without regard to persons' free choices, how is he good? That is the question. Because classical Christian free will theists believe in God's goodness and hell, they affirm libertarian free will. The only alternative is a God of power who is morally ambiguous. In fact, many free will theists ask, "If divine determinism is true and persons go to hell apart from freely chosen decisions and acts they could avoid, how is God different from Satan in terms of his purposes and intentions?" Satan, so it is usually believed, wants everyone in hell. The all-determining God of divine determinism wants some people to go to hell. Therein lies the difference. But is it sufficient to rescue God from looking like Satan?

Divine determinists take two approaches toward resolving this dilemma. First, some argue that God does not send anyone to hell arbitrarily. Rather, he simply allows some people to go to their deserved destiny in eternal condemnation and suffering. The problem remains. If God always saves unconditionally, why does he not save everyone? On what basis does he select some to spend eternity suffering everlasting punishment for decisions and actions they could not avoid? It cannot be on the basis of their character because, according to divine determinists, God saves some people apart from their freely developed character and apart from any freely chosen decisions or actions. Rather, he instills the saving qualities in them by his irresistible grace after selecting them unconditionally. Upon close examination the charge that this makes God arbitrary proves sustainable. There is no conceivable basis for his selections once the word *unconditional* comes into play. His selection of some to save and others to condemn is unavoidably arbitrary if it is totally unconditional.

Some divine determinists then say that God wishes he could save all but knows he cannot and therefore reluctantly and with grief saves some and allows others to pass into their deserved and predetermined eternal suffering in hell. But why cannot God save all? Why must he pass over some and allow them to suffer in hell forever? The frequently offered answer is "for his glory." In other words, according to some divine determinists, God's ultimate purpose in all of this is his own glorification; for that all of his attributes must be displayed without prejudice to any of them. One of God's attributes is justice, and that must be manifested as wrath. Therefore, hell is necessary for God's glorious attributes to be displayed which grieves him because of his goodness and love. This is, of course, to subordinate God's goodness and love to his glory and power. But more importantly, this entire line of argument (which is necessary to explain why hell is necessary) diminishes the cross of Jesus Christ. *Was it not a sufficient display of God's justice and wrath?* Apparently not. Free will theists, however, believe it was. Hell is therefore completely unnecessary, which is why its existence is so tragic. It does not glorify God but is an expression of God's respect for those who freely resist the glory displayed sufficiently and fully in the cross of Jesus Christ.

The point of all this is not to engage in polemics against divine determinism but to explain the foundations of free will theism. From the perspective of free will theists, that view is the only viable alternative to a morally ambiguous, tyrant-like God who gets pleasure and glory out of the eternal suffering of the wicked. If divine determinism is true and humans do not possess liberty of will, they sin necessarily and suffer damnation necessarily; and that makes God (as free will theist Jacob Arminius said) the only real sinner. Of course, Christian divine determinists do not say this; they reject it most vehemently. But free will theists see the conclusion as the only good and necessary consequence of divine determinism including rejection of libertarian freedom. That is why they embrace free will theism and reject divine determinism. Even if it has problems of its own, they are less intense than those of divine determinism. Free will theists can live with the unanswered and perhaps unanswerable questions of that view; they cannot worship and serve a God who to them is barely distinguishable from the devil.

Classical Arminianism

It is time now to leave behind the exposition and defense of free will theism in general and turn to classical Arminianism which is the best-known and most influential form of Protestant classical free will theism. Jacob Arminius was a Dutch theologian who died in 1609 at the height of his career and the controversy swirling around his teaching.[8] He was a minister of the Reformed Church of the Netherlands (then called the United Provinces,

---

8. For Arminius's biography see Carl Bangs, *Arminius: A Study in the Dutch Reformation,* 2nd ed. (Grand Rapids: Zondervan, 1985).

of which Holland was the leading province). Arminius denied divine determinism and affirmed libertarian free will. His written works, almost all of which expound his free will theism and defend it against Calvinistic critics, fill three huge volumes in English translation.[9] He was not aware of introducing anything new into the stream of Christian theology or Protestantism. He personally affirmed the Heidelberg Catechism, which was the only binding confessional statement for ministers of his church. He also unequivocally embraced and upheld the sole supreme authority of the Bible and made all of his arguments on the basis of scriptural exegesis aided by tradition and reason. Although some uninformed critics have tried to put Arminius into a heretical corner, they have failed; he consistently denied every heresy thrown at him and held firmly to all the orthodox doctrines of Protestant Christianity.

Arminius's followers called themselves The Remonstrants; and they published, among other things, a document known as *The Remonstrance,* which set forth their beliefs about sin, grace, free will, and related matters. To this day the denomination founded by Arminius's followers exists in The Netherlands; it is known as The Remonstrant Brotherhood and is a charter member of the World Alliance of Reformed Churches. Clearly, then, true, historical, classical Arminianism is not antithetical to Reformed Christianity; it is a subspecies of it. Arminianism was picked up by John and Charles Wesley among others, who, with their Calvinist friend George Whitefield, led the Great Awakening in England. The earliest Baptists were Arminians ("General Baptists"), and many Baptists have been Arminian down through the centuries. Methodism, founded by the Wesleys, is Arminian in its theology. So is Pentecostalism, the entire Restorationist movement (Churches of Christ/Christian/Disciples of Christ) and the Holiness Churches (Nazarene, Free Methodist, Wesleyan, Salvation Army, and a host of other churches that believe in "entire sanctification"). Arminianism, then, is a major branch of the Protestant tradition and has always played a significant role

---

9. *The Works of James Arminius,* trans. James Nichols and William Nichols (Grand Rapids: Baker, 1996).

in evangelical revivals and evangelical alliances and cooperative movements such as the National Association of Evangelicals.

Classical Arminianism wholeheartedly affirms God's omnipotence and omniscience (including exhaustive and infallible foreknowledge) as well as salvation by grace through faith alone. It also affirms libertarian free will and rejects unconditional election and irresistible grace. Its model of God is intensely personal; the God of Arminian theology is interactive with human persons who can affect God because God gives them the power to do that. The God of Arminian theology is a self-limiting God who does not exercise all the power he has. He does not control everything in meticulous fashion but extends to human beings the power to resist his will and his grace. According to Arminian theology, then, history is a mixture of God's will and human resistance to and cooperation with it. God does not always get his way even though no creature can act apart from God's consent and cooperation. Arminius and faithful Arminians have always affirmed divine sovereignty and providence. These are not in dispute. What is in dispute is determinism. God chooses not to rule by controlling everything and everyone to the exclusion of creaturely free will but chooses to rule by including even creaturely resistance into his plan and purpose and overcoming it through persuasion and mercy. In the end, however, hell is real against God's desire. It is necessary because some people misuse the good gift of free will to their own destruction. To them God says, "Not my will but thine be done."

In all of these areas and in many other ways, Arminianism builds on and assumes classical free will theism; it is a subspecies of that. Not all free will theism is distinctively Christian. One can find examples of free will theism (just as one can find examples of divine determinism) outside Christianity. Arminianism is Christian free will theism; it shares that perspective on God and God's relationship with creatures with the earliest (especially Greek) church fathers and the Catholic reformer Erasmus and the radical Reformers (the Anabaptists). It is also distinctively Protestant in that it not only affirms the basic doctrines of ecumenical Christianity but also wholeheartedly embraces and teaches the classical Protestant doctrines of *Sola Scriptura* (Scripture as sole supreme authority for faith and practice), *Sola Gratia et Fides* (salvation by grace through faith alone) and the priesthood of every believer. Some critics, approaching Arminianism from a divine determinist perspective (e.g., Calvinism), argue that it is not authentically Protestant because it adds at least one "good work" to faith alone in salvation. That is, they accuse Arminianism of being Semi-Pelagian if not Pelagian.[10]

Arminius himself went out of his way to turn aside these accusations and prove his theology did not succumb to heresy or give any ground to works righteousness. Later Arminians such as John Wesley and his nineteenth-century Methodist followers (theologians Richard Watson, William Burton Pope, Thomas O. Summers, John Miley, and others) vehemently denied these charges of heresy and heterodoxy and worked assiduously to demonstrate their commitment to belief in human depravity, the divine initiative in salvation, salvation by grace through faith alone, and other key components of Protestant orthodoxy.[11] Classical Arminians follow Arminius's teachings on these matters; some revisionist Arminians such as some of the later Remonstrants and many twentieth-century liberals in theology including mainline Methodist thinkers departed from Arminius's biblical fidelity and adherence to the great tradition of Christian orthodoxy and classical Protestantism.[12]

Arminius and all his faithful followers reject three points of the famous "T.U.L.I.P." (Total Depravity, Unconditional Election, Limited Atonement, Irresistible Grace, and Perseverance of the Saints, i.e., "the eternal security of believers") scheme of sin and salvation, a five-point model which was developed in the midst of

---

10. Pelagianism is the ancient heresy of self-salvation by good works and Semi-Pelagianism is the idea that even sinful, fallen people can initiate salvation by exercising a good will toward God apart from a supernatural impartation of grace.

11. Because of limitations of space here, I will refer readers to my book *Arminian Theology: Myths and Realities* (Downers Grove: InterVarsity, 2006) for detailed evidence of these and other Arminians' orthodox Protestant credentials.

12. Here I treat Arminianism as classical Arminianism and strictly avoid revisionist Arminianism which I do not consider true Arminianism at all. (Examples would be twentieth-century Methodist theologians influenced by the Boston Personalism of B. P. Bowne and Edgar Sheffield Brightman and also theologians who have adopted process theology.)

the controversy between the Arminians and high Calvinist theologians before, during and after the Synod of Dort in 1618/1619. At that time Arminius's followers, the Remonstrants, were condemned as heretics and thrown out of the Reformed churches and the United Provinces (only to return later). The Reformed divines (ministers) of the Synod of Dort affirmed these five points of what they considered sound Reformed theology, while the Arminians rejected Unconditional Election, Limited Atonement, and Irresistible Grace. Contrary to popular belief, the Arminians did not reject total depravity or perseverance. At least not all of them did. Arminius himself never settled into a definite belief about the security of the believer; he said Scripture wears "both aspects" (namely, possible apostasy and security in grace). Most of the Remonstrants came to embrace the possibility of apostasy, but especially among even Arminian Baptists that has largely been rejected (except among Free Will Baptists). Virtually every faithful Arminian affirmed total depravity, including John Wesley in the eighteenth century. According to classical Arminian theology, every human person born of Adam's race comes into the world spiritually helpless even to exercise a good will toward God apart from God's supernatural prevenient grace.

The key doctrine of Arminianism (beyond rejection of the distinctive notes of high Calvinism) is prevenient grace. It is not unique to Arminianism, but Arminius and his followers gave it special pride of place in their theology in order to combine total depravity as spiritual helplessness with free will. The idea that Arminians believe people naturally possess free will to exercise a good will toward God is false; Arminius rejected that and so have all true Arminians.[13] According to classical Arminianism whatever good a person has, including ability to exercise a good will toward God (for example, responding to the proclamation of the gospel with repentance and faith), comes from God. Apart from God's preparing and assisting grace, no person (except Jesus Christ who was not depraved) can initiate a relationship with God or receive the saving grace of God through repentance and faith. Arminius believed in a work of God prior to conversion

13. Again, I refer skeptical or interested readers to the evidence I marshal for that in *Arminian Theology: Myths and Realities*.

that is partially regenerative; the broken and depraved will of the fallen person is enslaved to sin until God's prevenient grace reaches him or her (most often through the proclamation of the gospel) and restores moral ability to hear and respond positively to the message of the gospel with repentance and faith.

A person who does respond with repentance and faith unto conversion is then regenerated by the Holy Spirit and justified by God through the death of Jesus Christ. That person is then also united with Christ and given the Holy Spirit for sanctification. This *ordo salutis* (order of salvation) makes clear that grace precedes and enables salvation. Prevenient grace includes conviction, calling, illumination, and enablement. Without it no descendent of Adam except Christ can do anything spiritually good; one cannot "reach out to God" for salvation, nor can one respond to the gospel with saving faith. Thus, the person who is saved cannot boast because all of the power comes from God; all the saved person did was freely accept and not reject the free grace of God. Indeed, he or she must make a free decision, but it is not a good work; it is only nonresistance to God's saving work. Can the saved person boast just a little because he or she made the right decision? Arminians point to a beggar who is on the verge of starvation and receives a gift of food or money that saves life. Can that person boast of accepting the life-saving gift? Hardly. So it is with salvation; even though the person being saved must freely accept and not reject grace, he or she has no ground for boasting because all of the ability came from God.

Critics, including many Calvinists, want to know where prevenient grace is found in the Bible. Where is Trinity found in the Bible? Where is the doctrine of Christ's two natures found in the Bible? Many crucial doctrines are developed out of the scriptural materials even though they are not explicitly named or stated there. They are found "between the lines," so to speak, because what the Bible does say necessarily implies them. Arminians see prevenient grace in Philippians 2:12–13: "Work out your own salvation with fear and trembling. For it is God who is working in you, [enabling you] both to will and to act for His good purpose" (HCSB). The directive to "work out your own salvation" refers to receiving the gift of saving grace through repentance and faith; "God who is working in you" refers to prevenient and assisting grace that goes before and makes possible free human reception of the grace of God. Throughout Scripture people responded to the call of God; it is always because God enabled them to do it. This is the Arminian alternative to irresistible grace; prevenient grace can be and often is resisted. But wherever faith is found prevenient grace is found before it.

Who receives prevenient grace? Even classical Arminians do not fully agree on the answer. John Wesley seemed to believe that God is an equal opportunity Savior. He saw prevenient grace as universal in some measure. Even the "savage" has a conscience and some light of nature which are both instruments of prevenient grace. Arminius himself hinted that God's Word may be present and active (prevenient grace) where it is not explicitly called such. However, Arminius and some of his followers have tended to restrict the reach of prevenient grace to the reach of the gospel; this is why evangelism and missions are so important. The proclamation of the gospel is the channel of prevenient grace; faith comes by hearing and hearing by the Word of God. Whenever and wherever people hear (or read) the gospel message of God's love in Jesus Christ, their hearts are softened and liberated, and they are enabled to receive salvation. Charles Wesley expressed the concept in a hymn ("And Can It Be That I Should Gain") without the term "prevenient grace" but referring to it:

> Long my imprisoned spirit lay
> Fast bound in sin and nature's night;
> Thine eye diffused a quickening ray,
> I woke, the dungeon flamed with light;
> My chains fell off, my heart was free;
> I rose, went forth and followed Thee.

For Wesley the "quickening ray" is prevenient grace that liberates people from the shackles of bondage to sin and gives them the freedom to respond to God's call and to the gospel with faith.

Thus, for Arminians, free will is a gift of God. One interpretation held by many Arminians is that God has bound himself so that normally he depends on human partners to diffuse this "quickening ray" among the prisoners in the dungeon. Evangelists are diffusers of that ray among the masses of depraved people. Other Arminians believe Christ's death itself diffused the ray of prevenient grace, and they or others may point to the universal presence of the Holy Spirit and of the Logos of God (John 1) as examples of prevenient grace. In any case, according to classical Arminianism, God foreknows who will respond positively to prevenient grace, and they are the ones he predestines to be conformed to the image of his Son and to be with him in heaven (Rom 8:29). The "elect" are simply the community (not individuals by themselves) of God's predestined (because foreknown) people.[14]

What model of God does classical Arminianism assume? Arminianism is not conscious of offering any novel model of God; Arminians simply believe their view of God is the historic Christian one continuous with the early church's concept of God. However, it is fair to say that it differs from some other models of God both old and new. First and foremost, the Arminian model of God highlights and underscores the personal nature of God and of God's relationship with creatures (especially humans). *Personal* in this model means "interactive." That is, God is not strictly immutable or impassible; God is capable of being affected by humans because he opens himself to that. God makes room in his life for humans without losing anything of himself. God freely chooses to allow his people to influence him so that he does not do all of the deciding and acting; he is not the all-determining reality because he invites and enables humans to help determine some of reality.

At the same time, in spite of God's self-limitation for the sake of personal relationships and human partnership, God retains his transcendence and holiness. God is not human or creaturely or finite. God's power, knowledge, and wisdom are unlimited even if he limits his exercise of special power for the sake of human

---

14. For a complete account of the Arminian view of election, see William Klein, *The New Chosen People: A Corporate View of Election* (Grand Rapids: Academie, 1990).

involvement with him in determining in a limited way how things go in the world. Many, if not most, Arminians are classical Christian theists. Certainly that was true of Arminius himself. He affirmed all the classical attributes of God as developed by the early church fathers and the medieval scholastic theologians such as Thomas Aquinas.

A crucial question is whether God can be the providential Lord of history bringing it to its ultimate consummation in his kingdom without exercising absolute, meticulous control of every twist and turn of every molecule and every thought of finite minds. Some divine determinists believe not. If even one maverick molecule exists, so some say, God is not Lord of the world. Then God is not God. Arminians disagree. In their model of God, everything that happens down to the least vibration of an atom is allowed by God but not necessarily caused or controlled by God. God concurs with every decision and action creatures make and do, but he does not cause all of it or control all of it. God governs without control just like a parent of a late adolescent governs the maturing child without controlling him or her. There are consequences and the household will survive the adolescent's acts of rebellion because of who is in charge. But the adolescent may resist and do terrible things that bring grief and sometimes chaos for a time. But like a good parent, and to an even greater extent because of his omnipotence, God will keep faith with his creation and use his power in all its forms to hold onto it and bring it to his predestined outcome. Human resistance is real but not determinative.

Reflective Arminians admit that their model of God and God's relationship with creatures raises some problems and questions and that perhaps not all of them can be resolved. What exactly is free will? Can an effect (viz., a free will decision or action) be without a cause? Can persons act contrary to their strongest motives? How can God guarantee that his will be done if people have free will to resist and even contradict God's will? Arminians simply believe that in every case the question can be turned around and made harder to answer or that another question can be raised in the case of divine determinism. If God's will is always already being done on earth as in heaven (as divine determinism implies) why did Jesus teach his disciples to pray, "Thy will be done on earth as it is in heaven?" If free will is consistent with determinism (as compatibilism says), how is the person who does what he or she cannot avoid doing responsible? Would any jury convict a person of murder if they knew the person could not have done otherwise—even if they wanted to murder the victim? Who made them want to? If God is the all-determining reality, does he determine even the sinful motives that drive people to commit acts of unspeakable evil? If so (and how can one escape that conclusion?), how is he not the author of sin and evil? Arminians simply cannot live with the problems of divine determinism; they can live with the problems of free will theism in the light of divine revelation, tradition, reason, and experience.

CHAPTER 6

Responses to Roger E. Olson
"The Classical Free Will Theist Model of God"

Response by Paul Helm

Roger Olson provides the reader with a synoptic view of Arminianism, concentrating his attention so much on the importance of indeterministic human freedom that there is a danger of altogether forgetting the doctrine of God. His choice of approach underlines the fact that in Arminianism one distinctive view of human freedom drives everything else. But he also fails to address areas of difficulty that emerge from his broad brush discussion. In my remarks I shall concentrate on three of these.

Divine Foreknowledge

Although Olson stresses how much Arminianism and openness theism have in common, one matter they do not have in common is the extent of God's knowledge. Arminianism holds that God knows the future, that he foreknows it in every detail, and that what he ordains is on the basis of what he foreknows. His ordination is an endorsement of what he foreknows. But if he foreknows matters with what Hasker has called simple foreknowledge, then he has no choice in the matter: His ordination of it follows logically from his simple foreknowledge of it. Olson does not dwell on this distinguishing feature of his position. He does not tell us how it squares with scriptural presentations of divine foreknowledge and ordination, nor does he reveal how such foreknowledge is consistent with the human freedom he cherishes. The little he says on this possibly commits him to backwards causation, as when he notes, "God simply knows the future because it will happen; his knowing future free decisions and actions of creatures does not determine them. Rather that they will happen determines God's knowing them because God has decided to open himself up to being affected by the world." In fact this appears to be backwards causation, the causal agent of which is something that does not exist at the time that it is causally efficacious! He does not even venture an opinion of his own on this, except to turn down the idea of middle knowledge while endorsing Alvin Plantinga's argument in *God, Freedom and Evil*.[1] Olson's omission here is not perhaps surprising because it is not easy to see how the two can be shown to be consistent, or given the many arguments purporting to show their inconsistency, how they can be shown not to be inconsistent.

Divine Foreknowledge and Relationships

Much of Olson's discussion of human freedom and its consequences is indistinguishable from that of openness theists such as Sanders—each is a free will theist. So Olson stresses, as does openness theism, how important libertarian freedom is for establishing genuine human-divine relationships: "The personal God of the Bible who enters into real relationships with people in which God suffers (as in his relationship with Hosea) presupposes that God is not the all-determining reality." But as we have already noted, there is one crucial difference between Arminianism and open theism: God's meticulous foreknowledge: "Classical free will theists believe that God foreknows the entire course of the future as well as its end; God is omniscient in the

---

1. Plantinga's argument is in fact a rebuttal of one argument against the compatibility of divine omniscience and human indeterministic freedom, that from God's essential omniscience. He does not claim to have demonstrated the consistency of divine omniscience and human indeterministic freedom, nor (in that place) to respond to other arguments against the compatibiity of divine omniscience and human indeterministic freedom. Elsewhere, in his "On Ockham's Way Out," he offers a response to the argument from the necessity of the past in *The Concept of God*, ed. Thomas V. Morris (Oxford: Oxford University Press, 1987).

biblical and traditional sense. Every true proposition is known exhaustively and infallibly by God." Open theists, having a very anthropomorphic conception of God, make a great deal of the fact that on their conception of things a divine human relationship is very like a relationship between humans. Each is able to reciprocate with the other as each together faces an open future. This is made into a major selling point of their position: God is a friend, and he and his people face the future together, coping with the unexpected as best they can.

It cannot be like this with Arminianism since one of the partners in this "real relationship" is someone who knows precisely what his partner is going to do (by the exercise of his or her free will) before they do it. Does this not have a rather cramping effect on the interchange? And of course not only does God know exactly what his partner is going to do; he knows exactly what he himself is going to do in the light of what he knows his partner is going to do. It is all laid out in his mind's eye, part of his meticulous, simple foreknowledge. God therefore can do only what he knows beforehand he is going to do, and his partner can do (whether indeterministically freely or not) only what God knows beforehand that he is going to do. Olson uses the term "charade" of the Augustinian account of divine-human relationships. I believe that such a charge can be adequately answered. But suppose that it cannot be. Then the Arminians' account of divine-human relations has something of the charade about it too, does it not? And it is quite one-sided for Olson to say, along with Adrio König, that "apart from libertarian free will and with divine determinism God becomes an uncarved block or a force or a principle rather than the passionate, responsive God of the Bible."[2] If this is true. then it is also true of the all-knowing God of classical Arminianism. The truth of the matter is that *any* creaturely relationship with Almighty God is going to be unlike interpersonal human relationships, even when it has points

---

2. See Adrio König, *Here Am I: A Believer's Reflection on God* (Grand Rapids: Eerdmans, 1982), also cited in Olson's notes.

of similarity, and the Arminian together with the Augustinian ought frankly to recognize the fact. [3]

Olson goes on to say, "Every time Scripture says God repents or relents or changes his mind in response to human decisions or actions libertarian free will is taken for granted as divine determinism is denied." But if meticulous foreknowledge is affirmed, how can God relent or repent *in real time*? He knows beforehand that he will repent or relent. He certainly cannot be surprised by the emergence of some new fact or circumstance. He knows beforehand, for example, that the citizens of Nineveh will change their minds. And he knows beforehand that upon their change of minds he himself will pardon them. It may be that there is a way out for Olson here—to provide a convincing argument for the compatibility of divine foreknowledge and human freedom. But the prospects are not bright. The philosophical and theological highway is littered with the burnt-out remains of many such attempts. He, like Ware, is in something of an unstable position. And if he cannot provide a convincing reconciliation of divine foreknowledge and indeterminism, then Olson may find himself sliding inexorably either to openness theism (on the back of his inability to reconcile divine meticulous knowledge of the future with "real relationships") or (on the back of his commitment to meticulous foreknowledge) down the slope not to "divine determinism," a phrase I argue elsewhere in these Responses ought to be avoided, but to Augustinianism. Welcome, friend!

He thinks the best "biblical proof" of libertarian freedom of will lies in the attempt to square divine determinism with God's goodness in the face of sin, evil, and hell. But not so quickly! On the Arminians' view, God has before his gaze all the evil that will ever be committed. Let us suppose, as the Arminians claim, that much of this evil comes down to the exercise of libertarian choices. God sees the whole array of such choices and of their terrible consequences. More than that, presumably as the Creator and Sustainer of all that is, God holds in being libertarianly free perpetrators of evil. So these evil actions, let us suppose, are not

---

3. For a little more on this, see Paul Helm, "God in Dialogue," in *God and Time: Essays on the Divine Nature*, ed. Gregory E. Ganssle and David M. Woodruff (New York: Oxford University Press, 2002).

ordained by God in the way that the classical Calvinist under-stands the term *ordained*: they are not willingly permitted by him, so to speak. Nonetheless God knows the perpetrators of evil in every detail and helps them along. What does this do for the doctrine of God? What it does is to make God a willing accessory of every evil. Regarding the question of where evil is to be traced back to, Arminians and Classical Calvinists are in pretty much the same boat: each must trace evil back to Almighty God, for it is Almighty God who is (for the Calvinist) the ordainer of evil (though without being the author of sin) and for the Arminian he is the one who has willingly created the agents of evil, giv-ing them libertarian freedom, and, sustaining them in their evil courses, knows full well the bad use that they will make of their freedom. We can say of God, on this view, what Olson says of what he calls "divine determinism" and its relation to evil: "In some way, directly or indirectly, God willed it and rendered it certain."

As we have noted, Olson hangs rather loosely by scrip-tural evidence for his position. He asserts that the "rock of free will . . . is the revealed goodness of God throughout Scripture and especially in Jesus Christ." But we've just now seen the diffi-culties we are all confronted with in this area. What else is there? "Free will theists of all types point to experience to support their belief in libertarian free will. That we act freely at least some of the time is a matter of intuition." But isn't this a shaky basis on which to hold a Christian position of such fundamental impor-tance that it conditions the entire shape of Olson's theology, as can be seen from the passion with which he writes about God otherwise being indistinguishable from the devil?

In these circumstances, in which the chief difference between the Arminian and the Calvinist is certainly not that one provides a way out of the problems of evil while the other fails, the wiser course is to concentrate discussion upon the area that is central to an understanding of the Christian faith—the removal of the one specific evil that the Bible calls *sin*. Given that an appeal to liber-tarian freedom does not grant the Arminian a victory in the case of evil in general, it certainly does not do so in the particular case of sin. Here the scriptural evidence is much clearer, the evidence of the bondage of the will to sin, and the consequent need for God to act decisively in granting such grace as effectively brings life to the dead. That's no suitable basis for a Christian to continue to privilege libertarian freedom on the basis of experience and intuition and an appeal to the goodness of God. So the chief issue, and a much more profitable basis for discussion, is about the plight of man and the power of God. We turn finally to this issue.

The Two Freedoms

Olson distinguishes between libertarian freedom and freedom in the biblical sense. But he misses the point of the critique of Arminianism offered by the Augustinian. This is not that the Arminian fails to make the distinction but that the Arminians' adherence to the liberty of indifference entails that the agent and only the agent can admit the saving influences of divine grace into his life. That liberty is, in Olson's understanding, "part of the path to freedom," an "instrument." But in fact indeterministic freedom is the gatekeeper to the path, with the power to bar the entry of any unwelcome intruders.

So what is the Arminian to make of biblical testimony to the power of sin to bind the will? That in sin we are "helpless" (Rom 5:6), that we are hostile to God (Rom 8:7), that apart from Christ we can do nothing (John 15:5), that we have turned away (Rom 3:12), that we are dead in trespasses and sins (Eph 2:1 and Col 2:13), that our manner of life fulfils the inclinations of the flesh and thoughts (Eph 2:3), that we do not welcome the things of the Spirit of God (1 Cor 2:14), and that we serve divers lusts and pleasures (Titus 3:3). And that as a consequence, we need God's "drawing" (John 6:44) and making alive (Eph 2:5), the washing of regeneration and the renewal of the Holy Spirit (Titus 3:5), rescuing from the domain of darkness (Col 1:13), being set free by the Son (John 8:36). What is the cumulative impression of such language?

Of course, how people experience the liberating grace of God differs, but there are instances, such as the conversion of Saul of Tarsus, where it seems that the gift is "imposed" (Olson's word), though Saul at least gave no evidence of believing that he was being dealt with by "an arbitrary and seemingly tyrannical God," but by a good sovereign God showing amazing grace to the chief of sinners. It is not thus with what Olson calls Arminianism's "key doctrine," given "special pride of place" by Arminius and others, prevenient grace. This is, as he says, preparing and assisting grace, but it is not effective or effectual grace; it merely takes a person, wounded (but not dead) and out of focus (but not blind), to a place of equilibrium from where he can choose or refuse the overtures of grace. Once the person responds positively to such overtures he is regenerated not by the Spirit's sovereign movement like the wind (John 3:8) but by the person's own choice of whether to admit the Spirit into his life.

The pity is that Olson makes no attempt to root such Arminian ideas in Scripture. His answer to that challenge, "Where is prevenient grace to be found in the Bible?" is interesting. He retorts, "Where is Trinity found in the Bible? Where is the doctrine of Christ's two natures found in the Bible?" The answer surely is that these doctrines are found pervasively in the New Testament. And the Augustinians make a biblical case for the doctrine of effective grace. Why not the evangelical Arminian for prevenient grace? Instead everything has to fall before what one Puritan rather rudely called the "Dagon" of free will, which in turn, according to Olson, is rooted in intuition and is so obviously true that not a single biblical writer needs to state or to defend it. Olson amazingly concedes, "There is no chapter or verse that, taken alone, demonstrates conclusively that persons have libertarian free will."

Response by John Sanders

Roger Olson's chapter is an excellent essay delineating the main features of classical free will theism. As I say in my essay, Olson and I are members of the Hatfield free will family and differ sharply from the McCoy determinist family.[4] In fact, there

---

4. I discuss the many similarities and few differences between classical free will theism and open theism in my "Open Theism: a Radical Revision or Miniscule Modification of Arminianism?" *Wesleyan Theological Journal* 38, no. 2 (Fall 2003): 69–102

is only one issue about which we differ. I will comment on that disagreement later, but at this point I will highlight some of the issues that form the watershed between the free will and determinist theological positions.

Both classical free will and openness free will theisms draw upon the same root metaphors to describe God. God is Creator, Lover, and Savior. We do not deny that God is Judge and King, but we understand these via God's love. We emphasize God's relationality with his creatures and that God is affected by them. We reject strong immutability and impassibility. In contrast to the meticulous providence exercised by the God of theological determinism, we affirm that God exercises general providence in which God is in charge but does not control everything that happens. God has graced us with libertarian freedom which means that God takes risks that we will not do what he specifically wants us to do in a particular situation. In theological determinism God never takes any risks, and thus all evil is planned by God to manifest the divine glory; there is not pointless evil. In contrast, we free will theists believe evil is permitted by God because he refuses to renege on his gift of freedom. Thus, we appeal to the free will defense to extricate God from direct responsibility for evil.

When it comes to salvation, Olson and I agree that God grants humans prevenient grace which enables us to cooperate with God. Election is conditional, not unconditional; and grace is enabling, not irresistible. We believe that prayer may influence God and that God makes some of his decisions dependent upon our prayers. Theological determinists, on the other hand, believe that our prayers are the instruments by which God brings about what he has foreordained to occur: our prayers never affect God because none of God's decisions are dependent upon what creatures do or say. The position a person takes on these matters sends us down one side of the divide or the other. Clearly, Olson and I are on the free will side of the watershed with determinism on the other.

Olson provides a terrific discussion of common misconceptions of free will theism. I agree that genuine freedom lies in trusting God and that, in its ultimate sense, freedom is eschatological. Libertarian freedom is a lesser, though necessary, form of freedom required for love and moral responsibility.[5] Also, he correctly notes that the free will tradition predates Augustine and the determinist tradition. Hence, attempts to say free will theists get the notion of free will from the modern age are ill informed.

Olson and I agree that theological determinism does not get God off the hook of the problem of evil. We believe that the true divine glory is displayed in that God loves us even while we are ungodly (Rom 5:6). It seems to us that determinists such as Helm and Ware diminish the divine love and goodness rendering apropos John Wesley's statement that the love of the Calvinist's God is one to make the blood run cold. The God of theological determinism needs people to be damned for his glory because if all were saved then one aspect of the divine nature, God's justice, would not be fully manifested. Perhaps we should give the following title to a book about this needy deity: *God's Lesser Love: The Diminished God of Theological Determinism*.

Olson and I also are of one mind concerning God's control over world history. God is constantly involved in creation though rarely, if ever, overriding human free will. When humans sin, we thwart what God wants to happen in that particular situation. Yet God is faithful and does not give up on his creation and will ultimately bring creation to its predestined outcome in the eschaton. At this point Olson asks: "How can God guarantee that his will be done if people have free will to resist and even contradict God's will?" The answer for free will theists is that the predestined outcome involves the general nature of the eschaton—the rules by which his will operates and the nature of the people who will inhabit it—rather than lots of specific details about particular individuals. There are people who live out God's redemption in Christ Jesus, and God has predetermined that all those in Christ will ultimately be conformed to the likeness of the Son. This, in part, is why Olson and I believe that divine election is best understandable as corporate rather than as pertaining to individuals.

5. I discuss this in John Sanders, *The God Who Risks: A Theology of Providence* (Downers Grove: InterVarsity, 1998), 223–24.

In his essay Olson does not comment on divine timelessness. In my essay for this book, I argue that it is incompatible with the core beliefs of free will theism. I observe that the well-known Wesleyan theologian John Miley concluded that divine atemporality was incompatible with the core beliefs of free will theism. He reasoned that God could not be involved in the dynamic give-and-take relations with creatures that is a necessary aspect of free will theism. I see nothing in his essay that leads me to think he affirms divine timelessness, so we may be in agreement here as well.

The only point about which Olson and I disagree is whether God has exhaustive foreknowledge of the future actions of creatures with libertarian freedom. Yet even here we both agree that God's knowledge of what creatures do is determined by the creatures, not by God. That is, we agree on the crucial issue of the mode of divine knowledge, and we reject the theological determinist position that God's knowledge of what we do is absolutely independent of the creature. We reject, while determinists affirm, that God knows what we do because God determined we would do it. So, though Olson and I disagree on divine foreknowledge, we agree that whatever God knows about our actions, that knowledge is dependent upon the creatures doing those actions.

This is a point often overlooked by critics of open theism. Ware and others have failed to grasp that the mode of divine knowing is the same for proponents of simple foreknowledge and dynamic omniscience.[6] Helm, on the other hand, understands they are the same in this regard, which is why he takes issue with both views in his chapter, rejecting them because they make God's knowledge of what creatures do dependent upon the creatures. Some critics of open theism have claimed that the divide is between those who affirm exhaustive definite foreknowledge and those who do not. They claim that proponents of dynamic omniscience cannot be considered "Arminian" since Arminians affirm simple foreknowledge. Though this is a difference between

---

6. For elaboration on the fundamental similarities between simple foreknowledge and dynamic omniscience see Steven M. Studebaker, "The Mode of Divine Knowledge in Reformation Arminianism and Open Theism," *Journal of the Evangelical Theological Society* 47, no. 3 (September 2004): 469–80; see also Sanders, "Open Theism."

classical free will theists and open theists, it is not the crucial theological difference because, as Olson and Helm demonstrate, the watershed is between all forms of theological determinism and all forms of free will theism. The debate over the content of divine omniscience is not fundamental whereas the mode of the divine knowing—whether any of God's knowledge is dependent upon creatures—is fundamental.

Returning to the single point of disagreement between our positions, Olson writes:

> Classical free will theists believe that God foreknows the entire course of the future as well as its end; God is omniscient in the biblical and traditional sense. Every true proposition is known exhaustively and infallibly by God. But classical free will theists do not believe this reality robs the future of contingency or freedom. God simply knows the future because it will happen; his knowing future free decisions and actions of creatures does not determine them. Rather that they will happen determines God's knowing them because God has decided to open himself up to being affected by the world. But, according to classical free will theists (as opposed to . . . open theists), God does not learn anything.

Olson and I agree that God is fully omniscient in the sense that if something is real then God knows it. Where we disagree is over which propositions have truth value and what has ontological reality. In my essay I argue that the future does not have a present reality, it is not a thing, and it does not exist. If assertions about what creatures with libertarian freedom will do in the future have no determinate truth value then there is nothing to be known. God cannot be held at fault for not knowing what it is logically impossible to know.

Olson argues that God's foreknowledge of our future actions does not determine the actions. Rather, it is our future actions that determine God's foreknowledge. I am willing to grant that God's foreknowledge is not the cause of our actions. However, I do not believe that this escapes determinism. My former colleague,

William Hasker, has constructed an argument that claims only that foreknowledge entails determinism, not that foreknowledge entails that God causes our actions.[7] For example, if God eternally knows that I will have rice for lunch tomorrow, then it is not now in my power to do otherwise than have rice for lunch tomorrow. For if God eternally knows each and every action anyone does, then it is not now in our power to act differently from what God knows. If we could now do otherwise than what God knows, then God's knowledge would be wrong. Since God's knowledge is never wrong, it is never in our power to do otherwise than what God knows. But to deny that we can ever do otherwise is a denial of libertarian freedom because libertarian freedom is the ability to otherwise. Consequently, foreknowledge entails determinism. Again, this is not claiming that God's knowledge is the cause of our actions; it is only claiming that if we cannot do otherwise then we are not free in the libertarian sense.

Olson claims that "just because God 'sees' the future does not mean it is determined." In my essay I discuss the two main theories of time: the dynamic (A theory) and stasis (B theory). According to the stasis view, the past, present, and future each have equal ontological status which is why we can say that the future already has an existence and that is why God can know it. God knows reality; and if the future really exists, then God must know it. However, the stasis theory of time implies determinism because the book of time, which contains all events that ever occur, only contains what actually occurs, not possibilities of what might happen. That is, the book of the future contains no other possible futures. If the future is real, then there is a truth about each and every future action; and thus there is only one possible future. But if there is only one possible future, then it is not possible for me to have the ability to do one thing rather than another. In other words, I do not have the libertarian freedom to do otherwise than what is recorded in the book. The stasis theory easily explains how God could know the future, but it results

---

7. For the latest version of Hasker's argument see "The Foreknowledge Conundrum," *International Journal for Philosophy of Religion* 50 (2001): 97–114. An older version may be found in his *God, Time and Knowledge,* 64–74.

in determinism, which is why it cannot be accepted by free will theists.

Now Olson does not say whether he affirms either the dynamic or stasis theories of time. If one wants to be a free will theist, however, then one must affirm the dynamic theory. For the dynamic theory, the present has a special ontological status that the past and future do not possess. The past no longer exists, and the future does not yet exist. If the future does not exist, is not a reality, then there is nothing "there" for God to see. When Olson says that "God sees" the future, what exactly is this reality? Just as there is a "grounding objection" to the theory of middle knowledge, so this may be called the grounding objection to simple foreknowledge. What is the basis for this knowledge? How can it be foreknown? If the future does not already exist, then what does God foresee? A proponent of classical free will theism may legitimately say that he does not know how to answer this question, but it is still a problem.

My essay argues that since the dynamic theory of time is most amenable to the core beliefs of free will theism, free will theists are within their rights to say that the "future" does not exist, and this makes it possible for free will theists to affirm dynamic omniscience. This is precisely the route open theists take.

Moreover, I also raise some other problems for the theory of simple foreknowledge. For one, I cite John Miley who recognized a key problem that he confessed he had no answer for: How can God interact with us in reciprocal relationships if God has exhaustive definite foreknowledge? He argued that the core doctrines of the Wesleyan-Arminian tradition require reciprocal relations between God and humans. He argued that if belief in an interactive God is contradictory to foreknowledge then he would give up foreknowledge. He went on to say that belief in dynamic omniscience would not undermine any vital Arminian doctrines and would, in fact, free it from the perplexity of divine foreknowledge and human freedom.[8]

Another problem is whether simple foreknowledge implies that God previsions his own decisions and actions. Does God

---

8. John Miley, *Systematic Theology*, vol. 1 (New York: Eaton & Mains, 1892), 180–93.

learn of his own future actions? If so, is there a script that God must follow, and where did this script come from?

One other problem is that foreknowledge makes it difficult to explain certain types of biblical texts that Olson cites as important to his view. For example, he mentions that God sometimes changes his mind in response to what humans do. However, if God truly takes a different course of action because humans failed to do what he expected them to do, then it cannot be the case that God had certain and comprehensive foreknowledge of the future. I argue that the theory of dynamic omniscience better explains the two types of biblical texts that I call the "motifs of the open and closed futures." That is, some biblical texts portray God as knowing and predicting some future events while other biblical texts portray God as not knowing other future events. The dynamic omniscience view better handles such texts than does the simple foreknowledge view.

A major problem for the simple foreknowledge view is that it is providentially useless for God to have such knowledge.[9] That is, it does not do God any good to know what is going to happen in the future because he cannot change it from happening. That a doctrine is useless does not make it false, but it does render it less appealing. Many classical free will theists have claimed that simple foreknowledge gives God great providential control because if God "looks ahead" and sees that Billy Bob is going to do something that God does not want him to do, then God can take steps to prevent him from doing that act. Indeed, that would be a great advantage if God could do this; but, unfortunately, it is logically impossible. As Richard Swinburne points out: "What God already knows is beyond his making a difference to."[10] Just as we cannot change the past because it has already happened so God is unable to change anything about the future because it is, so to speak, "past" for him. Once God has knowledge of all that will happen, it is "too late" logically for God to change anything.

---

9. I have explained this problem at length in *The God Who Risks*, 200–6 and in "Why Simple Foreknowledge Offers No More Providential Control than the Openness of God," *Faith and Philosophy* 14, no. 1 (Jan. 1997): 26–40.

10. Richard Swinburne, *The Coherence of Theism*, rev. ed. (New York: Oxford University Press, 1993), 181.

Can a God with simple foreknowledge prevent sinners from being born or prevent certain evil choices? No. If what God *foreknows* is the *actual* world, then God foreknows the births, lives, and deaths of actual sinners. Once God has foreknowledge, he cannot change what will happen, for that would make his foreknowledge incorrect; and foreknowledge, by definition, is always correct about what is going to occur. God cannot make future actual events "deoccur." It is a logical contradiction to affirm that God both knows something will happen and that God knows he will bring it about that it not happen. Once God knows something as actual, he cannot make it the case that it not be actual.

Perhaps some illustrations will help make this clear. If God foreknows (has knowledge of the actual occurrence) that King Saul will freely choose to mistrust God, then God cannot intervene to prevent Saul from this mistrust. Such intervention would be pointless since God knows that, in fact, Saul will be disobedient. Moreover, if God knows that Saul will be a disobedient king, God cannot then refuse to make Saul king of Israel in the first place because that would mean his foreknowledge of Saul being the first king was wrong. Hence, God can see the evil coming before he creates the world but is powerless to prevent it. For another example, let us say that Mandie asks God whether she should marry Matthew or Jim, believing that God knows how everything will turn out. Mandie believes, for instance, that God knows for a fact whether Jim will be loving or abusive toward her and would advise her appropriately. The problem is that if God only knows truths, and God *knows* it as true that she actually marries Jim and that he actually will start out good but end up abusive, then God cannot change that from happening. Once God knows it as fact that she will actually marry Jim and be quite unhappy, then it is useless for God to give her the guidance to marry Matthew. It would be incoherent to claim that God, knowing the actual future and on the basis of this knowledge, changes it so that it will *not* be the actual future. A God who already knows the future cannot answer such prayers.

Classical free will theists affirm the theory of simple foreknowledge where God "sees" what is actually going to happen rather than what might happen. This is not the theory known as middle knowledge where God knows what would happen in various possible situations.

In Olson's paragraph quoted several paragraphs above he says that, unlike open theism, a God with simple foreknowledge "does not learn anything." Simple foreknowledge is the view that God "previsions" or "sees ahead" what we will actually do in the future. Prior to creation God first decided to create beings with libertarian freedom. After making that decision, God then "sees ahead" to find out what will happen in this particular world. At this point, just prior to actually creating, God *now* knows all that will happen in human history. Jack Cottrell, a well-known Arminian theologian who affirms simple foreknowledge, calls God's acquisition of this knowledge the "noetic big bang."[11] Now many though not all classical free will theists believe God is timeless. If God is timeless, then the terms *prevision* and *see ahead* are not understood temporally in the sense of one event followed in time by another event. Rather, they are understood in a logical order of explanation. That is, logically, but not in actual time, God makes a decision to create which precedes his knowledge of what will actually occur in this world. Until God decides to create a world in which some creatures have libertarian freedom, God does not foreknow what we will do. Logically speaking, once God decides to create, then and only then does God foreknow (learn) what we will do. Technically speaking, a God with simple foreknowledge acquires knowledge or learns even if he does so eternally.

In conclusion, I want to reiterate that the disagreement between the classical free will and openness free will positions is minor compared to our agreement on the watershed issue. Also, I am not averse to giving up my belief in dynamic omniscience. If classical free will theists can figure out how to answer the questions open theists have raised about simple foreknowledge such as (1) the explanation of particular biblical texts and (2) the philosophical problems (particularly the uselessness issue), then I am more than ready to affirm it. Even if that does not happen, the

11. Cottrell, "Understanding God: God and Time," paper presented at the Evangelical Theological Society, November 19, 2002.

debate between us remains a friendly dialogue between members of the free will Hatfield family and does not bear the acrimony and attempts at expulsion from broader communions that some members of the determinist McCoys have displayed toward open theists.

Response by Bruce A. Ware

Roger Olson's chapter serves very well to mark out many of the significant differences between free will theism and Calvinism, broadly understood. Even if I may differ with him on how he describes the Calvinist view throughout his chapter (I would prefer more charitable descriptions in many cases), the reader can easily and rightly detect that these traditions do understand and defend two models of God that are significantly different, even mutually exclusive, in many respects. And among these differences, I freely acknowledge that Olson's model of God has the advantage that it accords more easily with cultural values and human intuitions at certain points than does the Calvinist model. I have often told my students when teaching on the fundamental differences between Arminianism and Calvinism that if you decide this issue based on which view better matches both contemporary North American cultural values and latent intuitions, you'll likely end up with some version of free will theism. Calvinists hold the view they do for the simple reason that they are convinced that Scripture teaches its doctrines of God's comprehensive and meticulous sovereignty, the unconditional election of the sinners whom God graciously and from eternity chose to save, the effectual and ultimately irresistible grace of God that surely will bring all the elect to saving faith, and a notion of true and genuine freedom in which God's full sovereignty is seen as compatible with the moral responsibility attaching to choices and actions of the will. In each of these cases, admittedly, the Arminian view is more intuitive and thereby easier for many to grasp and accept. But *Sola Scriptura* reminds us that the doctrines we hold and advocate must align with the teaching of the entire Bible in all of its parts, regardless of whether those doctrines align also with contemporary cultural intuitions or beliefs. I will focus my response upon the two main areas Olson himself proposes are most crucial for free will theism, its view of free will as libertarian freedom and its view of God as universally loving.

Libertarian Freedom

One of the early central ideas that Olson discusses is the nature and purpose of freedom. It should be obvious to all that since his model is labeled "free will theism," the conception of freedom certainly must be one of the defining and centrally important notions within the model itself. He rightly declares that libertarian free will is held by all forms of free will theism (in fact, I have observed no detectable differences in how libertarian freedom is understood in process theism, open theism, Molinism or middle knowledge Arminianism, and classic Arminianism) and that libertarian freedom is fully incompatible with determinism. It is also clear that Olson describes libertarian freedom in a way that purposely distinguishes it from the kind of freedom understood within the Calvinist tradition. He writes, "Absolutely crucial to all forms of free will theism is the belief that persons only exercise free choice or liberty of decision and action when they could do otherwise than they do. A person who cannot do X instead of Y cannot be exercising free will when doing Y even if he or she wants to do Y. According to many divine determinists, all that is required for free will decision and action is doing what one wants to do even if one could not do otherwise. Free will theists reject this notion of free will as philosophical, speculative, and counterintuitive."

In response, I put forward this claim: libertarian freedom possesses an initial advantageous *prima facie* philosophical and intuitive legitimacy, yet under examination this legitimacy soon vanishes such that the Calvinist view of freedom—which I prefer calling "freedom of inclination"—alone can sustain careful and probing scrutiny. Without repeating the discussion on freedom in my chapter, I wish here first to acknowledge that the libertarian model does seem, on the surface, to describe accurately the experience we free agents have when we make what seems to be a free choice. For example, if we are considering the menu at a restaurant and eventually order the deluxe pizza, it seems clear to us that as we requested what we did, we surely could instead have selected a hamburger or the French dip. In other words, it seems intuitive that we could have chosen otherwise, and in fact, if we could not have chosen otherwise, we wouldn't have been free.

But what this surface analysis fails to notice is a definition of libertarian freedom that is sometimes hidden or implied. Not only is it the case that when we choose X, we could have chosen Y; it is also more precisely the case that at the moment we choose X, *all things being exactly what they are when we make the choice of X*, we could instead have chosen Y. Now, as one analyzes libertarian freedom more fully exposed, as it were, we can begin to detect a real problem. If it is the case that all of the factors present when I chose X would be exactly and identically the same such that, instead, given those very same factors I could have chosen Y, it follows that there is no way to distinguish just why I chose X over Y, or why I might instead have chosen Y instead of X. If all of the factors leading to my choosing X are identical to the reason that, instead, I might choose Y, then there is no explanation for the choice of X over Y or Y over X. Libertarian freedom, then, reduces to what Calvinists have long called a "freedom of indifference." If this libertarian view of freedom is correct (which, though, it cannot really be), libertarian freedom accounts for human free choice such that no explanation is forthcoming for why one made the specific choice one did and, hence, one must be quite literally "indifferent" to X or Y when one chooses X instead of Y or Y instead of X.

But of course, this is not the case! When we choose the deluxe pizza, while it is true that we have many options to choose from, something happens in our mind as we consider these options that gives a strongest desire for one menu item over the others. Hence, while it is true that had our strongest desire instead been for the hamburger, we could instead have ordered it, it stands to reason that since our strongest desire was for the pizza, we chose what we in fact most wanted. Given the reasons that went into forming the taste for pizza as the strongest desire, it would make no sense at all to say, as libertarians do, that when I chose the pizza, all things being just what they were, I could instead have chosen the hamburger. No, instead, since my strongest desire was for the pizza, this accounts precisely for why I chose the pizza *over* the hamburger. My freedom, then, is not a matter of being able to choose otherwise but a matter of being able to choose and act according to what I want most; freedom rightly understood is a "freedom of inclination."

Interestingly enough, Olson seems actually to sense that freedom is a matter of choosing what we most want, despite his formal rejection of this concept. In the paragraph following my previous quotation of Olson, he proposes that God was free—in the libertarian or noncompatibilist sense—when he created the world. But in describing God's freedom in creation, Olson writes, "Nothing within God or external to God caused him to create the world. Something inclined him to do it and he chose to do it, which is different from having to do it." My interest is in Olson's comment that "something inclined" God to create. If God has an inclination (he is more strongly inclined this way than another) to create, and he chooses to create according to this inclination, does it make sense to say that his freedom is precisely his ability instead to have done otherwise? In this case, would we not be saying (trying to keep libertarian freedom intact) that God could have followed a lesser inclination or gone against his true inclination in choosing instead not to create? How does it make sense to think of freedom as our ability to choose what we are not inclined to do, or to choose contrary to our strongest inclination? Indeed, it makes no sense. Here, as with all decisions, various factors are at work giving rise to a strongest inclination, and freedom is constituted precisely not with the ability to choose contrary to that inclination but rather to choose in accordance with it. In short, when God created, he did what he most wanted, and in this he was free.

I have devoted a fair bit of attention here simply because the free will theist believes that he surely has the philosophical high ground with his notion of libertarian freedom. But the truth is that this notion is deeply flawed, and upon examination it fails truly to account for why we, and God, make the choices that we do. Since, as Olson makes clear, libertarian freedom is essential to the free will theist position; and since it fails as an operational conception to account for the actual working of a free will, one has strong reason to call the model as a whole into question.

The Love of God

As important as libertarian freedom is to free will theism, Olson makes clear that the primary basis for this model is not its view of the freedom of the will but its view of God. In a very important section, Olson writes, "Classical Christian free will theism arises not so much from a desire to elevate free will as from a desire to do justice to God's character as loving kindness—not only toward a portion of humanity (or even creation) but toward all (John 3:16–17). Libertarian free will is not an idol erected to exalt humanity; it is rather a necessary protection of God's goodness. Without it God would be virtually indistinguishable from the devil."

Permit me two brief responses. First, as with every aspect of the Calvinist view of God, Scripture's teaching must be accepted whether or not our cultural intuitions align with that teaching. Olson's view of the universal and equally distributed love of God, while fitting well with our contemporary culture, expresses only one aspect of the Bible's teaching on the love of God. Yes, there truly and biblically is a sense in which God loves all people in the entire world equally, and Olson is correct, in my judgment, to cite John 3:16 in support of this notion. But a far richer and more prevalent conception of God's love throughout Scripture is his particular and selective love for his own people, his elect (see Eph 1:4–5; 5:25–27). Though this category of particular and selective love is stronger in Scripture than its presentation of God's universal and impartial love, yet defenses of free will theism usually fail to acknowledge and incorporate this teaching in their presentations.

To cite just one vivid example, in Isaiah 43, God's comfort and source of hope for the people of Israel is his commitment to them even at the cost of other peoples' lives. Isaiah 43:3–4

(HCSB) reads: "For I the Lord your God, the Holy One of Israel, and your Savior, give Egypt as a ransom for you, Cush and Seba in your place. Because you are precious in My sight and honored, and I love you, I will give human beings in your place, and peoples in place of your life." In what is clearly a reference to the exodus from Egypt, God draws the lesson from this event that it was his particular love for Israel that led him to deliver them by means of bringing death to the Egyptians. And when one considers afresh just how the exodus from Egypt took place, it is clear that this account from Isaiah gets it exactly right. After all, was it necessary for God to bring death to the firstborn in every Egyptian household in order to deliver his people? Of course not, yet it is clear from back in Exodus 4:21–23 that God intended from the outset to deliver Israel only through and not apart from the death of the firstborn in Egypt. No doubt a major part of the reason for this was to demonstrate his grace on Israel. Although the Israelites were as guilty as the Egyptians before God (see Ezek 20:4–10), yet God favored these guilty Israelites, his own people, by providing a means by which the angel of death would "pass over" their homes through the shed blood of the lambs, thus sparing what otherwise would be the shed blood of their own firstborn children and livestock. So, although Israel deserved the same death brought to the homes in Egypt, God loved Israel and so spared them, while he executed his just wrath against Egypt. Could equal judgment have been given to both, or equal mercy be shown to both? Yes, but what God wanted Israel to learn was his special love for them. As Isaiah 43 puts it, because Israel was precious in God's sight and because he loved them, he gave other people in their place and in exchange for their lives. While this may be difficult for our cultural sensibilities, and while it conflicts directly with the free will conceptions of who God must be and how God must act, the teaching of the Bible here is not unclear. A model of God that does not account both for his general and universal love for all along with his stronger and deeper particular and selective love for his chosen people simply is not dealing rightly with the Scripture.

Second, I find it utterly audacious for Olson and other free will theists to charge the God of Calvinism with being "virtually indistinguishable from the devil" (a charge Olson makes in different forms at least three times in his chapter). My main concern is not the pejorative nature and polarizing effect this language has on discussion among those who claim to be Christians, when the tradition of Augustine, Martin Luther, John Calvin, Jonathan Edwards, George Whitefield, William Carey, Hudson Taylor, George Mueller, Adoniram Judson, Charles Spurgeon, John R. W. Stott, and J. I. Packer is tarred with such a despicable depiction. Mainly, I worry deeply for Olson and others who think the way that they do when it well may be the case that the view of God they find indistinguishable from Satan turns out to be the true and living God of the Bible.

Where we agree is this: The true and living God despises wickedness, and there is no evil in him (Ps 5:4). We agree that God is light, and in him there is no darkness at all (1 John 1:5). But a fundamental place where we disagree is God's relation to evil. The Calvinist stands squarely on Scripture's teaching that this God who is light himself nonetheless "forms light and creates darkness," and this God who hates wickedness is nonetheless the God who "causes well-being and creates calamity," for as God himself declares, "I, the Lord, do all these things" (Isa 45:7). Yes, God is good, yet God is fully and meticulously sovereign. Yes, God loves all, yet God savingly loves those whom he has chosen. Yes, God hates evil, yet God ordains all the evil that occurs for the fulfillment of his good and wise purposes, to the glory of his great name. The whole counsel of God's Word must be accounted for, and when one does, one finds the free will model one-sided— a partial understanding of the God of the Bible which, since it is partial, is also deeply flawed. The whole picture of God is needed from the whole of Scripture. In the end, free will theism's view of God fails to give us this full and reliable portrait.

CHAPTER 7

Divine Providence and the Openness of God

JOHN SANDERS

When I was a young Christian, I was taught that our prayers of petition could influence what God decided to do. Not that God has to do what we ask but that God graciously decides to take our concerns into account in formulating his responses, just as he did with Moses and others. However, in college I was assigned some standard evangelical theology books that described the nature of God as "impassible" (could not be affected by creatures in any way) and "strongly immutable" (could not change in any respect). My spiritual life was thrown into a quandary—either I had been incorrectly taught that my prayers could affect God or the theology books were wrong on these points. This uncertainty led me to an examination of Scripture from which I concluded that God genuinely responds to us. The search for a theology of prayer led me into other areas of providence and so, for more than two decades, I have reflected upon Scripture, theology, philosophy, and spirituality concerning these matters

My conclusion is that we can actually affect God. Hence, what most evangelicals live out in piety is correct as is their emphasis on a personal relationship with God. In my view, the free will theological tradition (which includes Arminianism), rather than the tradition of theological determinism, is more consistent with this sort of piety and with scriptural teaching. Yet free will theism needs some modifications in order to provide a more biblically faithful and logically consistent account of God's relationship with us. Openness of God theology attempts to accomplish this task.

Openness of God—a Definition

According to openness theology, the *triune* God of love has, in *almighty* power, created all that is and is *sovereign* over all. The Father, Son, and Holy Spirit have eternally loved one another; love has always been an aspect of reality.[1] Love had always been internal to God and in deciding to create others, the divine love flowed externally. In *freedom* God decided to create beings capable of experiencing his love, and it was God's desire for us to enter into reciprocal relations of love with God as well as with our fellow creatures. In creating us the divine intention was that we would come to experience the triune love and respond to it with love of our own and freely come to collaborate with God toward the achievement of his goals.

Second, God is almighty in that he has all the power necessary to deliver and care for us. However, God has chosen not to override our free will and make us love (which would not be love anyway). Instead, God restrains the full use of his power. God has not given up or lost power; he simply chooses not always to exercise it to its fullest extent.[2] God has, in *sovereign freedom,* decided to make some of his actions contingent upon our requests and actions. God elicits our free collaboration in his plans. Hence, God can be influenced by what we do, and God truly responds to what we do. God genuinely interacts and enters into dynamic give-and-take relationships with us. That God changes in some

---

1. We believe that love is the primary characteristic of God because the triune Godhead has eternally loved before creatures existed. Divine holiness and justice are aspects of the divine love toward creatures. Love can even be experienced as divine wrath when God responds to his beloved's destruction of herself and others.

2. Some open theists speak of God's "self-limitation" in this regard, but it is preferable to say God "restrains" the use of his power.

respects implies that God is temporal, working with us through time. God, at least since creation, experiences duration.[3]

God decided to make some of his decisions contingent upon our actions because God is love and love does not force its way (1 Cor 13:4–7). This made it possible for us to misuse our freedom and commit sin, which brought grief to God (Gen 6:6). We experience something of what God does when we choose to have children. When you open yourself in this way, you open yourself to suffering; you become vulnerable to being grieved. In spite of our sin, God has chosen to endure our lack of love. However, divine forbearance does not mean that God is blind to the evil infecting us. Rather, God evaluates our situation and takes the steps necessary to try to prevent the beloved from destroying herself and bring about reconciliation. God's wisdom is adept at overcoming obstacles that hinder the divine project. God is competent and resourceful in working with recalcitrant sinners. Despite the fact that humanity failed to love God and others as God intended, God remains *faithful* to his intentions by enacting a plan of redemption.

Third, the only *wise* God has chosen to exercise general rather than meticulous providence, allowing space for us to operate and for God to be creative and resourceful in working with us. God has chosen not to control every detail that happens in our lives. Moreover, God has flexible strategies. Though the divine nature does not change, God reacts to contingencies, even adjusting his plans, if necessary, to take into account the decisions of his free creatures. God is endlessly resourceful and wise in working toward the fulfillment of his ultimate goals. Sometimes God unilaterally decides how to accomplish these goals, but he usually elicits human cooperation such that both God and humanity decide what the future shall be. God's plan is not a detailed script or blueprint but a broad intention that allows for a variety of options regarding precisely how his goals may be reached. What God and people do in history matters. If the Hebrew midwives

---

3. It is not essential for open theists to take a stand on whether God was temporal prior to creation. Even if God was eternally temporal, God did not experience metric (measured) time until the creation. See Nicholas Wolterstorff's discussion in *God and Time: Four Views*, ed. Gregory Ganssle (Downers Grove: InterVarsity, 2001), 233.

had feared Pharaoh rather than God and killed the baby boys, then God would have responded accordingly, and a different story would have emerged. Moses' refusal to return to Egypt prompted God to resort to plan B, allowing Aaron to do the public speaking instead of Moses (Exod 4:14–16). What people do and whether they come to trust God make a difference concerning what God does. God does not fake the story of human history.

Finally, the *omniscient* God knows all that is logically possible to know. I call this quality "dynamic omniscience" in that God knows the past and present with exhaustive definite knowledge and knows the future as partly definite (closed) and partly indefinite (open). God's knowledge of the future contains knowledge of what God has decided to bring about unilaterally (that which is definite), knowledge of possibilities (that which is indefinite) and those events that are determined to occur (e. g., an asteroid hitting a planet). Hence, the future is partly open or indefinite and partly closed or definite. God is not caught off guard since he has foresight, anticipating what we will do. Also, it is not the case that just anything may happen, for God has acted in history to bring about events in order to achieve his unchanging purpose. Graciously, however, God invites us to collaborate with him to bring the open part of the future into being. We call this the "openness of God" because God is "open" to what creatures decide to do and because God has left most of history open to multiple possible futures.

The Divide

The knowledgeable reader will note that most of the beliefs espoused by open theists are also affirmed by other free will theists such as the Eastern Orthodox and the Arminians. This is due to the family resemblance shared by proponents of free will theism when it comes to theologies of salvation, providence, anthropology, and impetratory prayer (entreaties that God, indeed, responds to). In fact, open theists have nothing to add to the vast majority of theological stances taken and explanations of various biblical texts propounded by their free will theistic forebears. For example, open theists can utilize the same range of views put forward historically by free will theists in order to explain the nature of election or texts such as Romans 9–11. This also explains why the vast majority of criticisms leveled against open theists by theological determinists are the same old arguments against Arminianism.[4] The "Hatfield" free will theistic family has been in a feud with the "McCoy" theological deterministic family for 16 hundred years.

The watershed separating these two families is whether one affirms that God is ever affected by and responds to what we do. Does God tightly control everything such that what God wants is never thwarted in the least detail? Does God ever take risks? Is God ever influenced by what we do, or does everything work out precisely as God eternally foreordained? Free will theists such as John Wesley and C. S. Lewis are on one side of this divide, and theological determinists such as John Calvin and John Piper are on the other.

Free will theists affirm that God, in sovereign freedom, decided not to control tightly human affairs by initiating meticulous providence. Instead, God exercises general providence, granting us libertarian freedom (the ability to do otherwise than we did even in the same circumstances). Hence, God took the risk that history would not go exactly as he desires. Humans can rebel or become collaborators with God by either accepting or rejecting divine initiatives. Given the type of world God decided to create, he cannot guarantee that everything will go precisely the way he would like. For free will theists God is weakly immutable in that the *character* of God does not change, but God can have changing plans, thoughts, and emotions. God is also weakly impassible because God is affected by and responds to our prayers and actions though he is not overwhelmed by emotions as we are apt to be.[5]

Theological determinists affirm that God exercises meticulous providence, controlling everything that happens down to the smallest detail. Consequently, the divine initiatives in every

---

4. Roger Olson makes this point in his *The Mosaic of Christian Belief: Twenty Centuries of Unity and Diversity* (Downers Grove: InterVarsity, 2002), 196.

5. Most of the early church fathers were free will theists who affirmed weak immutability and weak impassibility. See the outstanding study by Paul Gavrilyuk, *The Suffering of the Impassible God: The Dialectics of Patristic Thought*, The Oxford Early Christian Studies series (New York: Oxford University Press, 2004).

instance are always fulfilled; God never takes risks. Humans have compatibilistic freedom (you are free so long as you act on your strongest desire) so God is able to guarantee that whatever he wants done will be done by ensuring that each of us always has the particular desire God wants us to have at any moment. Those theological determinists who care about logical consistency hold that God is strongly immutable (never changes in any respect, such as in emotions) and strongly impassible (never affected by us).

Given these fundamental differences, the theological Hatfields and McCoys are not going to reconcile anytime soon. Profitable discussions, however, do take place within each family and that is what open theism is about. It is an internal dialogue among free will theists about the best way to affirm the core beliefs and values in the family heritage. Open theists think that two beliefs, customarily affirmed by free will theists, need to change in order to better carry on the family line. Later discussion will address these issues, but a brief word is needed here. Both areas concern God's relationship to time. A longstanding debate among free will theists has been whether God is *atemporal* or *temporal*. The majority view has been that God is timelessly eternal, that God either does not experience time at all (timeless) or that God experiences all time at once (simultaneity). A minority of free will theists have said God experiences temporal succession: God is everlasting in that he always was, is, and will be. Open theists side with this minority view within the free will family.

The second disagreement is about whether God has exhaustive definite foreknowledge of future contingent events. Though all free will theists affirm divine omniscience (God knows all that is knowable), they disagree about what constitutes truths. They differ over foreknowledge, not omniscience. Most free will theists affirm what is known as "simple foreknowledge" by which God, so to speak, "looks ahead" and "sees" in exhaustive detail exactly what we are going to do in the future. Open theists affirm dynamic omniscience in which God also "observes" what we do but does so temporally rather than timelessly.

Both views agree that whatever is knowable, God knows it. They simply disagree as to what is knowable. Both views agree that God does not determine or write the script of the future. Rather, they both hold that God "sees" or "observes" what free creatures do. It is fundamental to free will theism that God not determine our free actions. This is an important point, for it identifies the divide between free will theism and theological determinism. Though the simple foreknowledge view agrees with theological determinism that God has exhaustive definite foreknowledge, the mechanism by which God comes to possess such knowledge is different in each case.[6] In simple foreknowledge God "observes" what we will actually do without determining what we do. However, in theological determinism God does not passively observe what will happen. Rather, God foreordains or determines what we will do, and that is why he knows what will happen. The radical difference between the means by which God has foreknowledge in these two views is related to the divide between free will theism and theological determinism regarding evil, salvation, and prayer. The dynamic omniscience and simple foreknowledge perspectives share the same views on evil, salvation and prayer in opposition to theological determinism.

Divine Providence in the Openness Model

Most evangelical Christians believe that our lives make a difference to God and that our prayers and actions can affect God. Also, everyone agrees that our actions affect our fellow creatures. God has created a highly relational and interdependent world. Open theism highlights the reciprocal give-and-take relations between God and creatures as well as the interdependent

---

6. Many critics of open theism have failed to understand this connection to the free will tradition, claiming that the watershed is between those who affirm exhaustive definite foreknowledge and those who do not. They claim that proponents of dynamic omniscience cannot be considered Arminian since Arminians affirm simple foreknowledge. Though this is a difference between the views, it is not the crucial difference. For elaboration on the fundamental similarities between simple foreknowledge and dynamic omniscience, see Steven M. Studebaker, "The Mode of Divine Knowledge in Reformation Arminianism and Open Theism," *Journal of the Evangelical Theological Society* 47, no. 3 (September 2004): 469–80; and John Sanders, "Open Theism: A Radical Revision or Miniscule Modification of Arminianism?" *Wesleyan Theological Journal* 38, no. 2 (Fall 2003): 69–102.

relations between creatures. God decided to place great responsibility upon humans to care for creation and for one another. History does not develop solely on the basis of what God decides; rather, God has given us a say-so in what transpires. God sovereignly decided that it was "good" to make much of what happens in history dependent upon us when he delegated a significant part of the caretaking to us (Gen 1:26–28). God will hold us accountable in our role as his appointed caretakers (Matt 25:14–30). Consequently, the New Testament writers call upon the followers of Jesus to collaborate with God to overcome evil powers, to make God's gift of reconciliation a reality among the nations, and to reclaim aspects of creation defiled by our sin.

For these reasons the openness of God model emphasizes human responsibility. God has chosen to rely on us in many areas of life. Because the future is not wholly fixed or determined, the story of God and humanity is more like a "create your own adventure book" than a completed novel. Moreover, the story is not authored by a single individual but by hosts of individuals in relation to one another. It is a group project. To change metaphors, life with God is more like playing jazz than a symphony. Though jazz has structure, there is a great deal of improvisation within it because the players have to respond to one another. Jazz requires careful listening between the players in order to collaborate toward the production of the song. The members take turns between playing the solo lines and playing backup. In a band one famous musician might get the headlines. Yet the musician does not produce music without the other members. We might picture God as the band member with the "name recognition" who has chosen not to play without our participation.

Let us now apply this approach to a number of topics in order to see how divine providence functions in the openness model.

Prayer

There are many different types of prayer, but I wish to examine only prayers of petition since they highlight the issue of divine response. The book of James says that we "do not have, because [we] do not ask" (4:2). A widely accepted understanding of this is that God might not give us some good things *because* we fail to ask for them.[7] God will only bring some things about if we ask him because he desires an interdependent world and prayer is one means of fostering our dependence and concern for one another. Dallas Willard affirmed this when he wrote, "God's response to our prayers is not a charade. He does not pretend he is answering our prayers when he is only doing what he was going to do anyway. Our requests really do make a difference in what God does or does not do."[8]

This does not mean, however, that we receive whatever we request. Though we may prevail upon God, God can also prevail with us, getting us to change our minds. In this way prayer is a dialogue, opening windows of opportunity for the Spirit to work in our lives. Our failure to pray means that particular desires of God may not be realized because we fail to ask. If God's bringing about a certain state of affairs is contingent upon our prayer and our prayer is the result of our free will, then God is taking a risk that some particular good may not come about.

Prayer for one another is an important factor in the way God has chosen to build Christian community. Some of the things God wants to do for others depend upon my prayers. This is no different from God wanting to feed the poor through me. If God has chosen to depend upon me to feed them or me to pray for others, then it is irresponsible of me to claim that it is God's fault for the state they are in. Certainly, God can act unilaterally, but he has ordained that the structures of the world that he established at creation continue to operate and so God continues to place great responsibility on us to be our brother's keeper. Furthermore, God does not need input from us to enlighten him about a situation. Yet in grace God desires our input because that is the kind of relationship he wants.

---

7. For a thorough study of this position, see Vincent Brummer, *What Are We Doing When We Pray? A Philosophical Investigation* (London: SCM Press, 1984).

8. Dallas Willard, *The Divine Conspiracy: Rediscovering Our Hidden Life in God* (San Francisco: HarperSanFrancisco, 1998), 244. Willard comments about divine foreknowledge on 244–53. However, he is not clear on whether he means (1) that God could have determined all future events (no libertarian freedom) and thus had exhaustive foreknowledge of them (what proponents of dynamic omniscience believe) or (2) that God could know the future actions of creatures with libertarian freedom but somehow chooses not to.

If the future is open because some of God's decisions are dependent upon our prayers and some of God's plans can change, then the sort of prayer described here makes sense, and it lends urgency to our prayers for one another. The situation is much different, however, in theological determinism where God is never affected by what we do. If we do not pray for someone, it is because God never decreed that we would pray for them. God does not truly respond to our prayers according to this view. Rather, as Jonathan Edwards put it: "Speaking after the manner of men, God is sometimes represented *as if* he were moved and persuaded by the prayers of his people; yet it is not to be thought that God is properly moved or made willing by our prayers. . . . he is self-moved. . . . God has been pleased to constitute prayer to be antecedent to the bestowment of mercy; and he is pleased to bestow mercy in consequence of prayer, *as though* he were prevailed upon by prayer."[9] Theological determinism rejects the common evangelical belief that our prayers affect God. Instead, our prayers are the eternally decreed means by which God brings about his eternally decreed ends.

Salvation

In the openness mode, the triune God of love seeks to establish relations of love with his creatures which results in the creatures loving one another. Unfortunately, creation has miscarried for sin has spoiled God's intention. Nonetheless, God refuses to give up on us and so seeks to redeem his creation. God's redemptive love is most clearly manifested in the life, death, and resurrection of our Lord Jesus Christ. As creatures we are solely dependent upon divine grace to initiate the reconciliation necessary to restore the broken relationship. As sinners we are on the run from God; but, like the good parent he is, God seeks after his lost children. Though our hearts are calloused from sin, the Holy Spirit provides enabling grace which empowers us to repent. Enabling grace is a necessary, though not sufficient, condition for our salvation. In order for reconciliation to take place, both sides must freely desire the restoration of the relationship. The

9. "The Most High a Prayer-Hearing God," *Works of Jonathan Edwards,* vol. 2, 115–16 (emphasis mine).

Holy Spirit empowers us through the gospel story of Jesus to see God's stance toward us as one of love that beckons us to return home. But our acceptance of restoration is not manipulated or determined by the Spirit. God waits on us to respond freely to his grace.

This approach is part of the standard affirmation of conditional election by free will theists. Though Jesus' atonement is for everyone and God desires to save all, some reject God's grace. God gives all an opportunity to be redeemed, but God cannot guarantee that all will, in fact, be redeemed unless he forecloses on the free will he gave us. God is the initiator and provider of salvation, yet he will not restore the broken relationship without our free consent. Hence, divine election to salvation is contingent upon our free acceptance.

Regarding sanctification, at any particular time we may, or may not, exhibit the degree of holiness that God wishes us to have. God has given us everything we need for a life of godliness (2 Pet 1:3–11), and we may use these gifts to grow in Christlikeness and service to God. However, we may also fail to use them and thus grieve the Holy Spirit for not being what God intends us to be. We cannot achieve personal holiness without the Spirit's help, and the Spirit will not make us holy without our free participation. Again, this view is different from theological determinism in which the degree of holiness we have any one moment is precisely the degree God wants us to have at that moment so God could never be grieved over us.

As for perseverance, open theists follow the traditional teaching of free will theists that it is possible for genuine believers to apostatize. The Arminian tradition interprets the warning passages in the New Testament (e.g., Heb 6:4–6) to be genuine warnings to actual Christians. The Christian life is an ongoing relationship with God in Christian community. Though salvation may begin at a particular point, salvation is not a one-time event but an ongoing relationship. Because it is an ongoing relationship, God takes the risk that we will decisively and ultimately break off the relationship.[10] We can rest assured that God will do

---

10. All free will theists face the question as to whether our free will implies that we might fall away in heaven. A brief response is that we will freely ask God to confirm

everything he can within the structures he established, to keep this from happening. Our faithfulness may waver, but God's does not. God's faithfulness is not dependent upon our faith.

Guidance

Though some free will theists believe that God has a blueprint for every decision we make, such as which college to attend or which career to take up, open theists believe that no such blueprint exists. Rather, God has an overarching goal for our lives that is clearly stated in Scripture: to be like Jesus. The issue then becomes whether we are seeking to be like our Lord in our actions and attitudes at whatever college we attend or whichever career we choose. For example, there are usually several good careers we could select. Though some may be more suited to our gifts and personality, for most people there is no single "best" one. We need never have anxiety that due to our past decisions we must now settle for "second best." There are usually several good options for us, and God is interested in the path we most want. God is resourceful and is able to take many routes to achieve his goals.

In making such decisions we are to seek wisdom from the Holy Spirit, who typically provides it through the body of Christ. We seek counsel from Christians we respect as we deliberate, and we trust the Spirit to help us examine the alternatives. The Bible speaks a great deal about seeking divine wisdom and little about reading the so-called signs in our circumstances. The wisdom approach to guidance implies that we can at times fail to understand God's wisdom or, if we do understand it, we might reject it. This is true for all free will theists, not just open theists, because we believe that humans can thwart God's desires in particular situations.

Free will theists, as opposed to theological determinists, believe that there are chance events and accidents. Because God does not meticulously control everything that happens, we should not attempt to read most events as messages from God.

---

our characters in such a way that we never choose to sin. For elaboration see my "The Assurance of Things to Come," in *Looking to the Future,* ed. David Baker (Grand Rapids: Baker, 2001), 281–94.

Many people, for example, used to believe that lightning striking your house was a sign from God, and they accused those who placed lightning rods on their barns and houses as lacking faith. If you are a good employee and are fired, it most likely has nothing to do with God's trying to get your attention. Certainly, God will try to help us exercise virtues in such situations, and God will work to bring good out of them, but we need not see it as a sign from God. Such events are usually the result of other factors, some of which have little or nothing to do with us.

Some critics of open theism claim that a deity without exhaustive definite knowledge of the future could not guide us properly. If by this they mean that everything will not necessarily turn out well in the end, then they are correct. But no free will theist believes God can guarantee that our lives will turn out for the best. Perhaps the critic believes that a being who knows precisely what is going to happen has the ability to forewarn us in order to prevent something terrible from happening. For instance, say that Beth is considering marrying Harry, and Beth believes that God knows everything that will happen in the future. Let us also suppose that in the future God knows that Harry will become addicted to gambling and alcohol, which will lead to their financial ruin and physical abuse of Beth. Beth may think that if God knows that will happen, then God would guide her to decline an engagement to Harry. However, that is not possible if God possesses the type of foreknowledge most Arminians affirm, that of simple foreknowledge. According to this view God, prior to creation, figuratively "looks ahead" and sees everything that will occur in history. What God observes is what will *actually* happen, not what might happen. If so, what God sees is Beth's unhappy marriage to Harry since that is what will factually occur. Since God's foreknowledge is always correct, God cannot guide Beth away from Harry.[11]

Gregory Boyd tells the story of a woman he met who was angry with God because she believed God had intentionally guided her

---

11. For a fuller account of why simple foreknowledge is useless for divine providence, see John Sanders, *The God Who Risks: A Theology of Providence*, rev. ed. (Downers Grove: InterVarsity, 2006): section 6.7.3 (6.5.3 in first edition) and my "Why Simple Foreknowledge Offers No More Providential Control than the Openness of God," *Faith and Philosophy* 14, no. 1 (January 1997): 26–40.

into an abusive marriage.[12] From a young age she wanted to be a missionary in Taiwan; and when she went to college, she met a young man who shared that same goal. For three years they attended church together and prayed together. They consulted with their parents, pastor, and friends, after which they felt it advisable to marry. After college they married and then attended a missionary training school together. However, at this time her husband had an affair with another student. When confronted, he repented, but then the affair resumed. After a while he became physically abusive to his wife and then divorced her. Several of her friends told her what Job's friends had told him—that God intended this horrible set of events to teach her a lesson.

According to theological determinism, God did indeed meticulously control all these events in order to achieve some desired end. However, according to the openness model, God did not intend for her to be abused since God intends good, not evil. Instead, God was grieved that she was treated as she was and worked to change her husband. For openness, God's guidance at any particular point is based on his wisdom which includes exhaustive knowledge of the past and present and anticipatory beliefs about the future. At the time of their engagement, her fiancé was a godly person with a passion for ministry so the prospects were good that they would have a healthy marriage and ministry. However, because of free will, he gave in to temptation and resisted the promptings of the Spirit even after he was found out. Through a series of choices, he became what he had not been when they were dating. God's guidance had not been wrong. What was wrong was the husband's misuse of his free will. Fortunately, God is resourceful and redemptive and so is ready with other options for her life. God is guiding us with the best wisdom at any point in time, but God's wisdom might guide us to a change in direction should someone misuse their freedom by sinning.

The openness conception of God calls believers to be collaborators with God in redeeming the world. It gives significance to our lives. God calls us to love and care for one another. It gives

---

12. Gregory Boyd, *God of the Possible* (Grand Rapids: Baker, 2000), 103–6.

urgency and motivation to activities such as prayer for others, care for the environment, healing the sick and aiding the poor. This model of providence allows us to see the Christian life as a journey, an adventure, in which we interact with God in reciprocal give-and-take relations. As such, it comports well with the way most Christians actually live their lives.

Suffering and Evil

The problem of evil is a difficult challenge, and a range of Christian responses to it have been developed. Free will theists devised what is commonly called the "free will defense." Open theists make use of this approach as well, and it may be explained as follows.[13] God's purpose in creating was to bring forth beings who could respond to his love by loving God in return as well as establishing loving relationships and social structures among creatures.[14] This implies that God did not want moral evil to arise; it was not part of his plan. The Scriptures attest that God is implacably opposed to moral evil and that his heart breaks over the sinfulness of his creatures (e.g., Gen 6:6; Isa 2:10–15; Eph 4:30). The Father, Son, and Holy Spirit are portrayed as standing opposed to the harm we bring on one another. The world simply is not the way God wants it to be; creation has miscarried. For open theism, there is no "happy fall" (*O felix culpa*) into sin. Evil is not part of a divine blueprint ordained by God.

It may be asked whether God can create free beings and *guarantee* that they never do evil. The answer is yes if God creates us with compatibilistic freedom, for then God simply has to ensure that we have the proper desires in order to guarantee that we "freely" never commit evil. If God creates us with libertarian freedom, God could still guarantee that we never do evil if God can do the logically impossible. However, if, as open theists affirm, God cannot do the logically impossible and God creates

---

13. For other discussions about evil by open theists, see Gregory Boyd, *Is God to Blame?* (Downers Grove: InterVarsity, 2003); Gregory Boyd, *Satan and the Problem of Evil: Constructing a Trinitarian Warfare Theodicy* (Downers Grove: InterVarsity, 2001); and William Hasker, *Providence, Evil, and the Openness of God*, Routledge Studies in the Philosophy of Religion (New York: Routledge, 2004), chaps. 1–5.

14. Proponents of the free will defense sometimes emphasize the intrinsic, as opposed to instrumental, value of libertarian freedom. I have tried to avoid doing so.

us with libertarian freedom, then God cannot guarantee that we will always do what is good.

Since God desires relationships of love and since these cannot be coerced, the divine love is vulnerable to being rejected due to our use of libertarian freedom. Since God enacts general rather than exhaustive control, the possibility exists that what God wants to happen in any particular situation may not happen. God's intentions can be thwarted by our actions. God simply cannot guarantee that we will act in loving ways toward one another. God is solely responsible for creating a world with the conditions in which the failure to love was a *possibility*. But God is not responsible for evil actually occurring.

Some object that God, like a human parent, ought to act more often to prevent harm and suffering. After all, what parent would stand by and allow her child to be assaulted? Though God is in some respects like a human parent, God is not completely like a human parent for God is uniquely responsible for upholding the ontological, moral, and relational structures of the universe. God has a role that is unlike the role of any human. Even in our own lives we play different roles. For instance, though I have responsibility for the health of my children, it is not my role to prescribe drugs for them or perform surgery on them. In his role as the one who established and sustains the project, God cannot also bring it about that he abandons the very conditions for the project. The Almighty could veto any specific human evil act, but if he made a habit of it, this would undermine the type of relationships he intends. God cannot prevent all the evil in the world and still maintain the conditions of fellowship intended by his purpose in creation.

But could not God allow only those people to come into existence whom he knows would love and trust him? Not in the open theist view, because they affirm dynamic omniscience. Accordingly, God did not know prior to creation that an individual would become a child abuser or a CEO who rips off his company.[15] Nevertheless, most open theists hold that God does intervene at times in specific situations. Some people are healed,

---

15. The same is true for a deity with simple foreknowledge (see note 11 above).

for example. Why then, does God not heal all? Does God play favorites? The God of open theism would certainly anticipate that something dreadful was about to happen, and God has the power to prevent it, so why does God not prevent it? This is a difficult question for open theists as well as for all theists who hold that God has the ability to intervene, but a number of responses are available.

Though none of us has any claim or right to a special act of God, for God is not at our beck and call, the question of divine favoritism remains if some people receive protection or healing and others do not. In order to establish that God was showing favoritism or was acting arbitrarily, however, we would have to have access to all of God's knowledge and intentions, and that simply is not possible. Additionally, in my opinion, God is much more active than we can ever identify; but most of his work, like an iceberg, goes unseen by us. God may be doing much in any given situation even if we do not detect it or if it is not the sort of help we desire.

Furthermore, free will theists, in contrast to proponents of meticulous providence, can say that one reason for God's not intervening in a particular situation is his unwillingness to interfere with the libertarian freedom of the people involved. Some open theists believe that God might occasionally override the free will of a human while others believe that God never does this. A question arises for those open theists who believe God does occasionally violate human freedom: why does not God do so more often to bring about a better world? David Basinger replies that we cannot know the extent to which God is already doing this. Perhaps, he says, God has already maximized the extent to which he may profitably violate human freedom.[16]

We also affirm that God is at work in many ways. Human lives are affected by "behind the scenes" human and nonhuman forces that seek to undermine God's program. Whether we think of these powers as demonic beings, as the open theist Gregory Boyd does, or as malevolent social forces, the point is the same: God is hard at work keeping creation from disintegrating. These

---

16. David Basinger, *Divine Power in Process Theism: A Philosophical Critique* (Albany, NY: State University of New York Press, 1988), 63.

forces demand God's competence, wisdom, and power to keep creation going in the direction he intends without overturning the very rules of the game he established at creation. We believe that God is doing all he can, short of rescinding his original gifts of freedom to his creatures, to prevent what evil he can and, for that evil that does occur, God works to bring good out of those situations (Rom 8:28).

Moreover, open theists, as opposed to theological determinists, can say that God in no way wants the evils of this world. They are not part of a detailed plan by which absolutely everything works out for a specific greater good. It is not God's desire for creation that a young child contract a painful and incurable bone cancer. God's intention for creation did not include evils such as rape, terrorism, corporate theft, or abuse of the natural environment. Such evils are gratuitous or pointless, for they were not intended with the purpose of attaining a greater good.[17] Theological determinists sometimes claim that such evils are for the purpose of helping us learn a lesson. Though free will theists can certainly affirm that God works to bring good out of evil situations and that we may, indeed, learn something from our suffering or the suffering of others, it cannot be held that God always succeeds in such efforts. We simply do not always respond in virtuous ways to suffering. Some of us become embittered, hateful, and further perpetrate violence on others. Though some of us respond in redemptive ways to evil, not all of us do. Given our libertarian freedom, God cannot guarantee that a greater good will arise out of each and every occurrence of evil.

Open theists are under no illusions that they have the perfect solution to the problem of evil. Every response to the problem of evil has difficulties. Nonetheless, open theists believe that the approach stated above yields some beneficial practical results. For instance, a woman who has been abused by her husband need not believe that it was "God's will" that she suffer so. God did not ordain such evils for her to learn some lesson. This should relieve a great burden from many people who have been taught that everything that happens to us is part of the divine blueprint

---

17. See William Hasker, "The Necessity of Gratuitous Evil," in *Providence, Evil, and the Openness of God*, 58–79.

for the greater good. A fair number of people in church are angry at God though it is considered improper to confess it. The anger arises because people have been told to believe that God ordained their cancer or the death of a daughter for some unknown and difficult to grasp good. However, if God did not ordain such evils, then we need to think of God's relationship to such events differently. We are free to grieve such losses and work to redeem what we can from them.

Biblical Support for Open Theism

Open theists provide a wide array of biblical and theological reasons in support of this understanding of providence. However, most of these reasons are the same ones used to defend any version of free will theism so I will focus more narrowly on the types of evidence used to support the two key modifications of free will theism made by open theists.

In this discussion only an overview of the kinds of biblical texts proponents of open theism use to support their position is possible.[18] Before we examine this material, let me state at the outset that other well-informed Christians interpret these texts differently. The reading I give these texts is not the only possible one. Theological determinists have been interpreting these passages of Scripture, as well as those on election and atonement, differently from free will theists for centuries. A straightforward appeal to scriptural teaching will not settle the matter.[19] We do not have a universally objective and neutral approach to Scripture so appeals to scriptural texts, though necessary, will not settle this dispute. My claim is only that the open theist's way

---

18. For more see Terence Fretheim, *The Suffering of God: An Old Testament Perspective,* Overtures to Biblical Theology (Philadelphia: Fortress, 1984); Sanders, *The God Who Risks,* rev. ed., chaps 3 and 4; Richard Rice, "Biblical Support," in Clark Pinnock et al., *The Openness of God: A Biblical Challenge to the Traditional View of God* (Downers Grove: InterVarsity, 1994), 22–50; Boyd, *God of the Possible,* 53–87.

19. For elaboration on this point, see my "No Way to Settle the Matter: The Criteria We Use to Develop Different Models of God," in *And God Saw That It Was Good: Essays on Creation and God in Honor of Terence E. Fretheim,* ed. Fred Gaiser (Word and World supplement, 2006); and John Sanders and Chris Hall, *Does God Have a Future? A Debate on Divine Providence* (Grand Rapids: Baker, 2003), 124–29.

of understanding how such biblical passages portray God is the justifiable one.

The Bible portrays God as authentically responding to His people's petitions.

When God called Moses to be the one to lead the Israelites out of Egypt, Moses gave God several reasons why he was inadequate for the task (Exod 3–4). In response God attempted to satisfy Moses' felt needs. At one point God switches to plan B by allowing Aaron to do the public speaking instead of Moses. In another text God had the prophet Isaiah announce to King Hezekiah that he would not recover from his illness. However, Hezekiah prayed and God responded by sending Isaiah back to announce that God had changed his mind; Hezekiah would recover and not die (2 Kg 20). Such texts reveal divine flexibility, and God's use of various ways of achieving his agenda based upon human responses.

John Goldingay concludes from his study of the Hebrew Bible that God does not operate with a blueprint:

> The First Testament story never talks about God having a plan for the world or a plan of salvation or a plan for people's individual lives, and the story it tells does not look like one that resulted from a plan. . . . The story does not give the impression that from the beginning God had planned the flood, or the summons of Abraham, or the exodus, or the introduction of the monarchy, or the building of the temple, or the exile. . . . It portrays these as responses to concrete situations.[20]

The New Testament exhibits something of the same. Mark 2:5 portrays Jesus' healing of a paralyzed man because of the faith of his friends. He responded to the faith of this small community by granting their request. People's faith, or lack of it, deeply affected Jesus and his ministry. Mark says that Jesus could not perform many miracles in Nazareth due to the lack of faith by the people in the community (6:5–6). It is not that their unbelief tied God's hands, but it did seriously alter what Jesus would

---

20. John Goldingay, *Old Testament Theology*, vol. 1 (Downers Grove: InterVarsity, 2003), 60.

have done had they been more receptive to his message. Not only did the response of the community affect what Jesus did; it also disturbed him for "he was amazed at their unbelief" (6:6 HCSB). Oftentimes, what God decides to do is conditioned upon the faith or unbelief of people. As James says, we have not because we ask not (Jas 4:2).

The Bible portrays God as being affected by creatures and as sometimes being surprised by what they do.

Genesis 6:6 says that God was grieved because humans continually sinned. Why would God grieve if God always knew exactly what humans were going to do? It makes no sense to say that a timeless being experiences grief. Also, the biblical writers, when describing God's speeches, use words such as *perhaps* and *maybe*. God says "perhaps" the people will listen to my prophet, and *maybe* they will turn from their idols (e.g., Ezek 12:1–3; Jer 26:2–3). Furthermore, God makes utterances such as "If you really change your ways and your actions . . . I will allow you to live in this place" (Jer 7:5,7 HCSB). Such "if" language, the invitation to change, is not genuine if God already knew they would not repent. According to theological determinism God specifically ordains everything that happens; God is in total control as to how the people will respond. If so, why would God use conditional language since God is the one in control of whether the people repent? It would seem, then, that such utterances were disingenuous on God's part. If theological determinism is true, then all such portrayals of God in the Bible do not inform us as to what God actually is like, and they do not describe to us the way God relates to us as he actually does. Nicholas Wolterstorff says that if God does not relate the way the Bible describes in the texts cited above, then we "would have to regard the biblical speech about God as at best one long sequence of metaphors pointing to a reality for which they are singularly inept, and as at worst, one long sequence of falsehoods."[21]

Many today admit that God experiences changes in emotions, but these same people also affirm that God possesses exhaustive

---

21. Nicholas Wolterstorff, "God Everlasting," in *God and the Good*, ed. C. J. Orlebeke and L. B. Smedes (Grand Rapids: Eerdmans, 1975), 181–203.

and definite foreknowledge of future contingent events. They claim that God knows from all eternity that, for instance, Saul will disobey God at a particular point in history. Nevertheless, they also claim that God experiences a genuine change in emotion from joy to grief over Saul. It is questionable whether it is coherent to affirm both that God has always known of this event and that God now has changing emotions about that event. Furthermore, Fretheim notes that "the texts say that God was provoked to anger at a particular historical moment, and not that some previous divine provocation was realized."[22]

Moreover, God says, "I thought Israel would return to me but she has not" (see Jer 3:7; cf. 32:35) and that he had planted cultivated vines and so did not expect them to produce "wild grapes" (Isa 5:1–4). In these texts God is explicitly depicted as not knowing with certainty the specific future. Of course, God knew all the possible reactions of the people, but the people did not respond in the way God thought most probable. A related case is when God gave King Zedekiah two possible courses of action with a resulting outcome of each (Jer 38:17–23). It does not seem from the text that the future was as yet determined. If God knew it was determined, then why give Zedekiah options? Similarly, God repeatedly sent Elijah to call King Ahab to repentance, but the king refused to do so. Was God playing a cat-and-mouse game with Ahab? If God foreknows from the moment he gives the invitation that it will be pointless, then God is holding out a false hope. On the other hand, if God is genuinely inviting the people to change, then the future is not yet settled.

Scripture mentions occasions where God "consults" with certain people of faith in deciding the course of action God will take. God does this with Abraham concerning judgment upon Sodom (Gen 18) and Amos (chapter 7) regarding judgment upon Israel. God, in freedom, decides not to decide without consulting these figures of faith or, as with Moses (Exod 32:14), decides to change his decision in response to Moses' intercession. Finally, God asks questions regarding an indefinite future. God agonizes over what to do with his sinful people (Hos 6:4; Jer 5:7). When

---

22. Fretheim, *Suffering of God*, 42.

God asks, "What am I going to do with you?" God is seeking a response from the people. By asking such questions, God puts a decision to the people, and judgment is not yet inevitable.

Other support is derived from those predictions in Scripture which either do not come to pass at all (Jonah 3:4; 2 Kg 20:1) or do not come to pass exactly as foretold. For example, Jacob's blessing is qualified by Esau's blessing (Gen 27:27–40); Joseph's dream of his parents bowing down to him does not happen (Gen 37:6–9); and neither Jacob nor Joseph's brothers believe they have to do what the dream predicts (37:8, 10).[23] A detailed prophecy that is not fulfilled in the way stated is the destruction of the city of Tyre (Ezek 26). Even allowing for hyperbole, two aspects of the prophecy are clear: (1) King Nebuchadnezzar of Babylon is specifically named as God's intended agent to destroy Tyre and (2) the city would be utterly destroyed and would never be inhabited again. Nebuchadnezzar did try to destroy Tyre, but he failed, and the city was continuously occupied for hundreds of years. We know this because God himself admits that the prophecy failed and so he revised it (29:17–20). God acknowledges that Nebuchadnezzar tried very hard to take the city but was unsuccessful so God said that instead of Tyre he would give Egypt to Nebuchadnezzar as payment for his services. Jeremiah also declares that Nebuchadnezzar would conquer Egypt (Jer 46:25–6) and that the Egyptian city of Memphis would be burned to the ground and remain uninhabited (46:19). Even these revised prophecies, however, did not come to pass since Nebuchadnezzar never conquered Egypt.

In his study of this prophecy, Kris Udd asks: "Why would God declare the destruction of Tyre by Nebuchadnezzar, if his foreknowledge meant that he knew when giving the prophecy that it would not come true?"[24] A God with exhaustive foreknowledge should be 100 percent correct in the details.[25] This problem has

---

23. For detail on this see Terence Fretheim, *The Book of Genesis*, The New Interpreter's Bible (Nashville: Abingdon, 1994), 601.

24. Kris Udd, "Prediction and Foreknowledge in Ezekiel's Prophecy Against Tyre," *Tyndale Bulletin* 56, no. 1 (2005): 35. See also, Thomas Renz, "Proclaiming the Future: History and Theology in Prophecies Against Tyre," *Tyndale Bulletin* 51 (2000): 17–58.

25. It is common for people to claim that the predictions in Scripture are all fulfilled in exacting detail. A more helpful approach to prophecies that are unfulfilled or only par-

led to a number of imaginative interpretations of the text which shall not detain us here.[26] Proponents of dynamic omniscience explain such "failed" prophecies as divine intentions that are implicitly conditional (if God decides not to act unilaterally). Thomas Renz put it well when he said, "Prophetic predictions are not historiography before the event but a proclamation of God's purposes" that are flexible and revisable in light of changing human situations.[27] Consequently, God did not deceive, nor was he wrong since he was not declaring what would in fact be the case but what he desired to be the case.

For open theists predictions fall into one of the following three categories:

1. God may utter predictions based on his determination to unilaterally bring an event about. In this case, the issue is whether God has the power to do it, not whether he has foreknowledge. For example, God promises to bring about the eschaton.

2. God may predict a future event based on inferences from his exhaustive knowledge of past and present. In this type of prediction God states what he believes is the most probable state of affairs to materialize. A case of this type is the prediction of the destruction of Tyre by Nebuchadnezzar.

3. God may declare what he wants to happen. Such statements may be in the form of what looks like an unconditional prediction when, in fact, it is conditional since most predictions are conditional in nature even if not stated conditionally.[28] God declares that some event will happen but does not state that it will not occur if or unless certain other events come to pass. The classic

---

tially so is by S. Brent Sandy, *Plowshares and Pruning Hooks: Rethinking the Language of Biblical Prophecy and Apocalyptic* (Downers Grove: InterVarsity, 2002).

26. See Udd, "Prediction and Foreknowledge," 37–39 and Daniel Block, *The Book of Ezekiel Chapters 25–48*, New International Commentary series (Grand Rapids: Eerdmans, 1998), 147–49.

27. Renz, "Proclaiming the Future," 17.

28. This is the view of Walter Kaiser and Moises Silva. See their *An Introduction to Biblical Hermeneutics* (Grand Rapids: Zondervan, 1994), 148–49.

example of this is the prediction in Jonah that Nineveh would be destroyed (see also Jer 15 and Ezek 12:1–3).

The Bible portrays God as testing people in order to discover what they will do.

God put Abraham to the test and afterward said, "Now I know that you fear me" (Gen 22:12). God put the people of Israel to the test to find out what they would do (Exod 15:25; Deut 13:3). After the sin of the golden calf, God asked the people to "put off your ornaments that I may know what to do with you" (Exod 33:5). Why test them if God eternally knew with certainty exactly how the people would respond? One could say the testing was only for the benefit of the people since it added nothing to God's knowledge, but that is not what the texts themselves say.

Commenting on such texts John Goldingay Wrote:

> He limits his knowledge to be able to genuinely listen. . . . No doubt God could know everything, including everything about us, whether we are willing for this or not. . . . But even God's supernatural knowledge of us comes about through discovery, through "searching out," rather than because God possesses this knowledge automatically (e.g., Pss 33:15; 139:1–6). God does not seem to have looked into their minds to discover what their reaction will be. . . . Perhaps there would be something abusive about looking into our minds all the time, like a parent reading a child's journal. One would do that only in exceptional circumstances. Instead God lets people reveal who they are.[29]

The Bible portrays God as changing his mind as he relates to his creatures.

God announced his intention to destroy the people of Israel and start over again with Moses, but Moses said that he did not want to do that and so God did not do what he had said he was going to do (Exod 32). It is not that God had to do what Moses wanted. Rather, it is that Moses has become a "friend" of God such

---

29. Goldingay, *Old Testament Theology*, 136–37. See also Michael Carasik, "The Limits of Omniscience," *Journal of Biblical Literature* 119, no. 2 (Summer 2000): 221–32.

that God values what Moses desires. Sometimes God made promises that were stated in unconditional terms, but God changed his mind due to human rebellion. For instance, God had promised Eli in unconditional terms that his descendants would be priests forever in Israel. But after the horrible exploitation of the priestly office by his sons, God changed his mind and removes the line from the priesthood (1 Sam 2:30). Another illustration of this occurs with King Saul. The Bible says that God's original plan was to have Saul and his descendants as kings forever in Israel (1 Sam 13:13). In other words, there would have been no Davidic kingship. Later, due to Saul's sin, God changed his mind and rejected Saul and his line (1 Sam 15:11, 35).[30] Though Samuel and Saul pled with God to change his mind back to the original plan and go with Saul and his sons, God declared that he would not change his mind back to the original plan (1 Sam 15:29). If God always knew that he was never going to have Saul's line be kings, was God deceitful?

God's changing his mind is an important theme in the Hebrew Bible; the words that suggest or even state specifically that he does so appear about three dozen times.[31] Moreover, the statement that God can change his mind is added on to the great creedal formula of the divine nature (Exod 34:5–7), which says that God is "compassionate. . . gracious, slow to anger, and rich in faithful love and truth, maintaining faithful love to a thousand [generations], forgiving wrongdoing, rebellion, and sin." This formula is quoted in whole or in part a dozen times in the Hebrew Bible, demonstrating its importance for disclosing Yahweh's character. Two of these quotations (Joel 2:13 and Jonah 4:2) add a key phrase to the list: "God repents" (*nicham*) of carrying out threatened punishment. Divine change of mind here appears alongside divine grace and love as a key characteristic

---

30. See Terence Fretheim, "Divine Foreknowledge, Divine Constancy, and the Rejection of Saul's Kingship," *Catholic Biblical Quarterly* 47, no. 4 (October 1985): 595–602.

31. Hebrew Bible scholar Terence Fretheim has done the most exegetical work on the divine change of mind texts. In addition to the article cited in the previous note, see his *The Suffering of God* and "The Repentance of God: A Key to Evaluating Old Testament God-Talk," *Horizons in Biblical Theology* 10, no. 1 (June 1988): 47–70; and "The Repentance of God: A Study of Jeremiah 18:7–10," *Hebrew Annual Review* 11 (1987): 81–92.

of God. David Allen Hubbard remarks: "So dominant is this loyal love, so steeped in grace . . . and mercy . . . that it encourages Yahweh to stay open to changes in his plans. . . . God's openness to change his course of action . . . has [in these two passages] virtually become one of his attributes."[32] This is what the God of Israel is like: a God who loves and sometimes changes his mind as he relates to changing human situations.

There is a give-and-take quality to these texts. If God is affected by creatures and is responsive, as these texts indicate, then God has a before and after—succession—in his experience. God is temporal and has a history. However, one may try to explain all of these texts about divine change of mind in terms of law. That is, if the people sin, then God threatens punishment; and if the people repent of their sin; then God withdraws the threatened punishment. This would mean that God did not really change his mind at all since it only amounts to God saying that his punishments are conditioned upon what humans do; and since God knows what they will do, God was never going to punish the people in the first place. It only "looks to us" like God changed his mind, but God did nothing of the sort. This is the way Calvin, for instance, understood these texts.

Open theists propose that there are two types of texts in Scripture relevant to divine foreknowledge. The first type may be called the "motif of the open future" in which God is portrayed as not possessing exhaustive definite foreknowledge (God tests people, changes his mind, and switches to alternative courses of action in response to human actions). In the other type, the "motif of the closed future," God is portrayed as declaring that a specific event will occur no matter what the people do, as in, for example, the Babylonian exile (Isa 42:9, 44:28). In order to resolve the tension between such texts, some interpreters claim that we must subordinate one motif to the other. They argue that those who hold that God changes his mind, switches to plan B, or comes to know something that God did not know previously, diminish God. They claim that the "clear" teaching of Scripture is that God knows every detail of what will happen in the future—the

---

32. David Allen Hubbard, *Joel and Amos*, Tyndale Old Testament Commentary (Downers Grove: InterVarsity, 1989), 35, 58.

future is completely definite for God—so the motif of the closed future is the "literal" truth about God whereas the Scriptures indicating an open future are "metaphorical." In other words, only one scriptural motif is true.

Proponents of the dynamic omniscience view believe there is a better way of handling these two motifs of Scripture. They claim that some aspects of the future are definite or settled while others are indefinite or not determined. If God decides to unconditionally guarantee that some event will happen, then that future event is definite, and God knows it as such. Since most events are not determined by God (he has given us freedom), these are indefinite, and God knows them as indefinite (possibilities). Both motifs are true. God can declare the future with certainty regarding those events that are determined, and God can be grieved, change his mind, or opt for plan B about those future events that are indefinite. Hence, divine omniscience contains both definite and indefinite beliefs. The future is partly open and partly closed because God decided reality would be that way. If God had wanted a completely closed future, God could have exercised theological determinism, and God would then possess exhaustive definite foreknowledge. However, open theists believe God decided not to create that sort of world. Hence, they are not reducing God because it is what *God* freely decided to bring about.[33] The openness model allows us to maintain that God is open to our prayers—sometimes allowing himself to be persuaded by them—that God has a rich emotional life, that God enters into reciprocal relations of love with us, and that he responds to us. It also allows us to maintain that God is faithful, steadfast, has the power to enact specific events of his choosing, and that the divine nature does not change. This model provides a coherent account of the biblical depiction of God, including both the motifs of the open and closed futures.

Before leaving the discussion about biblical support for open theism, I want to comment on my repeated statements that "the Bible portrays God." I am not taking these depictions of God

---

33. For a rebuttal to the charge of a diminished God, see my "On Reducing God to Human Proportions," in *Semper Reformandum: Studies in Honour of Clark Pinnock*, ed. Anthony Cross and Stanley Porter (Grand Rapids: Eerdmans, 2003), 111–25.

literally in the sense that my critics employ the word *literally* when they ask, "Why doesn't Sanders take the texts where God is depicted as having arms, wings, and nostrils literally if he takes the texts portraying God as having anger, disappointment, and changing his mind literally?" They say, "If you take one metaphor literally, then you must take them all literally." In my view the portraits of God in Scripture are *conceptual metaphors* which enable us to conceptualize (give meaning to) our experience of God in terms of concrete events or objects.[34] For example, when we say, "She shot my claims down," we are using the physical experience of warfare to understand argumentation. When we say, "I can't swallow that point," we are conceptualizing ideas in terms of eating. Conceptual metaphors depict the reality of our multifaceted relationship with God.[35] In the texts surveyed above, God is depicted as acting in common human ways. Broadly speaking, conceptual metaphors have three characteristics:

1. They are vehicles for understanding our world; they structure the way we think about life experiences.
2. They only partially map reality, for they do not say everything that can be said, and consequently they constrain our understanding. For instance, the apostle Paul speaks about the Christian community as a body; but since this conceptual metaphor does not communicate all of his understanding, he also speaks of believers as a building and as a farmer's field.
3. They are culturally constrained since not all cultures use the same conceptual metaphors to give meaning to our experiences of love, anger, success, failure, or truth. So, the biblical depictions of God convey the reality of God's relationship to us, but they do so in ways that cannot be nailed down without remainder.

---

34. On conceptual metaphor theory see George Lakoff and Mark Johnson, *Metaphors We Live By* (Chicago: University of Chicago Press, 1980) and Zoltán Kövecses, *Metaphor: A Practical Introduction* (New York: Oxford University Press, 2002).

35. I explain this use of conceptual metaphor theory more fully in the revised edition of my *The God Who Risks*, chapter 2.

Theological Support for Open Theism

The question arises: How do we maintain the core beliefs of free will theism? At its core free will theism affirms that God is a personal agent who experiences dynamic give-and-take relationships with his creatures. God changes in his relationships as he works with us in history, and God does not meticulously control all that happens. Such beliefs give rise to the doctrines of conditional election, resistible grace, and that our prayers can affect God. Without these core beliefs free will theism ceases to be. Open theists hold that divine timelessness and simple foreknowledge are incompatible with the core doctrines of free will theism while other doctrines do offer some compatability.

Divine timelessness is incompatible with the core beliefs of free will theism.

There are two major theories of time: the *dynamic* view (also called the "A theory," tensed or process) and the *stasis* view (also known as the "B theory," tenseless, or block).[36] For the dynamic theory, the present, or now, has a special ontological status because it exists in a way that past and future do not. The past no longer exists, and the future does not yet exist. Though we speak about "the future" as though it were an entity, it is really a conceptualization we use to understand our lives. The dynamic view involves change as we ordinarily conceive of it since things come into and go out of existence. At one point in time, the ark of the covenant did not exist, then it existed, and now it no longer exists. The stasis theory, on the other hand, holds that the past, present, and future have equal ontological status so every event exists timelessly (as God does). We can conceive of this by use of the spatial metaphor of a long block. The present would be at some point on the block while all past events would extend in one direction from the present, and all future events would extend in the other. All events exist timelessly in that they are always on the block.

---

36. For a discussion of these theories as they relate to God, see Gregory Ganssle, ed., *God and Time: Four Views* (Downers Grove: InterVarsity, 2001).

Increasing numbers of scholars are concluding that divine timelessness requires the stasis theory of time and that timelessness is incompatible with the dynamic theory. If divine timelessness requires the stasis theory and if the stasis theory implies determinism because there is only one possible future, then free will theists cannot affirm divine timelessness. The block, which contains the past, present, and future, is completely definite. What we call the "future" is already real even though it has different "temporal coordinates" from what we now experience. If the space-time continuum contains all events that actually happen, then what the Secretary General of the United Nations does on June 23, 2089 is in the continuum, and it cannot be changed. Consequently, libertarian freedom is undermined, which spells the end of free will theism. Hence, in order to maintain the core beliefs of free will theism, the dynamic theory of time must be affirmed, and divine timelessness must be rejected.[37]

Another significant problem is that a timeless being cannot perform many of the actions attributed to God by free will theists. For instance, a timeless God cannot literally be said to plan, deliberate, have changing emotions, adjust his plans, anticipate, respond, and change his mind.[38] All such actions require a before and an after. According to timelessness, there was not a moment when God was pleased with King Saul followed by another moment when he was grieved about Saul. A timeless experience is more like an abstract concept such as the number 5; it just *is* and does not change or have reciprocal relations with us. Hence, a timeless God is strongly immutable and impassible and so cannot be affected by us. Theological determinists such as John Calvin and Paul Helm understand this point, which is why they

37. Space does not allow me to provide arguments in support of the dynamic theory of time. For a fuller account of the position given here, see Nicholas Wolterstorff, "Unqualified Divine Temporality," in Gregory Ganssle, ed., *God and Time: Four Views* (Downers Grove: InterVarsity, 2001), 187–213; and William Hasker, "God Everlasting," in *God, Time and Knowledge*, 144–85; and J. R. Lucas, *The Future: An Essay on God, Temporality and Truth* (Cambridge, MA: Blackwell, 1989). These last two books address philosophical questions such as the truth status of statements about the future, modal logic, and other matters related to the nature of time.

38. This is shown by Norman Kretzman and Eleonore Stump, "Eternity," *Journal of Philosophy* 78 (1981): 429–58. There are those, however, who claim that a timeless God can experience changing emotions and give-and-take relations. It seems to me, however, that it is logically contradictory to affirm both.

do not interpret the biblical texts or the practice of prayer in ways that would imply change in God. The idea of reciprocal relations between God and creatures in which God responds and changes are problematic if God is timeless. Nicholas Wolterstorff points out that according to timelessness "none of God's actions is a response to what we human beings do; indeed, not only is none of God's *actions* a response to what we do, but nothing at all in God's life is a response to what occurs among God's creatures."[39] This is precisely the reason the influential nineteenth-century Arminian theologian John Miley rejected timelessness.[40]

Given the problems that divine timelessness and the stasis theory pose for free will theists, it seems best to reject these views and affirm divine temporality and the dynamic theory of time. Whereas timelessness and the stasis theory fit well with the doctrines of unconditional election, irresistible grace, and that our prayers have no effect on God, divine temporality and the dynamic theory fit well with the free will theistic doctrines of conditional election, resistible grace, and that our prayers can affect God.[41]

Furthermore, divine temporality resonates with the portrayal of God in the biblical narrative. There is no logical difficulty in saying that God has changing emotions and that he plans, deliberates, adjusts his plans, anticipates, suffers, or responds. Wolterstorff elaborates: "God the Redeemer cannot be [timeless]. This is so because God the Redeemer is a God who *changes*. And any being which changes is a being among whose states there is temporal succession. Of course . . . he is steadfast in his redeeming intent and ever faithful to his children. Yet, *ontologically*, God cannot be a redeeming God without there being change-

---

39. Wolterstorff, "Unqualified Divine Timelessness," 205. Paul Helm argues that there is a highly qualified way that a timeless God may be said to "respond," but Wolterstorff shows serious problems with Helm's claim (232–33).

40. John Miley, *Systematic Theology*, vol. 1 (New York: Eaton & Mains, 1892), 214–15.

41. It is commonly asked if divine temporality means that time is uncreated. We need to distinguish metric (measured time) from psychological or personal time. Prior to a physical universe, there are no bodies with distance between them so metric time begins at creation. Psychological time, the experience of consciousness, has always been part of God's life. Time in this sense is not a "thing"; it simply refers to the sequence of events in God's experience.

ful variation among his states."[42] We worship God for what he has done in history, not for being timeless. As the liturgy says, "Christ has come, Christ has died, Christ will come again."

Exhaustive definite foreknowledge is incompatible with the core beliefs of free will theism.

The dynamic and stasis theories of time have different understandings of the ontological status of the future, and this has immense significance for the foreknowledge discussion. If the future already ontologically exists (is real), then God must know it; but if it does not exist, then there is "no thing" to know. If the future is not real, then God is not ignorant of some reality, for there is nothing "there" to be known. Proponents of dynamic omniscience are sometimes accused of saying that "God does not know the future," but such a criticism is incorrect because the proposition misleads us into thinking that a reality called "the future" exists. Rather, what we call "the future" is simply our anticipatory understanding of what we believe will happen antecedently from the present. In other words, the accusation that we claim God does not know something begs the question, for it assumes a metaphysics that open theists reject. Again, if the future ontologically exists and God failed to know it, then it would be correct to say God did not know the future. So one must be aware that the critic is presupposing a theory of time that open theists reject. Since the dynamic theory of time is most amenable to the core beliefs of free will theism, free will theists are within their rights to say that the "future" does not exist, and this makes it possible for free will theists to affirm dynamic omniscience. This is precisely the route open theists take.

Open theists affirm the dynamic theory of time and hold that God has exhaustive knowledge of the past and the present and knows the future as partly definite (closed) and partly indefinite (open). When we say that "part" of the future is definite, it sounds as though we are talking about an entity, but this is not the case. Rather, it means God knows that some events are determined to occur; it is a matter of God's anticipatory knowledge not an

---

42. Wolterstorff, "God Everlasting," 182.

actual ontological entity. God knows, for instance, when the next solar eclipse will be, but the eclipse does not already exist. Yet the future is not completely settled, for there are multiple possible futures. It remains open to what God and humans decide to do. God knows as possibilities and probabilities those events which might happen in the future. God, together with creatures, creates the future as history goes along. Hence, God's omniscience is dynamic in nature. God knows all that can possibly happen at any one time and through his *foresight* and wisdom God is never caught off-guard. God is omnicompetent and endlessly resourceful as he works to bring his creational project to fruition. Divine knowledge is unsurpassable, and God will know exceedingly more about the possibilities regarding future contingent events and which of these possibilities are likely to occur than any creature. Also, an almighty being can choose to guarantee that specific events will occur that otherwise might not have happened. Regarding the future, God anticipates what we will do and plans his responses accordingly. In this view God is able to hear our prayers and respond to them, dispense guidance out of his unfathomable wisdom, and be flexible when necessary to adjust his plans as the situations change. God is involved with humans in dynamic give-and-take relationships, working with us to bring about the future.

Though John Miley affirmed divine temporality, he continued to affirm prescience (foreknowledge). However, he recognized a key problem that he did not know how to answer: How can God interact with us in reciprocal relationships if God has prescience? He argued that in order to adhere to the core doctrines of the Wesleyan-Arminian tradition it is necessary to affirm reciprocal relations between God and humans. He said that if belief in an interactive God is contradictory to prescience then he will give up foreknowledge. He went on to say that belief in dynamic omniscience would not undermine any vital Arminian doctrines and would, in fact, free it from the perplexity of divine foreknowledge and human freedom.[43]

---

43. See his *Systematic Theology*, vol. 1, 180–93.

Miley has raised two different problems here for free will theism. The first is the age-old debate as to whether foreknowledge implies determinism. If God knows that I will have eggs for breakfast tomorrow, am I free to have oatmeal instead? Open theists agree with theological determinists on this point: foreknowledge entails determinism.[44] Though many Arminians have sought to escape this conclusion, we do not find their reasoning persuasive. If exhaustive foreknowledge is incompatible with free will, then obviously free will theists cannot affirm it and continue to be free will theists.

The second problem Miley has raised is this: How can God interact with us in reciprocal relationships if God has exhaustive definite foreknowledge? According to the theory of simple foreknowledge, affirmed by most Arminians, God "sees" what is actually going to happen, not what might or might not happen. God's vision is about the actual world, not possible worlds. God knows in exhaustive detail every single event that will ever transpire in the universe.

If so, then how can God be said to interact, respond, suffer, or change his mind? Does simple foreknowledge imply that God previsions his own decisions and actions? If God possesses foreknowledge of his own actions, then the problem is to explain how the foreknowledge can be the *basis* for the actions when it already *includes* the actions. William Hasker explained: "It is impossible that God should use a foreknowledge derived from the actual occurrence of future events to determine his own prior actions in the providential governance of the world."[45] God would learn of his own future actions. This would mean that the language used to portray God in dynamic give-and-take relationships does not accurately depict God's relation to us. Biblical statements such as God regretted that he made Saul king (1 Sam 15:11) cannot mean what they say. If God actually changes his mind or goes to plan B because humans failed to do what he expected them to do, then it cannot be the case that God had certain and

44. William Hasker argues that exhaustive definite foreknowledge entails the rejection of libertarian freedom. For the latest version of his argument, see "The Foreknowledge Conundrum," *International Journal for Philosophy of Religion* 50 (2001): 97–114. An older version may be found in his *God, Time and Knowledge*, 64–74.

45. Hasker, *God, Time and Knowledge*, 63.

comprehensive foreknowledge of the future. The idea that God is affected by and responds to our prayers and actions is undermined if God has exhaustive definite prescience. Consequently, open theists claim that divine temporality and dynamic omniscience better uphold the core beliefs of free will theism.

The supposition that God intends evil is incompatible with free will theism.

Open theists are sensitive to the problem of evil. If such things as famines, wars, racism, and exploitation of children are not "all for the best" and are not sent by God, then we can understand that we are called by God to be collaborators with him against such evils. Consequently, to remain passive in the face of evil is to go against God. Instead, God wants us actively to combat and redeem evil. The open theist is free to challenge the status quo and must reject the notion that whatever is, is right in the sense that the world is precisely the way God wants it to be at any moment.

Some proponents of meticulous providence, however, claim that openness comes to the same conclusion regarding the mystery of why God intervenes in some situations and not others. Though both sides do appeal to mystery, they locate the mystery in vastly different places. Theological determinists locate the mystery in the heart of God (why does God intend each and every evil to occur?) while free will theists locate the mystery in the iniquity of human beings (why do we spurn God's grace?). Theological determinists believe that God providentially controls each and every action of humans including each aspect of each action.[46] God has an exhaustive blueprint for all things such that everything happens precisely the way God ordained it should happen. Though we call certain events accidents or tragedies since they seem to be evil from our vantage point, from God's perspective they are really necessary for achieving the greater good. There is no pointless evil. The openness position is quite different, for it is one thing to say that God, for reasons we don't fully understand, *allows* autonomous agents to do tragic and ter-

---

46. See, for instance, Paul Helm, *The Providence of God* (Downers Grove: InterVarsity Press, 1994), 104.

rible things. It is quite another thing to say that God deliberately plans and *intends* for all these evil things to happen so that in no single respect would God want the world to be any different than it actually is. To free will theists it seems that consistent theological determinists would say that God does not grieve over the rape of a little girl, for it is exactly what God wanted to happen. For open theists God does not want such evils, for he grieves over them and seeks to redeem them.

Though open theists do not claim to have the final word on the problem of evil, we do believe we have strengthened the free will defense in a number of ways. Open theism emphasizes divine risk taking more than has traditionally been the case. We believe that it is the most logically consistent form of free will theism when it comes to affirming divine passibility (God suffers with and for his creatures), divine temporality, and God's implacable opposition to evil. Also, because God has dynamic omniscience rather than either simple foreknowledge or middle knowledge God cannot be held responsible for creating a world in which he knew for sure that we would misuse our freedom and do so in the ways we have. Furthermore, God cannot be said to want the evil in the world. For these reasons open theists hold that this model provides a view that is both more faithful to the biblical narrative of God's actions and states of mind, is more logically consistent than other forms of free will theism, and yields fruitful ways in which to live the Christian life.

The biblical narratives amply demonstrate that events did not always go as God desired. God is not exercising exhaustive control over the world, but neither does he stand impotent before it. God's powerful love is demonstrated in a definitive way through the cross and resurrection of Christ. In the face of both moral and natural evil, Jesus stands fundamentally opposed to them and seeks to overcome them by suffering and resurrection. The resurrection is our sign of hope that the future will bring a transformation of our present conditions. Love and life triumphed over the forces of evil through the cross and resurrection. Suffering and death do not have the final word, for our relationships can continue after death. Moreover, the Holy

Spirit continues to work to redeem evil situations. God is not yet finished, and as long as God is working, there is hope that the future will be different from what we presently experience. These reasons give us courage to be God's fellow laborers in the struggle for *shalom*, working to extend God's victory over evil in every aspect of life.

Open theism coheres with relational theology.

The openness of God to his creation resonates well with relational approaches to theology.[47] One example of this concerns the revival of Cappadocian understandings of the divine nature toward the development of social trinitarianism in Western theology. To oversimplify, Western theology has typically begun with the oneness of God and the attributes that only God has such as simplicity, aseity, omnipotence, and omniscience. The Eastern Church, by contrast, has emphasized God's *triunity* (unity amid diversity) and relatedness in love as that which identifies God as God. Open theism affirms this trend in Eastern thought by highlighting God's relatedness, both internally and externally. Internally, the Father, Son, and Holy Spirit have always been dynamically related in love. This intra-Trinitarian relatedness provides a model for the God-world relationship. As a triune God, it is of the nature of God to be open to the other so God's openness to creatures does not represent a fundamental change in divine character. God is self-giving, making room for the other. Consequently, God does not exercise meticulous control of creatures but instead takes what we do into account in formulating his own actions.

This understanding of the divine nature also helps us see that the way of Jesus Christ is the way of God. The incarnation does not represent an aberration of God because self-giving love is what God is like. Consequently, the responsiveness, openness to others, and willingness to suffer in order to restore the broken relationship manifested in the incarnation confirm the portrait of God in the first testament.

---

47. For elaboration on this see my "Relational Theism in Contemporary Thought," in *The God Who Risks* (161–64 of the first edition).

Furthermore, Jesus is the definitive revelation of who God is, the "exact representation" of the divine nature (Heb 1:3). Jesus is the divine word who by his way of life displayed the true divine glory (John 1:14). We can even say that one who has seen Jesus has seen God (John 14:9). In Jesus, "the fullness of Deity dwells in bodily form" (Col 2:9 NASB). The Scriptures attest that Jesus Christ in his humanity is constitutive of the nature of God. Christians confess that God in Christ saved us, which means that the humanity of Jesus does not entail a surrender of deity. Instead, Christians are to define *divinity* in the light of Jesus' self-giving love, open to the other.

Open theism is a form of relational theology, and as such, it has been influenced by the critique of strong immutability and impassibility by other relational theologians. Also, significant relational theologians such as Jurgen Moltmann, Paul Fiddes, John Polkinghorne, and Keith Ward have rejected exhaustive definite foreknowledge in favor of the dynamic omniscience view.[48] These writers claim that exhaustive definite foreknowledge is incompatible with the notions that God is truly affected by and responsive to creatures. If God deliberates and even changes his mind at times, then divine temporality and dynamic omniscience readily make sense.

To sum up this section, there are a number of excellent versions of relational theology on the market, of which open theism is but one. Open theism coheres well with relational understandings of the trinity and Christology, and it upholds the core doctrines and practices of free will theism such as libertarian freedom, the free will defense, conditional election, and that our prayers affect God. Openness theology makes sense of the biblical depictions of God as changing his mind, testing to see what humans will do, and responding to creatures. Also, it provides a satisfactory explanation of the two scriptural motifs about the future as partially open and partially settled without subjugating one motif to the other. The affirmations of divine temporality and dynamic omniscience are attempts to revise free will

---

48. Their affirmation of dynamic omniscience is found in their respective essays in John Polkinghorne, ed., *The Work of Love: Creation as Kenosis* (Grand Rapids: Eerdmans, 2001).

theism in order to render it more biblically faithful and rationally coherent.

Clearing Up Some Misunderstandings

In order to clarify some of the ideas presented, I will provide brief responses to some common misunderstandings and criticisms.

1. Some claim that a God with dynamic omniscience cannot guarantee anything about the future. However, as theological determinists have long understood, it is not exhaustive definite foreknowledge that enables God to guarantee an event will occur. Rather, it is whether God has the almighty power to bring it about and open theism maintains that God has such power. If God wishes to guarantee that a particular event will happen, then God can do so.

2. It is sometimes said that open theism places "limits" on God. We believe that God restrains the full exercise of his powers in order to give us some degree of freedom. But that is God's choice and does not limit God. Some critics persist and say that the application of human logic to our understanding of God places limits on God. However, we use logical reasoning to understand what God has revealed to us all the time. For instance, if we read that God redeemed us in Christ, we do not take this to mean that God did not redeem us in Christ. If God can do the logically contradictory, then we could just as well say that God loves us and that God will damn every one of us. When I make this statement, my critics typically respond by saying that God would do no such thing since we can trust God's promises. In my experience virtually all those who claim that God is above logic also say that God cannot be dishonest. People who say this are, in fact, affirming the rule of noncontradiction since they believe that God cannot be both honest and dishonest. Also, if using logic to understand God places limits on God, then classical theists are guilty of doing so as well, for

they hold that God cannot feel pain or be affected by us. By using human reasoning, we do not claim to understand everything about God. We are finite beings so our knowledge is always less than complete. There is room for mystery and paradox in our theologizing, but logical contradictions pop the circuit breakers of our mind, shutting off any understanding of the divine.[49]

3. A few have claimed that open theism affirms "limited omniscience." This would be true if proponents of dynamic omniscience affirmed that there was an ontological reality known as "the future" of which God was ignorant. But that is not our position. As explained earlier, the metaphysical position upon which dynamic omniscience rests holds that there is no ontological reality called the future. The term "the future" refers to our beliefs about what we anticipate will occur after the present moment. The person making this criticism fails to realize that he presupposes a different metaphysical position (the future is an ontological reality) and then accuses us of not operating according to his position.

4. Some theological determinists say that open theists do not believe in divine sovereignty. We do. The issue is the kind of sovereignty that God has decided to practice. Theological determinists believe that God exercises meticulous providence: exhaustive control such that God's desires are never thwarted in the least detail. Open theists believe God exercises general sovereignty: he established the structures and limits of our freedom, but God has granted us the type of freedom which means that some of God's desires may be thwarted. The critic begs the question by assuming that her view of sovereignty is the only one.

5. Another misunderstanding is the equation of open theism to process theology. Both openness and process theisms affirm dynamic omniscience, but many orthodox

---

49. Paul Helm agrees with me on this. See his *The Providence of God* (Downers Grove: InterVarsity, 1994), 61–66. For further discussion see my "Mystery and Nonsense," in *The God Who Risks*, rev. ed. (2.4) .

Christian thinkers affirm dynamic omniscience and yet are neither open nor process theists. Also, process theology denies doctrines such as the deity of Christ, the Trinity, and that God can exist without a world. Openness, however, affirms all of these.

6. Others accuse open theism of going against church tradition. I have several responses. First, we do not take tradition lightly, but as Protestants we inherit a tradition that has sought continually to reform the tradition. Second, open theism arises out of a long-standing tradition in Christian theology known as free will theism. This tradition affirms conditional election, resistible grace, that our prayers can affect God, that some of what God does is contingent upon what we do or don't do, that God desires a dynamic give-and-take relationship with humans, that God places responsibility on us to carry out his purposes in creation, that God granted us libertarian free will and so took the risk that we might sin, and that God does not specifically intend the evil we do. Open theism is an attempt to make some modifications within this rich heritage. Third, though dynamic omniscience has certainly been a minority view in church history, it has been held and discussed throughout the history of the church, gained momentum in the nineteenth century, and presently has some significant proponents, particularly among Christian analytic philosophers.[50]

7. Some people have claimed that open theism will ruin piety and even destroy the church. However, thousands of people have written us testifying that their faith was

---

50. For elaboration and documentation see my *The God Who Risks*, 1st ed., 161–64 and the revised edition, "Proponents of Dynamic Omniscience," sec. 5.7. The information may also be found online at http://www.opentheism.info under the questions page. Millard Erickson, in *What Does God Know and When Does He Know It? The Current Controversy over Divine Foreknowledge* (Grand Rapids: Zondervan, 2003), chaps. 4–5, ignores the vast majority of the proponents of dynamic omniscience that I cite. Instead, he tries to argue that dynamic omniscience is in the tradition of people such as Celsus and Marcion. The problem with this argument is that both Celsus and Marcion held that a divine being must possess exhaustive definite foreknowledge in order to be God. Celsus said that Jesus lacked exhaustive definite foreknowledge and so could not be divine while Marcion claimed that the God of the Old Testament lacked it and so was not the true God. For documentation on this, see my *The God Who Risks*, rev. ed., secs. 5.7.

enhanced by open theism. Certainly affirmation of open theism would mean the demise of the piety practiced by theological determinists. Once again the critic begs the question by assuming his own form of piety is the only legitimate form. Also, it should be noted that the Anabaptists and the Wesleyans were accused of threatening piety and the church. Though these groups were a threat to certain forms of piety and church life of their day, they clearly had a piety that transformed their lives into godliness.

8. Some have found dynamic omniscience problematic because it implies that God did not eternally know which individuals would be redeemed. A God with dynamic omniscience would not be able to have such knowledge, but why is this necessary? Perhaps the critic believes the Bible teaches that God, prior to creation, elected those individuals who would be saved. Open theists, however, affirm corporate rather than individual election. To borrow a common Arminian line: "God elected the plan, not the man." Perhaps the concern is that a God with dynamic omniscience could not guarantee, prior to his decision to create, that even a single individual would come to faith. Certainly, theological determinism can guarantee that specific individuals would come to faith, but the theory of simple foreknowledge cannot do so. The reason is that, for simple foreknowledge, God's knowledge of what will happen in human history is logically antecedent to his decision to create a world with libertarian freedom. In other words, God decided to create this particular sort of world and then "saw" what would happen. Hence, prior to his decision to create, a God with simple foreknowledge could not guarantee that even one individual would come to faith. Free will theists, however, can say that God was not afraid to embark on a journey without such guarantees.

Conclusion

This chapter has sought to explain how providence is understood from an openness of God perspective and to provide some biblical and theological support for this view. As with the other chapters in this book, much has had to be left unsaid. One of the values of a book like this one is that it raises some fundamental issues that shape the way each of the authors reads Scripture and how they reason theologically. There is no easy way to resolve our important differences in hermeneutical method, theological background beliefs, and metaphysical positions. In his examination of the hermeneutical, theological, and philosophical presuppositions underlying the debate between open and classical theisms, Amos Yong concludes: "Each system interprets the Bible consistently and coherently within its presuppositional framework. . . . factors extraneous to the Bible itself determines how one reads and interprets the biblical text. . . with regard to the doctrine of divine omniscience in particular."[51]

For these reasons, though my chapter presents a case for an openness approach to divine providence, it cannot "prove" the case to the satisfaction of all rational Christians. Every view has problems, and sometimes we select a theological position because we are able to live with its attending problems whereas we are unable to live with what we perceive to be problems in another view. In fact, I believe that this is precisely what the responses to each chapter will show. Each author will find problems with the other proposals, and the problems mentioned will arise because of prior theological and philosophical commitments. I trust we can have a good conversation, but we will only get so far.

The openness of God approach to providence arises out of the free will theistic tradition and is, in fact, an attempt to solve a few perceived difficulties in this tradition. Roger Olson and I belong to the Hatfield clan because we both affirm the core doctrines and practices of the free will tradition. For example, we believe that God is affected by the prayers of his creatures, that

---

51. Yong, "Divine Omniscience and Future Contingents: Weighing the Presuppositional Issues in the Contemporary Debate," *Evangelical Review of Theology* 26, no. 3 (2002): 263. Yong does not take sides in the debate, and his is one of the best explanations of the underlying presuppositions.

240 — PERSPECTIVES ON THE DOCTRINE OF GOD

election is conditional, and that God takes risks because he does not specifically intend the evil we do. Paul Helm and Bruce Ware, on the other hand, are members of the McCoy clan since they affirm the core doctrines and practices of theological determinism. They believe in unconditional election, meticulous providence, and that God never takes risks because each of us always does specifically what God intends us to do. Additionally, these two clans differ on the type of freedom humans possess (libertarian verses compatibilistic). Given this divide between the clans, fruitful dialogue is more likely to take place within each clan than between them. In light of their reading of Scripture and their understanding of philosophical matters, open theists modify free will theism by exchanging divine temporality for divine timelessness and dynamic omniscience for simple foreknowledge. Perhaps free will theists will find better ways of resolving these difficulties than open theism provides. If so, I hope that the open theism proposal will have helped toward that end.

CHAPTER 8

Responses to John Sanders
"Divine Providence and the Openness of God"

Response by Paul Helm

Sanders's contribution contains some surprising statements. For example, God gives all an opportunity to be saved and in respect of the matters under discussion nothing can be settled by an appeal to Scripture (a somewhat fatalistic conclusion for an open theist), though he does give some weight to what he calls "common evangelical belief" in settling theological issues, as if something definite were denoted by that phrase. He does not seem to hold out much hope that the "same old arguments" between the free will family and the Augustinian family will be productive. Here the Augustinian can be more sanguine, believing that God may be pleased to work by the re-presentation of the biblical message of the plight of man and the power of God.

Much of Sanders's paper is taken up with highlighting those features of the biblical text that he believes favor open theism, but others have already addressed these issues.[1] Nowhere, as far as I can see, does he fairly and squarely address counterevidence; biblical statements of God's all encompassing knowledge and control, the election and predestination of the saints, the

---

1. For example, Bruce A. Ware, *God's Lesser Glory: The Diminished God of Open Theism* (Wheaton: Crossway, 2000); John Piper, Justin Taylor, and Paul Kjoss Helseth, eds., *Beyond the Bounds: Open Theism and the Undermining of Biblical Christianity*, (Wheaton: Crossway, 2003).

"golden chain" of Romans 8, and so on. However, I shall concentrate on four other issues concerning the concept of God: the respective theological methods of Augustinianism and free will theism, prayer to God, the contrast between the A-series and the B-series accounts of temporal order, and its implications for God's relation to time, particularly for the idea of divine responsiveness.

Theological Methods

Sanders gives great prominence to compatibilist freedom in his critique of the Augustinian or Calvinist doctrine of God, but there is a sense in which this is a red herring, despite Ware's enthusiastic adherence to it. It is a red herring for this reason. The philosophical doctrine known as compatibilism, which has its origin in paganism—in Stoicism if nowhere else—is not explicitly taught in Scripture. So insofar as anyone claims to follow the scriptural teaching on the knowledge and will of God in respect of his creation, one cannot consistently insist on compatibilism in that account. What one can do (that Augustinians typically but not universally do) is to express the opinion that of the two views, libertarianism and compatibilism, the latter best coheres not only with the biblical teaching on the divine decree but also with its teaching on the efficacy of grace as expressed in effectual calling. Libertarianism can only be regarded as being consistent with these teachings by being agnostic about the entire connection between God's will and the human will. Such agnosticism may be an uncomfortable and an unsatisfactory position, but it is not logically incoherent, and so it is a possible view for an Augustinian to take. Thus Augustinianism does not *entail* compatibilism.

Compatibilism is therefore a *theologoumenon*, a theological opinion, and nothing more. What matters more to the Augustinian is the biblical teaching respecting the extent and character of the divine decree and the nature of human brokenness due to sin rather than adherence to compatibilism at all costs. For supposing that opinion proved to be incorrect, either because of internal difficulties with compatibilism, or because there is an as yet undiscerned sense of freedom distinct from both libertarianism and compatibilism which better coheres with the biblical teaching than many Augustinians think that compatibilism does, or because of convincing reasons why one ought to tolerate a greater degree of mystery regarding the way in which the divine decree and effectual calling bear on the springs of human agency. Invoking compatibilism remains a human strategy, one that as it happens I share. But it is not part of the divine revelation. The doctrine of predestination, and the fact that human beings are in servitude to sin and spiritually dead (which *are* parts of the divine revelation), stand, whether or not compatibilism stands.

Similar remarks apply to determinism. Sanders regularly refers to "theological determinism," and this may give the impression that theological determinism is one species of determinism, along with physical determinism, psychological determinism, and so on. But this impression is wholly misleading. For it is a fundamental feature of any account of the relationship between divine and human action that it characterizes some aspect of the Creator-creature relationship, whereas the other determinisms are accounts of creature-creature relationships. Creator-creature relationships are unique, and this is one of the reasons that phrases such as "divine determinism" or "divine necessitarianism" do not occur in historical Augustinian discussions of their position but are of rather recent currency. "What God ordains," "the divine decree," "the divine will": these are the time-honored phrases. They enshrine the Pauline thought that God works all things after the counsel of his own will, but they do not identify a mechanism by which that divine working of all things is effected.

By contrast, in most accounts of free will theism, and certainly both with the version of Arminianism offered by Olson and (more especially perhaps) with its close relation, open theism, the position is altogether different. (Even Arminians such as David Hunt who are agnostic on the question of how it can be shown that God's foreknowledge is compatible with human libertarian freedom[2] are of course committed to libertarian freedom.) Here the philosophical doctrine *does* occupy center stage. Without such a doctrine the raison d'etre of free will theism disappears. And this is the point, as Sanders acknowledges in his book on providence; but as he and his Arminian brothers all too easily forget, libertarianism is also a philosophical doctrine derived from paganism but is now (in the case of Arminianism and open theism) exalted to the status of a Christian doctrine, of a concept underpinning a whole range of doctrines, not only the doctrine of God narrowly considered but also the entire spectrum of theological doctrines embraced within anthropology. Not only is it essential that human beings are libertarian, it is also vital that God himself is as well. (This is an ironic state of affairs, given open theism's claim to be biblical and not philosophical in its approach.)

Not only that, but in the case of Sanders's version of open theism, this central commitment to libertarianism has to involve other philosophical doctrines of an equally contentious nature, notably presentism, with respect to time. For according to Sanders's version of openness theism, God has no knowledge of the future to the extent that there is no truth of the matter with respect to much of the future.[3]

Prayer

Sanders cites James 4:2 and proceeds to argue that "God will only bring some things about if we ask him because he desires an interdependent world and prayer is one means of fostering our dependence and concern for one another." This contention seems reasonable enough. He goes on, "A widely accepted understanding of this is that God might not give us some good things because we fail to ask for them." This seems fair enough, too. But such an understanding should not then suggest that the

2. David Hunt, in "The Simple Foreknowledge View," writes, "What I am committed to defending in this chapter is the view that God simply knows the future (leaving open the question of how he does it)." See *Divine Foreknowledge: Four Views*, ed. James K Beilby and Paul R. Eddy (Downers Grove: InterVarsity, 2001), 67.

3. Incidentally, why openness has to commit itself to presentism is not clear. Richard Swinburne, who takes up a position in some respects similar to that of openness theism, nevertheless writes of God limiting himself with respect to his knowledge of the future. See *The Coherence of Theism* (Oxford: Clarendon, 1977), 176.

purposes of God are frustrated and fail because we do not pray. What Scripture in fact says in this connection is that God's people do not have because they do not ask (Jas 4:2), not that God has not because his people ask not. In view of this, the Calvinist is warranted in being a little more careful. If *desires* is another word for "decrees," then no, God's desires are not thwarted by our failure to pray. Such a failure is part of all that he works after the counsel of his own will (Eph 1:11). And if *desires* is a synonym for *wants*, then no again. What God wants is not denied to him by our failure to pray. But if *desires* is a reference to God's revealed will—what he commands his people—then certainly a failure to pray may involve disobedience.

However, if in decreeing an end God decrees prayers as a means to a decreed end, even as *the* means to that end, then it makes perfect sense to believe that "if I had not prayed for that end then that end would fail to be achieved" or even "if I were not to pray, then it would fail to be achieved." But of course, if the prayer is decreed as a necessary part of the fulfilling of an end, then if the end is decreed so is the prayer decreed.

The A Series and the B Series

Now, let us consider what Sanders has to say about God and time. He holds that divine timelessness is incompatible with the core beliefs of free will theism. But this is not a universally accepted view. From the time of Boethius onwards theologians have invoked divine timelessness in order to reconcile divine foreknowledge with libertarian freedom.[4] Further, in setting out this view and in dismissing timelessness, Sanders reveals some misunderstandings. For one thing, the terms "A series" and "B-series" (first coined by J. M. E. McTaggart) are not descriptions of two rival *theories* of time; they are simply names for different ways of understanding the temporal series. Further, the stasis theory, which uses the B-series account of the temporal series, the theory that all times are equally real, does not hold that "every event exists timelessly (as God does)." It is possible to hold that stasis theory and to deny that divine timelessness

4. See my response in this book to Roger E. Olson for more on this subject.

makes sense, and on one view the created order is timelessly created with time. The stasis theory holds that every event is tenselessly related to every other event; nevertheless on this account some events are earlier than other events, some simultaneous, and some later than others. Obviously so, if the stasis theory is a theory of *time*. The idea that God exists in time, and events occur in his life, can be straightforwardly incorporated into a stasis theory of time. It may be that divine timelessness requires the stasis theory, but it may not obviously follow that that theory alone entails determinism. Many, including Oaklander, think that it does not.[5]

Sanders may have misled himself on this point by thinking that according to the stasis theory what we call the "future" is already real. Not so, if by "already real" Sanders means "real now." On the stasis view what occurs in 2009 is not real now; the events that occur within that year are not occurring now. Rather it is real in 2009, and the events of 2009 occur then, some time later than those occurring in 2006 or 2007. So Sanders is incorrect to conclude that the stasis theory undermines libertarian freedom without addressing the arguments of Oaklander and others to the contrary. It may be that divine timeless eternity is incompatible with libertarianism, though many free will theists would disagree.

Divine Responsiveness

Finally, a word on divine responsiveness. Both Ware and Sanders are concerned about whether in the classical Augustinian or Calvinist view God's responsiveness is a genuine response, and even with the question of whether God can be in any sense said to be responsive. This concern with divine responsiveness also motivates Ware's concern for relationality and his proposed modifications of divine immutability. There are a number of separate issues here.

There is the question of how this relationality is conceived. Sanders writes as if it is one between two healthy, well-disposed adults, one of whom may, however, be "on the run" from the

---

5. For example, L. Nathan Oaklander, "Freedom and the New Theory of Time," in *Questions of Time and Tense*, ed. Robin Le Poidevin (Oxford: Clarendon, 1998).

other, but in general terms their relationship is a simple matter of "give and take," to love or not to love, as they freely decide. But this is not the biblical view, which regards the relationship between God and mankind as having broken down, and irrevocably broken down, unless there is a unilateral action from the Lord of life to remake it. For as I note in my response to Olson, according to Scripture men and women are dead, blind, deaf, and "far off." They need life, and sight, and to be brought near.

Then there is the question of whether God is responsive to the needs of his people, and finally the question of whether God's relations to his creatures are reciprocal. An affirmative answer to the second issue presumably entails an affirmative answer to the first, though not vice versa. So let's consider reciprocity and take the biblical refrain "When you call I will answer" (Pss 36:15; 86:7; 102:2; Isa 14:1; 58:9) as typifying such reciprocity. It would seem to follow that the refrain entails, "It will be the case that when at t1 you call then at t1 or later I answer." An upholder of divine timelessness does not have the least difficulty with that. He simply prefixes the words "God eternally decrees that . . ." to read, "God eternally decrees that when at t1 X calls then at t1 or later he himself will answer" (though we should not ignore those cases where God "responds" before he is called upon to do so, e.g. Isa 65:24). So God's actions are a response, and therefore there are elements in the life of God that constitute that response, namely his eternal decree to so respond, and the effect of that eternal decree in time. May such responses be part of a reciprocal arrangement? Of course. God may answer because his people call, and his people may respond when he answers. This is more complex to spell out, but no issue of principle is involved. Of course (a) "God eternally decrees that when at t1 X calls he will answer at t1 or later" is to be distinguished from (b) "God eternally decrees that when at t1 X calls, then at t1 or later God will decide what response to give and gives it," for that is straightforwardly inconsistent with an all-encompassing divine decree as well as with divine omniscience as classically understood. Sanders cites the objections of Nicholas Wolterstorff to (a), but those objections are to divine timelessness and its implications for responsiveness, not to the implications for responsiveness of an all-encompassing divine decree. It's possible to be a temporalist in respect of God's relation to time and nevertheless hold that God's decree is all-encompassing, and so to cite Wolterstorff's objections here is rather beside the point.

Response by Roger E. Olson

I certainly agree with my friend John Sanders that if he and I belong to a theological clan called "free will theism" and Bruce Ware and Paul Helm belong to one called "theological determinism," "fruitful dialogue is more likely to take place within each clan than between them." As a classical Arminian, I find much more common ground between my theology and Sanders's than between mine and Helm's or Ware's. And I agree with nineteenth-century Arminian theologian John Miley who said that dynamic omniscience (John's term for open theism's view of God's foreknowledge) would not undermine any vital Arminian doctrine. In fact, I would go so far as to say that I cannot see how it undermines any Christian doctrine. In my opinion, the furor over open theism among conservative evangelical theologians has been over the top; it borders on hysteria, especially since no crucial doctrine of the Christian faith is denied or undermined by it.

Having said all of that, however, I must go on to register some points of disagreement with my friend John and his open theistic account of God's foreknowledge. First, John's description could be read as implying that all Arminians agree that it is possible for genuine Christian believers to commit apostasy. In fact, the Arminian tradition is not monolithic in this regard. Arminius himself did not think Scripture sufficiently clear to decide; he admitted that it wore both aspects (eternal unconditional perseverance of true saints and possibility of apostasy of true Christians). Admittedly, most Arminians after Arminius have held to the Wesleyan view that apostasy is a real possibility. There is nothing intrinsic to the Arminian tradition that requires a classical Arminian to take one position on this question. Many prefer to leave the question unanswered and take with equal seriousness the biblical warnings against apostasy (e.g., Heb 6) and the biblical assurances of eternal security. My own experience tells me that the majority of Southern Baptists, for example, are Arminians (whether they call themselves that or not) who believe in eternal security.

Second, I am not yet convinced that "simple foreknowledge [is] incompatible with the core beliefs of free will theism." After all, what are the core beliefs of free will theism? I judge them to be God's posture of unconditional love toward creation (which does not preclude wrath and judgment in the face of unrepentance) and God's desire to have freely chosen relationships with human persons such that God and persons can affect each other. Arminians have traditionally believed and argued that contingently free decisions and actions of human persons cause God to foreknow them. This may be counterintuitive, but it is not, strictly speaking, illogical. In *God, Freedom, and Evil*[6] philosopher Alvin Plantinga presents a fifty-five-step syllogism, the last six of which (including substeps) convincingly demonstrate that exhaustive omniscience and human freedom (interpreted nondeterministically) are not logically incompatible. If that is the case, as I judge it is, then classical Arminians are warranted to continue believing in simple foreknowledge and noncompatibilist free will.

Sanders's weaker claim is that "divine temporality and dynamic omniscience better uphold the core beliefs of free will theism" than classical Arminianism's belief in simple foreknowledge. I am not as inclined to dispute this. Perhaps so. It certainly seems at times that the biblical narrative portrays God as facing a partly unsettled and uncertain (even to him) future. This is the implication in the stories about God's mental changes. At least in human experience, personal interactions that affect both parties seem to require an open (or partly unsettled) future. A human person who knows the future exhaustively and infallibly could hardly be said to experience mental changes. Whether that is true of a divine person is perhaps another question. And can a person lovingly interact with another person if the future of the

---

6. Alvin Plantinga, *God, Freedom, and Evil* (Grand Rapids: Eerdmans, 1977).

relationship is already absolutely known? Again, it is problematic from a human standpoint, but perhaps this is a case in which God is different.

I am not prepared at this point to adopt open theism even though I feel the force of John's (and other open theists') arguments, and I do not see what core doctrines of the Christian faith would be negatively affected by it. I have played an imagination game in my own mind (and in conversation with students and others) many times in which I pretend to believe in open theism. Then I examine what beliefs (other than simple foreknowledge) would necessarily be altered by that. So far I have not been able to determine that any would be. As an open theist, like current open theists, I would still believe in the divine inspiration of Scripture, the greatness and goodness of God (including all the attributes of God's majesty and power), the Trinity, creation out of nothing, the deity of Christ, salvation by grace alone through faith, and so on and so on. My Christianity would be substantially unaltered. And, as John argues, my belief about God's ability to be affected by my praying might have a firmer foundation.

So why am I not an open theist? Two factors hold me back from joining that club. First, I find some claims of Scripture incompatible with it. For example, Jesus' prophecy that Peter would deny him three times seems a case of exhaustive and infallible divine foreknowledge. (Whether Jesus knew this because he was God or God revealed it to him is irrelevant.) All the answers I've heard or read from open theists so far are less than fully convincing. Jesus (or God revealing Peter's future denial to him) seems to have had absolute prescience about something—a sin— that God himself could not have determined to happen, according to Arminian theology. Could it have been already settled by some factor internal to Peter at the time Christ foretold it? That seems unlikely especially when the detail about "three times" is considered. In other words, Jesus did not just know that Peter would deny him; he knew that Peter would deny him three times within a relatively brief time frame. This seems to be a case of absolute foreknowledge of a future libertarianly free decision and action. There are others in Scripture.

Second, I am not yet ready to affirm open theism (which is not to suggest I ever will be ready to affirm it) because I am puzzled about how the great tradition of Christian teaching could have missed such an important idea for nearly two thousand years. I know that one open theist claims to have found an early church theologian who believed something like open theism, but the only well-known person within the context of Christianity who taught it before the nineteenth century was Faustus Socinus, a radical reformer who was also anti-Trinitarian. Thus, between the New Testament and the Methodist theologian Lorenzo McCabe in the late nineteenth century, only one notable person associated with Christianity seems to have taught this, and he was a rank heretic! How could the entire church have been so wrong about something like the nature of God's foreknowledge? I do not believe tradition has a veto in these matters, however, and so I am willing to consider the possibility that the church was wrong. Scripture must settle the issue. But tradition at least gets a vote if not a veto, and that vote goes heavily against open theism.

Even some Arminians have declared open theism a heresy because it is foreign to the great tradition of Christian teaching. I disagree. Open theism would be a heresy if it blatantly contradicted the plain teaching of Scripture or if it presented a doctrine that absolutely contradicted the gospel. I judge that neither is the case. I find problems in its interpretation of Scripture while admitting that it has much scriptural support. And I know of no idea intrinsic to the gospel that it denies. I welcome John's version of open theism (as well as those of Clark Pinnock and Greg Boyd) into the Christian theological conversation especially as it is being presented humbly and as a *theologoumenon*—a hypothesis to be tested and not a new dogma to be adopted by everyone willy-nilly.

Response by Bruce A. Ware

John Sanders should be commended for writing a very fine explanation and defense of the openness view of divine providence. His lucid description of features of his model, his able defense through biblical and theological support, and his astute address of major objections that have been raised to the openness view commend this chapter as a clear and compelling treatment of the open view that Sanders espouses. As one who has interacted with openness literature for many years now, I gladly acknowledge that Sanders has done a superb job representing his own view, showing both a clear grasp of central issues and a maturity in his presentation that no doubt is the result of working hard on these issues over many years.

The excellent quality of this chapter's defense of the open view notwithstanding, it still is the open view. As such, it remains a position that will invite much critical scrutiny by fellow evangelicals both classic Arminian and Calvinist since it presents a view of God and God's relation to the world that has departed in some centrally important respects from all previous models of God held and advocated within the orthodox tradition of the church. I know that Sanders very much likes to uphold the openness view as one branch within the larger family tree of free will theists—"the 'Hatfield' free will theistic family" against the "'McCoy' theological determinist family," as he likened the debate. And while there is truth to this depiction at certain levels, it is also true that classic Arminianism stands with Reformed theology in affirming the exhaustive definite foreknowledge of God, a doctrine which both of these traditions (Arminian and Calvinist) view as indispensable to a theologically responsible, biblically faithful, and practically satisfying model of God and divine providence. So, while Sanders would like very much to have us all understand his rejection of exhaustive definite foreknowledge as simply his moving into a different set of rooms of the expansive free will theist home, others, including many classic Arminians, understand the openness proposal more as a move to a faraway and foreign country than to an upstairs apartment in the same home.

The "watershed" that Sanders describes, then, sets the divide between all free will theists on the one side and theological determinists on the other. In this sense open theism clearly stands with Arminianism and Molinism, but it also stands with process theism and Socinianism as well—the latter two movements of which all agree stand clearly and decisively outside the bounds of orthodoxy. But since many classic Arminians and Molinists have argued strongly against open theism and in doing so have stood with Reformed theologians in their vehement disagreement with this novel theological proposal, it seems to me that another watershed needs acknowledgement. It is the one between all of those who uphold the classic understanding of divine omniscience as including necessarily God's exhaustive and meticulous knowledge of every detail of what will happen in the future and those who deny classic divine omniscience, so defined, which includes Socinians, process theists, and openness proponents. Please understand: I am not suggesting that the open view is either Socinian or process, taken as a whole. Surely it is not. But it is true that the intentional rejection of exhaustive definite foreknowledge that separates open theism from Arminianism also aligns it, in this respect, with these other nonorthodox theological movements. While I gladly acknowledge the legitimacy of the divide that Sanders has proposed, I suggest that another divide of equal if not greater importance also exists. The denial of exhaustive definite foreknowledge is of much greater significance, with far more disturbing implications, than Sanders and others in the openness camp have ever seemed to understand.

In the remainder of my response, I will offer some brief comments on Sanders's proposal from biblical, theological, and practical perspectives.

Biblical Considerations

The denial of exhaustive definite foreknowledge is central and essential to the openness model, and Sanders endeavors to provide some of the basis for this denial from Scripture. Of course, all of the biblical support he offers would certainly weigh in heavily were it not for other clear, bountiful, and forceful biblical teaching that supports the opposite conclusion. Surely it is not the case that Scripture contradicts itself, nor would Sanders suggest this. Rather, he is as insistent as his evangelical critics that Scripture is consistent yet nuanced in its teaching regarding God's knowledge of the future. Sanders's solution is to see the teaching on God's definite knowledge of the future as limited and targeted, indicating certain aspects of the future that are both settled and known in advance to be so by God, while other passages indicate God's ignorance of the future as shown by his surprise when certain things happen, his testing to see what might take place, and his regret over things that have happened, all indicating God simply did not know and could not have known those aspects before they happened. But the whole of the evidence on this question taken together will not allow this conclusion. It is not the case that Scripture teaches that God merely knows some things future, leaving it open to conclude as well that he simply does not (and cannot) know other aspects of what is yet future. So much evidence, from so many texts and cases in the Bible, leads forcefully to the same conclusion that the church has uniformly affirmed over the centuries, viz., that God in fact foreknows all that will occur in the future. I have argued a portion of the case for this in chapters 4 and 5 of *God's Lesser Glory*,[7] and more recently, Steven Roy's *How Much Does God Foreknow?: A Comprehensive Biblical Study*,[8] has provided a compelling defense of exhaustive definite foreknowledge from Scripture. If the evidence on exhaustive definite foreknowledge were either minimal or weak, one would then be in a position to consider the openness proposal as a viable possibility, but if one concludes that the case for exhaustive definite foreknowledge is pervasive and strong, the openness approach simply fails.

Theological Perspectives

Theologically, the openness model seems unavoidably to emphasize two opposite themes, depending on the issue at hand. When the issue concerns the confidence that the believer can have that a God who doesn't know much about the future can be trusted to guide things now to accomplish what God knows

---

7. Bruce A. Ware, *God's Lesser Glory: The Diminished God of Open Theism* (Wheaton: Crossway, 2000).

8. Steven C. Roy, *How Much Does God Foreknow?: A Comprehensive Biblical Study* (Downers Grove: InterVarsity, 2006).

is best, we are assured that this God is highly intelligent and able to forecast well what will occur. As such we can be assured that we are in good and capable hands which have a firm grasp on reality and are guiding us into the future God alone knows is best. But when the issue instead is why such evil and horrid things happen in human history, instead we are told that God has granted people libertarian freedom over which, by definition, he cannot control, and so God simply isn't able to regulate a host of evil and wicked things that occur in human history. Further, God has built laws of nature into the created order which, again, he chooses for the most part not to control, so God simply isn't able to prevent natural disasters from occurring without making a mockery of the natural laws he has put in place. But most importantly, when God created the world and decided to give libertarian freedom to moral creatures and put laws of nature in the created order, he just didn't know how terrible things would often be. God's creation project was a huge risk, and even God simply couldn't know how things would go. Here, then, we are asked to understand God's lack of control over evil not only due to his decision to grant libertarian freedom and laws of nature to creation. More importantly, we are asked to give God a break, as it were, because he just didn't know how bad things often would be.

Isn't it interesting, then, that when the issue is whether we can trust God for the future, openness advocates appeal to God's great ability to see into the future and guide the present to God's wise and good ends. But when the issue is all of the evil that has occurred in the past, the same openness advocates appeal to God's vast ignorance and risk taking in his creating the world, along with his ongoing ignorance in advance of a host of developments that take place throughout human history. The duplicity here is simply not sustainable. And when push comes to shove, it seems clear that the stronger openness theme is the appeal to the divine ignorance in accounting for evil. After all, we have a long track record of evil, whereas we only have a guess about what might take place in the future. So at its foundation, it looks like the same God whose ignorance of the future when he created the world, the same God who took a huge risk back then at the beginning, is the same God we are asked to trust in today regarding our own personal futures as well as the future of the world as a whole. Just how openness proponents can reconcile this, I cannot comprehend. I only know that if I truly believed what open theism claims, I would despair.

Practical Issues

Because the knowledge, wisdom, and power of God are all subject to revision in the openness model, worship and prayer are both deeply affected. The openness model, it seems, calls into question the credibility of God as God. Certainly this claim reflects essentially what God himself through the prophet Isaiah has likewise concluded. The God of Israel challenges the gods of the ancient Near East to prove their deity by declaring what the future will be. If they truly are gods, they will be able to declare the future, and we should be able to consider their predictions and see when they are fulfilled. But of course they cannot do this, and because they cannot, the true God declares in no uncertain terms that they are not gods (Isa 41:21–24). Open theism's denial of God's exhaustive definite foreknowledge puts this movement in essentially the same position as those ancient Near Eastern gods who could not declare the future. And the effect then is the same effect now—such a god cannot truly be the God who reigns and who is to be worshipped above all. The diminished deity of open theism is not the God who is worthy of all praise, glory, honor, and worship. And how does one pray to this God who may not in fact have the best ideas about what should happen in the future? What confidence can the believer have in a God of such vast ignorance? Again, for every reassurance given about God's supposed vast and infinite intelligence, one cannot remove from one's mind this same God's track record of less than perfect divine guidance, and God's own horror about evil that he didn't anticipate happening. Can we truly put our lives in the hands of this God? Can we pray with confidence, and without qualification, "Your will be done"?

I'm grateful for John Sanders's clear and concise defense of the open view. But I hasten to say that I hope the day comes when openness proponents reconsider their own positions and return to the greater fold of those throughout the history of the church who have seen strong biblical support for, and taken great confidence in, the exhaustive definite foreknowledge of God. For the sake of the unity of the church, and for the glory of God's name, I pray that God will bring this to pass.

Author Index

Subject Index

Scripture Index

THE PERSPECTIVES SERIES

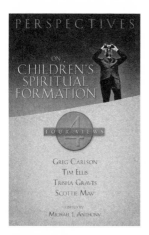

PERSPECTIVES ON CHILDREN'S SPIRITUAL FORMATION
Edited by Michael Anthony

ABOUT THE BOOK
A presentation of four views of children's spiritual formation and four related methods of Christian education. Contributors also respond to the other viewpoints. Chapters written by Greg Carlson, Tim Ellis, Trisha Graves, and Scottie May.

9780805441864
Paperback
352 Pages
$29.99

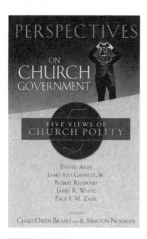

PERSPECTIVES ON CHURCH GOVERNMENT
Edited by Chad Owen Brand & R. Stanton Norman

ABOUT THE BOOK
The five predominant views of church government are presented in a point-counter point format. The contributors are James White, Daniel Akin, James Garrett, and Robert Reymond, and Paul Zahl.

9780805425901
Paperback
368 Pages
$19.99

THE PERSPECTIVES SERIES

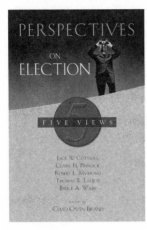

9780805427295
Paperback
352 Pages
$19.99

PERSPECTIVES ON ELECTION
Edited by Chad Owen Brand

ABOUT THE BOOK

Perspectives on Election presents five common beliefs on the doctrine of spiritual election that have developed over the course of church history. The contributors are Jack Cottrell, Clark Pinnock, Robert Reymond, Thomas Talbott, and Bruce Ware. According to Chad Brand, "The goal of this book is to add clarity to the discussion and to further the discussion, insofar as it is possible, in an amiable manner."

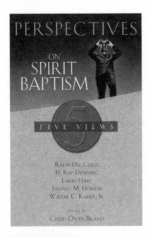

9780805425949
Paperback
352 Pages
$19.99

PERSPECTIVES ON SPIRIT BAPTISM
Edited by Chad Owen Brand

ABOUT THE BOOK

Through a dynamic array of positions and contributors, *Perspectives on Spirit Baptism* presents five common beliefs. Specifically addressed are Sacramental (Ralph Del Colle), Wesleyan (H. Ray Dunning), Charismatic (Larry Hart), Pentecostal (Stanley Horton), and Reformed (Walter Kaiser, Jr.).

THE PERSPECTIVES SERIES

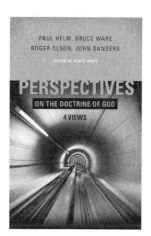

PERSPECTIVES ON
THE DOCTRINE OF GOD
Edited by Bruce A. Ware

ABOUT THE BOOK

Perspectives on the Doctrine of God presents four common beliefs that have developed over the course of church history. Its aim is to determine which view is most faithful to the Scriptures. Contributors include J. I. Packer, Bruce Ware, Roger Olson, and John Sanders.

April 2008
9780805430608
Paperback
320 Pages
$19.99

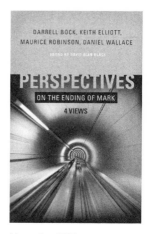

PERSPECTIVES ON
THE ENDING OF MARK
Edited by David A. Black

ABOUT THE BOOK

Because it is conspicuously absent from more than one of the early Greek manuscripts, the final section of the Gospel of Mark (16:9-20) remains a constant source of debate. This book will present the split opinions with a goal of determining which is more likely. The contributors include Maurice Robinson, David Alan Black, Keith Elliott, Daniel Wallace, and Darrell Bock, who responds to each view and summarizes the state of current research on the entire issue.

November 2008
9780805447620
Paperback
160 Pages
$19.99

ADDITIONAL ACADEMIC TITLES

PASSIONATE CONVICTION
Contemporary Discourses on Christian Apologetics

Edited by Paul Copan & William L. Craig

ABOUT THE BOOK

Is your heart on fire for God? This book brings together popular and heart-stirring presentations defending Christianity delivered at the annual conference on apologetics held in association with the Evangelical Philosophical Society, The C. S. Lewis Institute, and the Christian Apologetics program at Biola University. Contributors include J. P. Moreland, N. T. Wright, Francis Beckwith, Sean McDowell, and Gary Habermas.

9780805445381
Paperback
288 Pages
$19.99

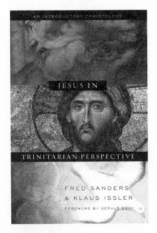

JESUS IN TRINITARIAN PERSPECTIVE
An Introduction to Christology

Edited by Fred Sanders & Klaus Issler

ABOUT THE BOOK

The Christian church has confessed this truth since the early centuries, but many modern theologies have denied or ignored its implications. To clarify the complex issue, these writers approach "post-Chalcedonian" Christology from a varity of disciplines – historical, philosophical, systematic, and practical. Contributors include Donald Fairbairn, Garrett DeWeese, Scott Horrell, and Bruce Ware.

9780805444223
Paperback
256 Pages
$24.99